Financial Modeling Using Quantum Computing

Design and manage quantum machine learning solutions for financial analysis and decision making

Anshul Saxena

Javier Mancilla

Iraitz Montalban

Christophe Pere

‹packt›

BIRMINGHAM—MUMBAI

Financial Modeling Using Quantum Computing

Group Product Manager: Reshma Raman

Publishing Product Manager: Apeksha Shetty

Senior Editor: Sushma Reddy

Technical Editor: Kavyashree K S

Copy Editor: Safis Editing

Book Project Manager: Kirti Pisat

Project Coordinator: Farheen Fathima

Proofreader: Safis Editing

Indexer: Manju Arasan

Production Designer: Prashant Ghare

Marketing Coordinator: Nivedita Singh

First published: May 2023

Production reference: 1300523

Published by Packt Publishing Ltd.

Livery Place

35 Livery Street

Birmingham

B3 2PB, UK.

ISBN 978-1-80461-842-4

www.packtpub.com

To my mother, Jeannette, and the memory of my father, Patricio, for teaching me the power of perseverance. To my beloved wife, Sandy, and my sons, Agustín, Francisco, and Máximo, for being the light of my life and a constant inspiration.

– Javier Mancilla

To my family, pets included.

– Iraitz Montalban

To my wife and my sons, who bring light and happiness to my world.

– Christophe Pere, Ph.D.

To my loving wife, Jyoti, who inspires me to do better every day, and to Dr. Richard Feynman, for everything quantum.

– Dr. Anshul Saxena

Contributors

About the authors

Dr. Anshul Saxena holds a Ph.D. in applied AI and business analytics. He has over 13 years of work experience across IT companies including TCS and Northern Trust in various business analytics and decision sciences roles. He has completed certification courses in Joint AI and Quantum Expert from IISC and Quantum Computing for Managers (BIMTECH). He is a SAS-certified predictive modeler and has undergone several T3 training courses arranged by IBM under its university connect program. He has also handled corporate training for companies such as IBM and TCS. Currently, he is working as a professor and consultant for various financial organizations. His area of interest includes risk analytics and the application of quantum physics in stock markets.

Javier Mancilla is a Ph.D. candidate in quantum computing and holds a master's degree in data management and innovation. He has more than 15 years of experience in digital transformation projects, with the last 8 years mostly dedicated to artificial intelligence, machine learning, and quantum computing, with more than 35 projects executed around these technologies. He has more than 8 certifications in quantum computing matters from institutions including MIT xPro, KAIST, IBM, Saint Petersburg University, and BIMTECH. He was also selected as one of the Top 20 Quantum Computing Linkedin Voices by Barcelonaqbit (a quantum organization in Spain) for both 2022 and 2023. Currently, he holds the role of quantum machine learning advisor and researcher for different companies and organizations in the finance industry in Europe and Latin America. Recently, he has been exploring the quantum gaming ecosystem and how to democratize quantum literacy.

Iraitz Montalban is a Ph.D. candidate at the University of the Basque Country and holds master's degrees in mathematical modeling from the same institution, in data protection from the University of la Rioja, and in quantum technologies from the Polytechnic University of Madrid. He holds the Qiskit Developer Certificate as well as other relevant certifications around agile frameworks and innovation adoption strategies for large organizations. He has spent more than 15 years working with data analytics and digital transformation, 7 of which were dedicated to AI and ML adoption by large organizations. As an assistant professor in several universities, he has contributed to creating big data and analytics curriculums as well as teaching on these topics.

Christophe Pere is an applied quantum machine learning researcher and lead scientist originally from Paris, France. He has a Ph.D. in astrophysics from Université Côte d'Azur. After his Ph.D., he left the academic world for a career in artificial intelligence as an applied industry researcher. He learned quantum computing during his Ph.D. in his free time, starting as a passion and becoming his new career. He actively democratizes quantum computing to help other people and companies enter this new field.

Additional contributor

Shadab Hussain works as a developer advocate (for data science and machine learning) at the London Stock Exchange Group and co-founded Quantum Computing India. He formerly worked as a data scientist for multiple startups and MNCs. He has around 5 years of experience in ML, analytics, and building end-to-end ML pipelines on the cloud using the agile framework, and has also gained expertise in quantum computing from institutions such as TheCodingSchool and IBM. He has also published a few research papers at national and international conferences and is presently investigating applications of quantum computing and machine learning in finance and healthcare.

About the reviewers

Santanu Ganguly has worked in quantum computing, cloud computing, data networking, and security for more than 23 years. He has worked in Switzerland and is now based in the United Kingdom, where he has held senior-level positions at various Silicon Valley vendors. He presently works for a quantum computing startup leading global projects related to quantum communication and machine learning, among other technologies. He has two postgraduate degrees in mathematics and observational astrophysics and has research experience, patents, and publications in quantum computing, silicon photonics, and laser spectroscopy. He is the author of the 2021 Apress publication, *Quantum Machine Learning: An Applied Approach*, and a reviewer of other books on the subject.

Jonathan Hardy has over 25 years of experience in financial services in areas such as lending, treasury, software development, management consulting, and project management, and is considered an industry-wide expert in intelligent automation and digital transformation. He holds an undergraduate degree from the University of Alabama in corporate finance, and an MBA in finance from Mercer University. He holds designations as a **Financial Risk Manager (FRM)** and a **Project Management Professional (PMP)** from the Global Association of Risk Professionals and the Project Management Institute respectively, along with credentials in agile project management and artificial intelligence as well. He was a founding member of an **Intelligent Automation (IA)** CoE at one major Fortune 500 company, while providing thought leadership in the startup efforts of another. He has been married for 20 years and is the father of two wonderful children. Please feel free to reach out on LinkedIn if you want to connect.

Alex Khan is an advisor, entrepreneur, and educator in quantum computing. He is the CEO of ZebraKet, a Canadian startup in supply chain optimization using quantum methods. He has had roles at Chicago Quantum, where he co-authored papers on portfolio optimization using D-Wave, at Harrisburg University where he taught quantum computing, and at QuantFi. He continues to be an advisor at QuSecure.

Alex is an experienced health IT executive. He has a BSME from Purdue University, an MSME from KSU, an MBA from Duke University, and a certificate in quantum computing from MITxPro. He is the author of *Quantum Computing Experimentation with Amazon Braket* and has been recognized by The Quantum Daily as one of the 126 advisors shaping the quantum computing industry.

Table of Contents

3

Quantum Finance Landscape 53

Part 2: Advanced Applications of Quantum Computing in Finance

4

Derivative Valuation 69

5

Portfolio Management   101

6

Credit Risk Analytics   133

7

Implementation in Quantum Clouds   165

Part 3: Upcoming Quantum Scenario

8

Simulators and HPC's Role in the NISQ Era   203

9

NISQ Quantum Hardware Roadmap   219

10

Business Implementation   239

Index   259

Other Books You May Enjoy   268

Preface

Welcome to the fascinating world of financial modeling through the lens of quantum computing. This book seeks to offer an enlightening exploration into the uncharted territory of quantum computing applications in the financial realm. Our journey begins with a comprehensive understanding of digital technology's limitations and how quantum computing serves to transcend these boundaries.

Within these pages, we delve into the nuances of **Quantum Machine Learning** (QML) and how its unique attributes can be harnessed to revolutionize various aspects of financial modeling. We will explore derivatives valuation, portfolio management, and credit risk analysis, laying bare the transformative potential of QML algorithms in these areas.

However, as with any technological implementation, simply understanding quantum technology doesn't ensure smooth sailing. Thus, this book also provides guidance on how institutions such as fintech firms and banks can navigate these project implementations, minimizing risks and ensuring successful, uninterrupted execution.

This book also elucidates the role of classical means and high-performance hardware in achieving a short-term quantum advantage. It further explores the potential evolution of noisy intermediate-scale hardware based on different provider strategies, emphasizing its long-term implications.

We have curated this material based on years of research and experience in quantum technology and financial modeling. The insights you will find here are the result of comprehensive research and extensive interviews with industry experts leading the field of quantum finance.

As per recent reports, quantum computing is poised to revolutionize the financial industry. As more institutions adopt this technology and the complexity of the financial models increase, understanding and successfully implementing quantum computing strategies will become a necessity rather than an option. This book aims to guide you through this transition, preparing you for the quantum leap in financial modeling.

Who this book is for

This book is for financial practitioners, quantitative analysts, or developers; looking to bring the power of quantum computing to their organizations. This is an essential resource written for finance professionals, who want to harness the power of quantum computers for solving real-world financial problems. A basic understanding of Python, calculus, linear algebra, and quantum computing is a prerequisite.

What this book covers

Chapter 1, *Quantum Computing Paradigm*, helps readers understand the challenges and limitations of digital technology and how quantum computing can help them overcome these.

Chapter 2, *Quantum Machine Learning and Optimization Algorithms*, considers how quantum machine learning utilizes qubits and quantum operations for specialized quantum systems to improve computational speed and data storage. This is done by algorithms in a program. This chapters explain how the quantum machine learning algorithm works in theory and in real life.

Chapter 3, *Quantum Finance Landscape*, helps readers understand the quantum finance landscape and the types of financial problems to which quantum computing principles can be applied.

Chapter 4, *Derivatives Valuation*, highlights that the valuation of derivatives is often highly complex and can only be carried out numerically—which requires a correspondingly high computing effort. This chapter examines the role of QML algorithms in derivatives valuation.

Chapter 5, *Portfolio Optimization*, considers portfolio management as the process of managing a group of financial securities and making ongoing decisions to meet investment objectives. Portfolio management also includes a number of steps, such as managing costs and risks, allocating assets, researching the market, and choosing securities. This chapter examines the role of QML algorithms in portfolio allocation.

Chapter 6, *Credit Risk Analytics*, outlines how credit risk is associated with the possibility of a client failing to meet contractual obligations, such as mortgages, credit card debts, and other types of loans. Minimizing the risk of default is a major concern for financial institutions. Machine learning models have been helping these companies to improve the accuracy of their credit risk analysis, providing a scientific method to identify potential debtors in advance. Learn how a QML algorithm can help solve this problem using real-world data.

Chapter 7, *Implementation in Quantum Clouds*, dicusses how the implementation of quantum machine learning and optimization architectures in productive environments, or as a backtest for current systems, is a crucial part to retrieve knowledge and start using this technology.

Chapter 8, *Simulators' and HPCs' roles in the NISQ Era*, highlights how classical means and in particular, high-performance hardware, have a key part to play in the delivery of short-term quantum advantage. In this chapter, we will explore some of the most relevant approaches in order to map the quantum-classical landscape comprehensively.

Chapter 9, *NISQ Quantum Hardware Roadmap*, demonstrates how Noisy Intermediate-Scale Quantum (NISQ) Hardware can evolve in various ways depending on the provider. Different approaches, ranging from fault-tolerant logical qubits to circuit knitting, could be among the early steps towards achieving fault-tolerant devices. In this chapter, we outline the key aspects of these approaches and their long-term potential.

Chapter 10, *Business Implementation*, underlines that knowing quantum technology does not guarantee that companies will successfully implement quantum computing with the lowest risk possible. In this chapter, we will provide helpful information for how fintech firms and banks can implement these kinds of projects without getting stuck half-way.

To get the most out of this book

Software/hardware covered in the book	Operating system requirements
Python	Windows, macOS, or Linux
Jupyter notebook	Windows, macOS, or Linux
Dwave Leap	Windows, macOS, or Linux
AWS Braket	Windows, macOS, or Linux
Azure	Windows, macOS, or Linux

If you are using the digital version of this book, we advise you to type the code yourself or access the code from the book's GitHub repository (a link is available in the next section). Doing so will help you avoid any potential errors related to the copying and pasting of code.

Download the example code files

You can download the example code files for this book from GitHub at `https://github.com/PacktPublishing/Financial-Modeling-using-Quantum-Computing`. If there's an update to the code, it will be updated in the GitHub repository.

We also have other code bundles from our rich catalog of books and videos available at `https://github.com/PacktPublishing/`. Check them out!

Download the color images

We also provide a PDF file that has color images of the screenshots and diagrams used in this book. You can download it here: `https://packt.link/1xxSu`.

Conventions used

There are a number of text conventions used throughout this book.

`Code in text`: Indicates code words in text, database table names, folder names, filenames, file extensions, pathnames, dummy URLs, user input, and Twitter handles. Here is an example: "Mount the downloaded `WebStorm-10*.dmg` disk image file as another disk in your system."

A block of code is set as follows:

```
import numpy as np

from scipy.stats import norm

t = 1.0 # year

K = 105 # Strike price

r = 0.05 # Riskless short rate

sigma = 0.25 # Volatility (stdev)

S0 = 100 # Present price
```

When we wish to draw your attention to a particular part of a code block, the relevant lines or items are set in bold:

```
[default]
exten => s,1,Dial(Zap/1|30)
exten => s,2,Voicemail(u100)
exten => s,102,Voicemail(b100)
exten => i,1,Voicemail(s0)
```

Any command-line input or output is written as follows:

```
$ mkdir css
$ cd css
```

Bold: Indicates a new term, an important word, or words that you see onscreen. For instance, words in menus or dialog boxes appear in **bold**. Here is an example: "Select **System info** from the **Administration** panel."

> **Tips or important notes**
> Appear like this.

Get in touch

Feedback from our readers is always welcome.

General feedback: If you have questions about any aspect of this book, email us at `customercare@packtpub.com` and mention the book title in the subject of your message.

Errata: Although we have taken every care to ensure the accuracy of our content, mistakes do happen. If you have found a mistake in this book, we would be grateful if you would report this to us. Please visit `www.packtpub.com/support/errata` and fill in the form.

Piracy: If you come across any illegal copies of our works in any form on the internet, we would be grateful if you would provide us with the location address or website name. Please contact us at `copyright@packtpub.com` with a link to the material.

If you are interested in becoming an author: If there is a topic that you have expertise in and you are interested in either writing or contributing to a book, please visit `authors.packtpub.com`.

Share Your Thoughts

Once you've read *Financial Modeling using Quantum Computing*, we'd love to hear your thoughts! Scan the QR code below to go straight to the Amazon review page for this book and share your feedback.

`https://packt.link/r/1-804-61842-X`

Your review is important to us and the tech community and will help us make sure we're delivering excellent quality content.

Download a free PDF copy of this book

Thanks for purchasing this book!

Do you like to read on the go but are unable to carry your print books everywhere? Is your eBook purchase not compatible with the device of your choice?

Don't worry, now with every Packt book you get a DRM-free PDF version of that book at no cost.

Read anywhere, any place, on any device. Search, copy, and paste code from your favorite technical books directly into your application.

The perks don't stop there, you can get exclusive access to discounts, newsletters, and great free content in your inbox daily

Follow these simple steps to get the benefits:

1. Scan the QR code or visit the link below

https://packt.link/free-ebook/9781804618424

2. Submit your proof of purchase
3. That's it! We'll send your free PDF and other benefits to your email directly

Part 1:
Basic Applications of Quantum Computing in Finance

This segment addresses the complexities of digital technology, its challenges, and the role of quantum computing in overcoming these limitations. It specifically highlights quantum machine learning, a technique that leverages quantum bits and operations to boost computational speed and data storage. Readers will gain a theoretical and practical understanding of quantum machine learning algorithms. The chapter also transitions into quantum finance, shedding light on its potential and illustrating the types of financial issues that can be tackled using quantum computing principles.

This part has the following chapters:

- *Chapter 1, Quantum Computing Paradigm*
- *Chapter 2, Quantum Machine Learning Algorithms*
- *Chapter 3, Quantum Finance Landscape*

1

Quantum Computing Paradigm

Quantum computers have shown the potential to be game-changing for large-scale industries in the near future. Quantum solutions (hardware and software), in their prime, have the potential to put humankind on planet Pluto with their optimized calculations. According to a Gartner report, 20% of organizations will be budgeting for quantum computing projects by 2023 (*The CIO's Guide to Quantum Computing*, `https://tinyurl.com/yrk4rp2u`). This technology promises to achieve better accuracy and deliver real-world experiences via simulations. This book delves into the potential applications of quantum solutions to solve real-world financial problems.

In this chapter, we will discuss various computing paradigms currently in the research phase. A chronicle of quantum computing is also curated and presented. Then, we will cover the limitations faced by classical computers and how these challenges will be overcome with the help of quantum computers. After that, the role of quantum computing in shaping the next generation of business is defined.

Later in the chapter, we will go through the basics of quantum computing. The types of hardware powering quantum computers are described in a subsequent section. We will also look into the potential business applications of this technology and how organizations can align their business strategy accordingly to harness their true potential.

The following topics will be covered in this chapter:

- The evolution of quantum technology and its related paradigms
- Basic quantum mechanics principles and their application
- The business applications of quantum computing

The evolution of quantum technology and its related paradigms

Computing paradigms can be defined as the significant milestones that have been achieved over the years. To say that computers have made the lives of humans easier is an understatement. On a daily basis, we need machines that can analyze, simulate, and optimize solutions to complex problems. Although the shapes and sizes of computers have changed over time, they still operate on the doctrines proposed by Alan Turing and John von Neumann.

In this section, we will study the evolution of quantum technology over the years. We will also study some of the technology's limitations in the face of certain business challenges.

The evolution of computing paradigms

Turing showed us the types of problems computers can solve, von Neumann built programmable computers, and Michael Moore's pioneering work in semiconductors made computers more capable. *Figure 1.1* shows the advancement of computing paradigms over the years, and their ability to affect growth in human history:

1821	Mechanical calculator	Has Enabled humans to migrate from mechanical devices to electronic devices with better accuracy in calculations.
1890	Punch-card system	Demonstrated first use case of large-scale computing by aiding in the US Census.
1936	Turing machine	Theoretical conceptual framework was laid down to solve large computational problems.
1941	Digital electronic computer	First time a computer was able to store information on its main memory.
1945	Electronic Numerical Integrator and Calculator (ENIAC)	First digital computer to perform large class of numerical problems through reprogramming.
1958	Integrated Circuit (IC)	Helped in the transition of enterprise-level computing to personal computing.
1976	Cray-1 Supercomputer	Aided 240 million calculations useful for large-scale scientific applications and simulations.
1997	Parallel computing	Multiple-CPU core was used to solve complex problems in a limited timeframe, enabling Google to form a better search engine.
2006	Cloud computing	Technology has enabled users to access large computational resources from remote locations.

2016	Reprogrammable quantum computer	Offers a better platform to solve complex simulation or optimization problems in comparison to classical computers
2017	Molecular informatics	Harnesses molecular properties for rapid, scalable information storage and processing.

Figure 1.1 – Evolution of computing paradigms

The evolution of computing technology has enabled humans to evolve from an agrarian society to an industrial society. Progress in computing prowess has catapulted society from bartering goods to building e-commerce platforms. *Figure 1.1* has given a conclusive summary of how computing technology has benefitted society through its progression from a device that merely performs calculations to the multifunction device in its present form. In the next section, we are going to assess the challenges faced by large-scale businesses and the limitations of current digital technology in addressing them.

Business challenges and technology solutions

Current digital technologies have advantages as well as limitations in providing solutions and insights in real time. The rise of numerous variables and their increasing complexity can affect decision-making in the real world. It is essential to have technology that is reliable and accurate, and fast-paced at the same time. The need for a reliable technology stack has prompted scientists worldwide to investigate technology that is beyond the reach of humans. The current challenges faced by large-scale businesses are as follows:

- **Faster task completion**: In the current era, where manufacturing firms are looking to achieve super-large-scale production capacity and efficiency, there is a need to build faster and more reliable systems. For instance, according to an exciting study by Artificial Brain (*How Artificial Brain is Building an Optimal Algorithm for EV Charger Placement Using Quantum Annealing and a Genetic Algorithm, Quantum Zeitgeist,* `https://tinyurl.com/bdep5eze`) regarding setting up charging stations within a 50-mile radius in the San Francisco Bay Area, around 8,543,811,434,435,330 combinations were possible. Now, how can this distribution be optimized when such a large number of combinations is possible? A quantum computer theoretically solved this problem in less than 3 seconds.

- **Content discovery**: With the advent of social media websites, a plethora of content is available to analyze. This content is available in different sizes and shapes, in the form of text and images. An organization would need a computer with superior computing power to explore this content. This special computing prowess was achieved through parallel computing and local optimization of the machines. However, much needs to be achieved in this field in order to mine real-time business insights from the underlying data. **Quantum natural language processing (QNLP)** is a promising technique to resolve problems in real time.

- **Lower administration costs**: It is always a good strategy to optimize costs. Automation of mega factories has provided the owners with a solution in the right direction. Large-scale automation comes with a set of problems of its own, but precision and real-time decision-making help to make it more accurate and reliable. Recently, BMW has come up with a challenge where competitors have to focus on solving problems based on pre-production vehicle configuration, material deformation in production, vehicle sensor placement, and machine learning for automated quality assessment. Based on the results obtained, Dr. Peter Lehnert, BMW Group's Vice President of Research and New Technologies Digital Car, commented: "We at the BMW Group are convinced that future technologies such as quantum computing have the potential to make our products more desirable and sustainable" (*Winners announced in the BMW Group Quantum Computing Challenge, AWS Quantum Computing Blog*, `https://aws.amazon.com/blogs/quantum-computing/winners-announced-in-the-bmw-group-quantum-computing-challenge/`).

- **Remote working**: The year 2020 played a pivotal role in the history of humankind. Due to the advent of COVID-19, humans have discovered that they can work from anywhere in the world. This has given rise to the demand for remote working from management and employees. Since there are some instances where you need higher computing power, remote working might not be feasible at all times. However, with most technologies going online and providing a real-time experience of working in the office environment through virtual and augmented reality and better connectivity, businesses can overcome this particular challenge. At the same time, it lowers the administration costs for management. It also helps in reducing storage costs further, which helps in reducing the unit cost for the company.

In order to perform a business task more efficiently and optimally, the business fraternity has started looking for technological solutions. Digital computing in its current state has helped businesses to achieve more efficiency via automation and augmented intelligence. However, current hardware technology has not been able to solve a few complex tasks, which can be associated with an abundance of data and the limitation of computing memory. The following section highlights the types of problems that can be solved by digital computing, and other problems that have generated the need to look beyond the current computing paradigm.

Current business challenges and limitations of digital technology

Digital computers are powered by **integrated circuits** (**ICs**), a technology that reached its peak in the 20th century. According to Moore's law, the number of transistors powering microchips will double every year. In 2021, IBM announced that it can fit 50 billion transistors into its 2 nm chip technology, which basically allows a chip to fit in a space the size of a fingernail. The presence of a large number of transistors has enabled the classical computer to perform large calculations and complex procedures that help in solving day-to-day problems much faster.

However, due to internal leakages and the miniaturization effect, classical gates (OR and AND gates) have been showcasing the quantum effect. Also, digital computers are traditionally unable to solve NP-hard problems (*Figure 1.2*). In layman's language, NP-hard problems are measured by the amount of time it takes to solve a problem based on the complexity and number of variables. An example of this, as discussed previously, is how to choose the optimum route out of the 8,543,811,434,435,330 combinations determined for charging station locations in the San Francisco Bay Area. While it would take years for a classical computer to solve the aforementioned problem, ideally, quantum computers can solve it in 3 seconds.

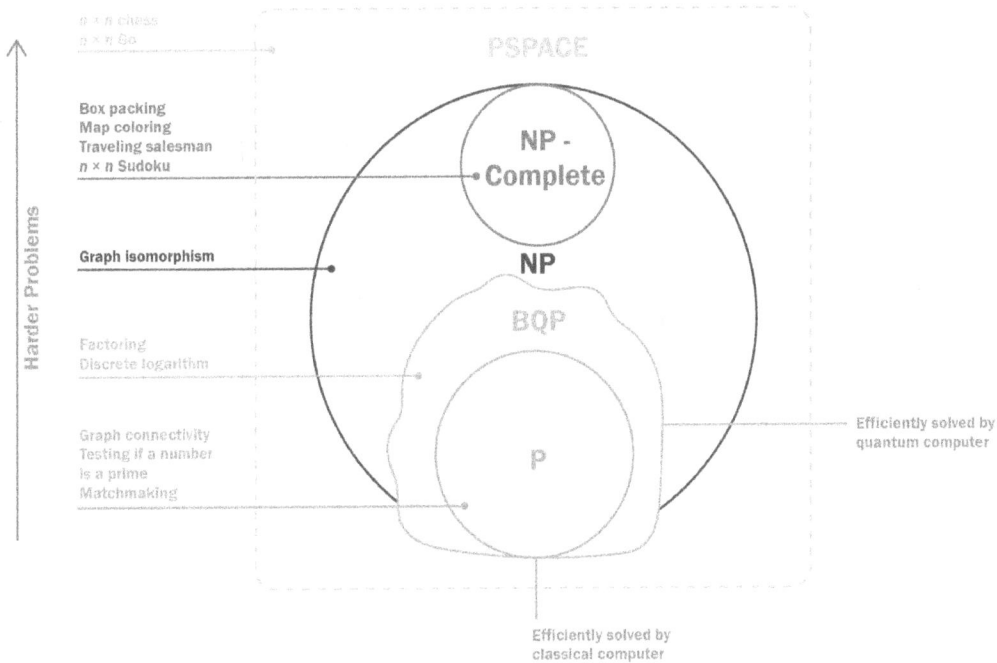

Figure 1.2 – Classification of NP-hard problems based on level of complexity

To understand the limitations of classical computers in a better way, imagine that you have to pick a portfolio of 100 penny stocks with a limited budget, and let's assume that the prices are discrete (for example, tick size on stock markets). Suppose you have to construct a portfolio in polynomial time (p = problems a computer can solve in a reasonable amount of time) and assume that it takes 100 steps (n = no. of inputs) to obtain an optimized portfolio or, in other words, n3 time. Theoretically, digital computers will solve the problem in three hours. This problem was easy to solve, and experts can easily verify the solution since we are dealing with stocks of the same class. Hence, we can confidently say that p-class problems are easy to check and solve. Now, the same problem but with a variation (a portfolio optimization of 100 stocks belonging to different risk classes in a limited time) will take around 300 quintillion years to solve, because although the solution is verifiable in a polynomial (n) timeframe, it is obtained in an exponential (NP) timeframe. This problem is classified as an NP problem. For an analogy, imagine a sudoku or tic-tac-toe problem: this is an NP problem for which it is difficult to obtain the solution (it takes exponential time), but easy to verify in polynomial time.

Following on from the preceding discussion, four types of NP problems that are deemed difficult to be solved by digital computers are as follows:

- **Simulation**: Computation simulation is modeling a natural world or physical system into a virtual scenario to understand its outcome and impact in advance. For instance, after the subprime crisis of 2008, financial institutions must run a stress test on their underlying assets and their crossholdings to predict the scenario in which the next financial crash could occur. According to one estimate, assessing the probability of a financial crash for a simple network of 20-30 institutions, having exposure in equity, derivatives, fixed income securities, and risk exposure to each other, would take 13.7 billion years, as calculated by a digital computer. This is the estimated time of running a simulation problem that is deterministic in nature and hints at solving a problem's complexity in n steps in p time, which will not work using current digital technology and thus requires an advanced system to give a faster turnaround.

- **Optimization**: Optimization refers to improving the efficiency of an existing algorithm to reduce time complexity. Suppose you have to build a portfolio of 1,000 stocks belonging to 10 sectors. Your client, an international hedge fund, will have to generate several scenarios based on market conditions and thus look for an efficient frontier. These scenarios need to be updated in real time, adjusting themselves based on the risk tolerance limit defined for the portfolio. The classical computer may be able to solve the puzzle using parallel computing, but this might not be the most cost-effective and time-effective strategy. This problem underlies a need for an efficient computer to solve the puzzle in real time.

- **Pattern recognition**: The pattern recognition method uses underlying data to discover hidden patterns and trends using machine learning algorithms. However, recent advances in GPU and related technology have enabled programmers to meet with decent success in understanding and uncovering hidden patterns in the given data. In financial fraud, however, the complexity of human behavior makes it difficult for machine learning algorithms to understand the patterns. Theoretically, a computer able to comprehend data in real time can help decode the patterns of financial fraud more successfully.

- **Cryptography**: Providing a secure channel for customers to do transactions online in this e-connected world is a foremost priority for banks in the 21st century. All over the world, banks use **Rivest, Shamir, and Adleman (RSA)** technology based on linear factorization. The recent development of computing prowess hints that such encryption can be easily broken using quantum computers.

To summarize, it will suffice to say that with the limitations observed in current technology, it is time to explore new computing paradigms that can help solve the problems faced by the business fraternity at large and help the industry bring in innovations and creativity.

Basic quantum mechanics principles and their application

Quantum computers use principles and theories (such as quantum field theory and group theory) to describe the quantum mechanics phenomenon. Quantum mechanics principles, such as superposition, decoherence, and entanglement, have been utilized to build processors that process and relay information at exponential speed. The following section maps the quantum computer's evolution journey and briefly describes quantum mechanics principles.

The emerging role of quantum computing technology for next-generation businesses

For a long time, advances in digital computers at economies of scale have suppressed the development of other computing paradigms. Moore's law (*Figure 1.3*) has predicted exponential growth and advancement in the microprocessor. However, the presence of a large amount of data collected over decades of computing advancements has put a limitation on computing power, storage, and communication. To overcome the limits of the current architectures, we must overcome challenges such as finite memory, self-programmable computers, large number factorization, and faster microprocessors.

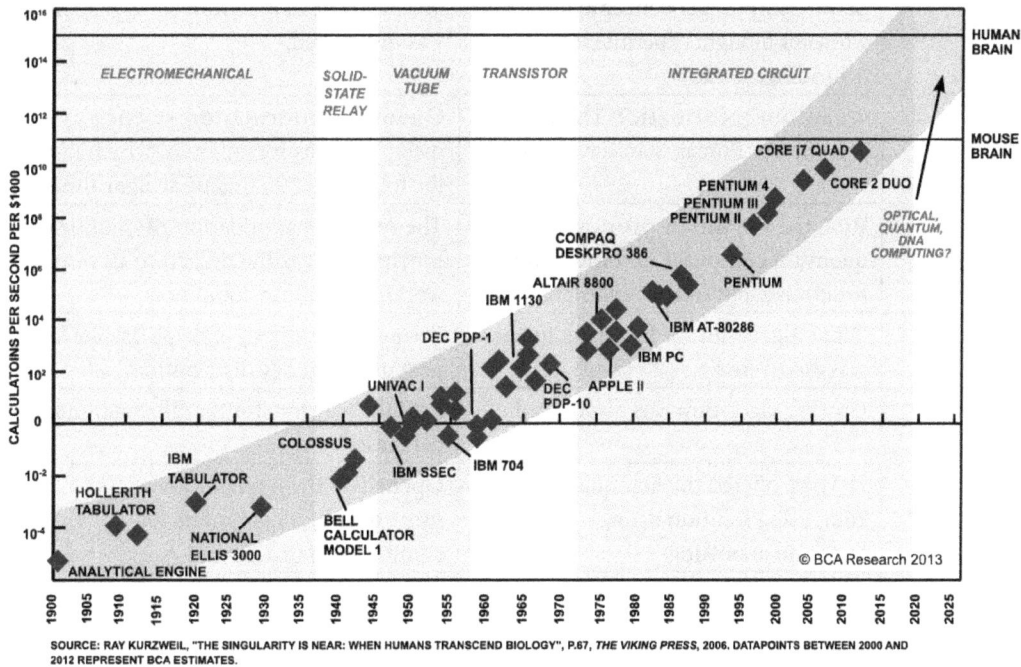

SOURCE: RAY KURZWEIL, "THE SINGULARITY IS NEAR: WHEN HUMANS TRANSCEND BIOLOGY", P.67, *THE VIKING PRESS*, 2006. DATAPOINTS BETWEEN 2000 AND 2012 REPRESENT BCA ESTIMATES.

Figure 1.3 – Transistor number growth according to Moore's law

Looking at the current limitations of digital computers due to their fundamental principles and assumptions, there is a need for new computing paradigms to emerge. To solve the problems related to various domains related to climate, process automation, industry mechanizations, and autonomous systems, there is a need to overcome the current challenges. Quantum computing, molecular computing, nature-inspired algorithms, and synergistic human-machine interaction (Computer's Special Issue September 2016 Examines "Next-Generation Computing Paradigms," IEEE Computer Society, `https://tinyurl.com/4b5wjepk`) are the current areas of interest and innovation in the pursuit of overcoming the aforementioned challenges. *Figure 1.4* charts the journey and impact of the quantum-computing paradigm from theoretical to practical application:

Year	Phenomenon	Effect
1905	Photoelectric effect was discovered by Albert Einstein and discovery of photon took place.	Laid the foundation to discover quantum behavior in atomic particles.
1924 to 1927	Max Born coined the term Quantum Mechanics and Heisenberg, Born, and Jordan discovered matrix mechanics.	Discovery of quantum mechanics principles, which were harnessed to produce the quantum processor.
1935	Erwin Schrödinger conceptualized and wrote his thought experiment known as Schrödinger's cat.	The principle of quantum entanglement was discovered.
1976	Quantum information theory was proposed by Roman Stanisław Ingarden.	Quantum Information science as a discipline was formulated, which laid the foundation for quantum algorithms.
1981	Richard Feynman proposed that a quantum computer had the potential to simulate physical phenomena.	The practical application of quantum mechanics was harnessed to develop working quantum computers.
1994	Shor's algorithm for factoring integers was discovered.	Formulated the basis of cryptography for post quantum key distribution.
1996	Grover's algorithm was discovered.	Laid the way for storing information in database form.
2011	D-Wave offered the first quantum computing solution using quantum annealing.	Opened up the possibilities of using quantum computers for commercial purposes.
2019	Google claimed quantum supremacy.	Showed a use case of quantum supremacy that can help in better encryption.
2021	IBM unveiled the first 127-qubit quantum computer named Eagle.	Facilitated faster processing of the complex NP-hard problem.

Figure 1.4 – Journey from quantum mechanics to quantum computing

As you can see from the evolution point of view (*Figure 1.4*), quantum technologies are making rapid strides to overcome problems such as accurate simulation, efficient optimization, and correct pattern recognition. Once researchers can overcome the related problems that limit current users, and implement quantum technology to solve day-to-day problems, one can see how the industry-wide adoption of quantum technology can solve large-scale problems.

The next section describes some of the common terminologies and principles of quantum mechanics used in building and operating quantum computers.

From quantum mechanics to quantum computing

Deciphering the quantum mechanics principles involved in quantum computing is an uphill task for a layperson. This section describes each quantum mechanics postulate in easy-to-understand language, explaining how it is involved in the quantum computing mechanism.

Postulate	Definition	Usage	Further Reading
Qubits	The qubit is a basic unit of quantum information stored on a two-state device encoding information in 0s and 1s) ·	Facilitates faster processing of information for complex processes like simulation and optimization.	What is a qubit? (quantuminspire.com)
Quantum State	Quantum state is the position and value of attributes (change and spin) of atomic particles obtained naturally or induced by creating physical environments (e.g. laser and heat).	Used in processing and transforming information using qubits in a controlled environment.	Superposition and entanglement (quantuminspire.com)
Quantum Superposition	It refers to a phenomenon that tells us that quantum superposition can be seen as the linear combination of quantum states.	This property makes it hard for a system to decrypt quantum communication and thus provides a safer way to transfer information.	Superposition and entanglement (quantuminspire.com)
Quantum Entanglement	Quantum entanglement refers to the linking of two particles in the same quantum state and the existence of correlation between them.	Facilitates the ability of a system to do calculations exponentially faster by more and more qubits.	Superposition and entanglement (quantuminspire.com)

Quantum Measurement	A set of mathematical operators to understand and measure the amount of information that can be recovered and processed from qubits.	Useful in understanding the complexities of quantum mechanics.	Quantum measurement splits information three ways - Physics World.
Quantum Interference	It refers to the ability of atomic particles to behave like wave particles, thus resulting in information or the collapse of qubit state thus leading to quantum coherence or dechorence.	It measures the ability of quantum computers to accurately compute and carry the information stored in them.	What is quantum mechanics? Institute for Quantum Computing (uwaterloo.ca)
No Cloning Theorem	The "**no cloning theorem**" is a result of quantum mechanics that forbids the creation of identical copies of an arbitrary unknown quantum state.	The no cloning theorem is a vital ingredient in quantum cryptography, as it forbids eavesdroppers fom creating copies of a transmitted quantum cryptographic key.	The no cloning theorem – Quantiki

Figure 1.5 – Quantum computing glossary

The postulates mentioned in *Figure 1.5* have enabled computer scientists to migrate from classical to quantum computers. As we will see in subsequent sections, postulates such as quantum interference and the no-cloning theorem have enabled quantum technologies to come to the fore, and laid the basis for achieving faster, more efficient, and more accurate computational power. The following section will look at technologies fueling innovations in quantum computing paradigms.

Approaches to quantum innovation

In its current form, quantum computing relies on a plethora of technologies to expand its footprint. It will take years for quantum computers to fully reach their commercial potential. However, when they work in hybrid mode (in tandem with classical computers), they are expected to produce much better results than in standalone mode. Let's have a look at the technologies that make them tick:

- **Superconducting**: This technology takes advantage of the superposition property of quantum physics. Information is circulated by two charged electron currents flowing in opposite directions around the superconductor, and then exchanging the info stored in the qubit while entangling each other. This technology needs the quantum computer to be operated at extremely low temperatures.

- **Trapped ions**: An ion is a charged atom (Ca+ or Br+). Suppose a piece of information is coded on this charged atom. The atom is transported from state 0 to state 1 by emitting an energy pulse. This charged atom will carry the information and be decoded with the help of lasers. These ions are trapped in electric fields. Information coded is interpreted using a photonic unit and then passed on using optic fibers.

- **Photonics**: This technology uses photons to carry information in a quantum state. Using current silicon chips, the behavior of photons is controlled, and the information is transmitted over the circuit. Due to its compatibility with existing infrastructure and chip-making capabilities, it shows promise to achieve great success.

- **Quantum dots**: Quantum dots are small semiconducting nanocrystals made up of elements such as silicon and cadmium. Their size ranges from 2 to 10 nm. The physical implementation of a qubit involves exchanging information via charged qubits in capacitive states. Due to its conducive conditions, photonics is less error-prone.

- **Cold atoms**: Cold atoms use a ploy similar to trapped ions, where atoms are cooled below 1 mK and then used as an information highway to bounce off the information. Lasers are programmed to control the quantum behavior of cold atoms, and to then leverage them to transfer data.

To understand the milestones achieved by each technology, we will take the help of DiVincenzo's criteria. In the year 2000, David DiVincenzo proposed a wish list of the experimental characteristics of a quantum computer. DiVincenzo's criteria have since become the main guidelines for physicists and engineers building quantum computers (Alvaro Ballon, *Quantum computing with superconducting qubits*, PennyLane, `https://tinyurl.com/4pvpzj6a`). These criteria are as follows:

- **Well-characterized and scalable qubits**: Numerous quantum systems seen in nature are not qubits; thus, we must develop a means to make them act as such. Moreover, we must integrate several of these systems.

- **Qubit initialization**: We must be able to replicate the identical state within an acceptable error margin.

- **Extended coherence durations**: Qubits will lose their quantum characteristics after prolonged interaction with their surroundings. We would want them to be durable enough to enable quantum processes.

- **Universal set of gates**: Arbitrary operations must be performed on the qubits. To do this, we need both single-qubit and two-qubit gates.

- **Quantification of individual qubits**: To determine the outcome of a quantum computation, it is necessary to precisely measure the end state of a predetermined set of qubits.

Figure 1.6 helps evaluate the promises and drawbacks of each kind of quantum technology based on DiVincenzo's criteria:

	Superconducting	Trapped Ions	Photonics	Quantum Dots	Cold atoms
Well-characterized and scalable qubit	Achieved	Achieved	Achieved	Achieved	Achieved
Qubit initialization	Achieved	Achieved	Achieved	Achieved	Achieved
Extended coherence durations	99.6%	99.9%	99.9%	99%	99%
Universal set of gates	10-50 ns	1-50 us	1 ns	1-10 ns	100 ns
Quantification of individual qubits	Achieved	Achieved	Achieved	Achieved	Achieved

Figure 1.6 – DiVincenzo's criteria

On various parameters, technologies such as superconducting and trapped ions are showing the most promise in overcoming the challenges of quantum technology. While supergiants such as IBM and Google are betting on such technology to develop their quantum computers, new-age start-up technologies, including IQM and Rigetti, are exploring others that are more compatible with the current infrastructure.

In the next section, we will detail the applications and technologies associated with the quantum computing ecosystem.

Quantum computing value chain

Quantum computing technology is still in its infancy. If we have to draw parallels from a technology point of view, in 1975, most of the investors were investing in hardware firms such as IBM, HP, and later Apple, to make sure that people would be able to migrate from mainframe to personal computers. Once the value from hardware had been derived, they started paying attention to software, and firms such as Microsoft came into prominence. According to a report published by BCG, 80% of the funds available are flowing toward hardware companies such as IonQ, ColdQuanta, and Pascal. Key engineering challenges that need to be overcome are scalability, stability, and operations.

Several companies and start-ups are investing in quantum computing. Countries such as the USA ($2 billion), China ($1 billion), Canada ($1 billion), the UK (£1 billion), Germany (€2 billion), France (€1.8 billion), Russia ($790 million), and Japan ($270 million) have pledged huge amounts to achieve quantum supremacy. It has been speculated that quantum solutions, including quantum sensors, quantum communication, and quantum internet, need huge investments to help countries in achieving quantum supremacy. McKinsey has pegged the number of quantum computing start-ups at 200. Also, according to PitchBook (market data analyst), global investment in quantum technologies has increased from $93.5 million in 2015 to $1.02 billion in 2021. A few well-known start-ups that have attracted huge investments recently are Arqit, Quantum eMotion, Quantinuum, Rigetti, D-Wave, and IonQ.

Figure 1.7 shows the potential application of quantum technologies in different fields based on the types of problems solved by quantum computers:

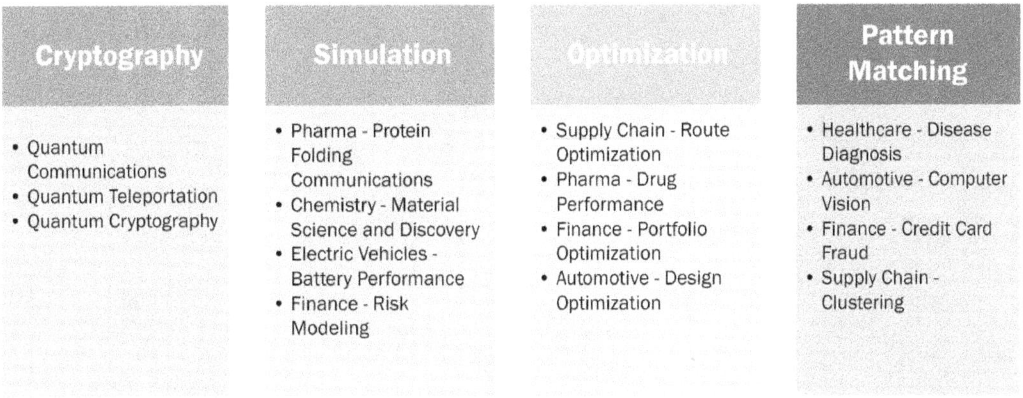

Cryptography	Simulation	Optimization	Pattern Matching
• Quantum Communications • Quantum Teleportation • Quantum Cryptography	• Pharma - Protein Folding Communications • Chemistry - Material Science and Discovery • Electric Vehicles - Battery Performance • Finance - Risk Modeling	• Supply Chain - Route Optimization • Pharma - Drug Performance • Finance - Portfolio Optimization • Automotive - Design Optimization	• Healthcare - Disease Diagnosis • Automotive - Computer Vision • Finance - Credit Card Fraud • Supply Chain - Clustering

Figure 1.7 – Application of quantum computing

The following technologies are helping companies to create the value chain for end users in the quantum realm:

- **Quantum computing**: Quantum computing refers to developing software and hardware technologies using quantum mechanics principles.

- **Quantum key distribution (QKD)**: QKD, or quantum cryptography, provides a secure way for banks and other institutions to exchange encryption keys. It uses principles of quantum mechanics to secure the communication channels.

- **Quantum software and quantum clouds**: Quantum software, or programming languages such as Qiskit, provide a medium for end users to interface with system hardware and perform complex computing operations including simulation, optimization, and pattern recognition.

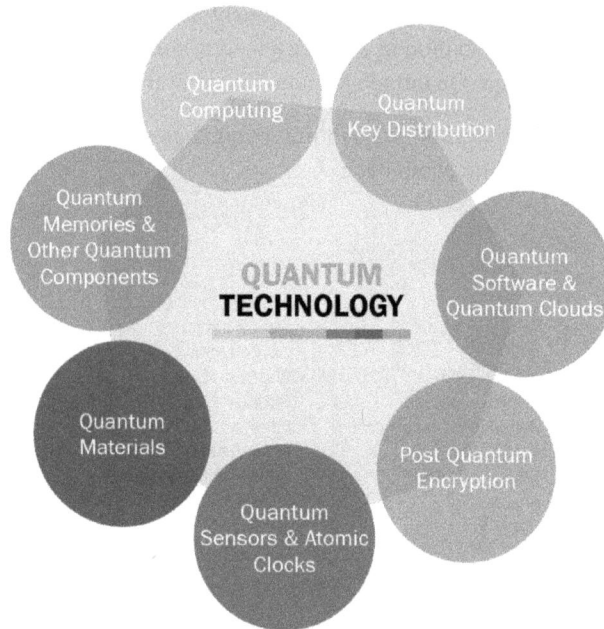

Figure 1.8 – Quantum technology

- **Post-quantum encryption**: One of the key research areas that have prompted countries to invest billions of dollars is the hunch that current encryption software will be susceptible to quantum algorithms. They need algorithms that can secure these channels further.

- **Quantum sensors and atomic clocks**: These terms refer to the development of laser and trapped-ion technologies to control the atomic behavior of molecules. This has prompted researchers to develop use cases where next-gen technologies such as quantum sensors will be useful in the early detection of natural calamities, including tsunamis and earthquakes.

- **Quantum materials**: Quantum materials refers to the cluster of world-class technologies that help capture and manipulate elements' quantum properties for industrial usage.

- **Quantum memories and other quantum components**: These devices carry information in qubit form via photons. It is complex technology that is still under development and is expected to overcome the memory barriers defined by current limitations.

As observed in *Figure 1.8*, the quantum computing ecosystem is vast. It has multiple facets such as quantum materials, memories, and sensors, empowering the user to collect and analyze data more effectively.

In the following section, we will look at the companies powering the revolution in quantum technologies.

The business application of quantum computing

Although it is still in its infancy and yet to achieve a commercial application, quantum technology holds much promise. In the near future, quantum computers will be able to help accelerate the pace of solving complex problems in conjunction with classical computers. In this section, you will learn about the business applications of this wonderful technology.

Global players in the quantum computing domain across the value chain

According to a McKinsey report (Quantum computing funding remains strong, but talent gap raises concern, `https://tinyurl.com/5d826t55`), quantum technology has attracted a total investment of $700 million from various governments and funding agencies. The promise shown by this technology has prompted the industry to fund ongoing research in various universities and labs. D-Wave was the first company to pioneer the quantum computing solution in 1999, through quantum annealing. Since then, other companies such as IBM have built a robust community of researchers and end users alike to propagate the use of quantum computers. The following is a brief list of the companies doing pioneering work in the field of quantum technology:

- **IonQ** (NASDAQ: IONQ): IonQ was founded in 2015 by Christopher Monroe and Jungsang Kim. IonQ has received total funding of $432 million. IonQ builds quantum computers based on ion trap technology. It provides quantum computers as **Platform as a Service** (**PaaS**) to service providers.

- **Rigetti** (NASDAQ: RGTI): Rigetti Computing was founded in 2013 by Chad Rigetti. It has currently received funding of $500 million. Rigetti has developed a quantum computer based on superconducting technology.

- **Quantum Computing Inc.**: Quantum Computing Inc. focuses on providing software and hardware solutions to the end user. It is also focusing on developing business use cases for companies, thus showcasing the potential of quantum computing in the near future.

- **Archer** (ASX: AXE): Archer is an Australian company that is conducting research on developing a quantum computer at room temperature. It was founded by Dr. Mohammad Choucair. It aims to produce a quantum computer that can have a widespread reach.

- **D-Wave** (coming soon via SPAC merger): D-Wave is credited with introducing the world's first quantum computer for commercial use. It uses the quantum annealing technique to develop quantum solutions for the end user. It offers a limited but powerful piece of technology with 5,000 qubits of quantum computer at its disposal, which has a lot of potential business applications.

- **Quantinuum**: Quantinuum was formed as a result of a merger between Cambridge Quantum and Honeywell Quantum Solutions. While the primary focus of Cambridge Quantum was on developing the operating system and software for quantum computers, Honeywell has focused primarily on developing the quantum computer using ion trap technology.

Global players across the value chain in the quantum computing domain include giants such as IBM, Microsoft, and Google, and well-funded start-ups such as Rigetti, IQM, and Quantinuum. These companies have invested in different types of technologies (hardware as well as software) to catapult the research in this technology domain.

In the subsequent segment, we will evaluate the roadmap provided by different technology giants to achieve full-scale quantum supremacy.

Building a quantum computing strategy implementation roadmap

Building quantum advantage to solve real-time business problems is the end goal of many companies operating in the quantum realm. This technology is perceived to aid companies in solving large-scale problems. Recently, BMW has commissioned a million-dollar challenge to discover a solution to its inventory scheduling problem using the **AWS Amazon Braket** platform. In *Figure 1.9*, you can chart the route that could potentially lead to the era in which quantum supremacy can be achieved, and see how we can solve more problems using quantum computing:

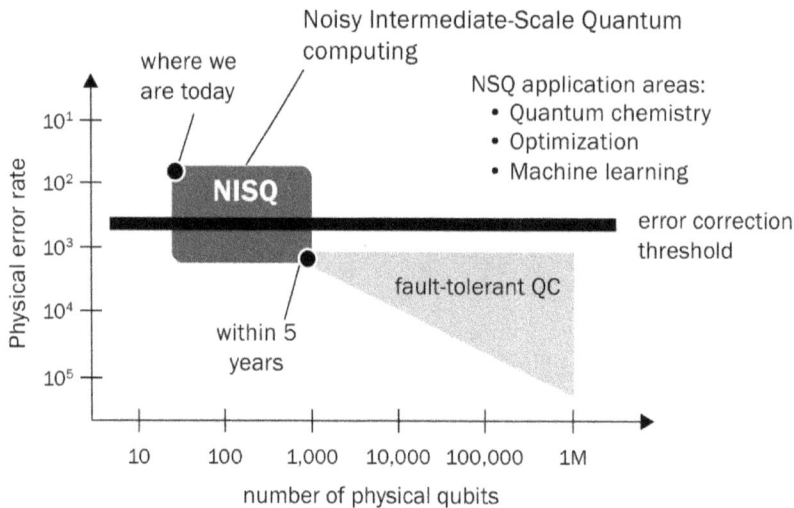

Figure 1.9 – Quantum computing era

Broadly, the quantum era can be divided into three parts:

- **Noisy intermediate-scale quantum** (**NISQ**): This era is marked by the availability of a lesser number of good-quality qubits (<50 to 100) to solve real-world problems. The word *noisy* refers to the tendency of the qubits to lose their quantum state due to disturbances. It is expected that the current technology setup will be able to come out of the NISQ era by 2030.

- **Broad quantum advantage**: IonQ has defined the broad quantum advantage as the advent of the era where quantum computers are available for developers and end users to solve real-life problems. Based on the consensus developed by industry practitioners, 72-qubit systems will start aiding the industry in solving commercial-grade problems. Thus, it will be possible in the future to access the platform enabled by demonstrating high-level application programming and HMI functions.

- **Full-scale fault tolerance**: This era refers to large-scale quantum computers that have achieved two-qubit gate fidelity of 99.5%. By 2040, it is expected that the existing efforts will help in solving the problem of **decoherence** (leakage of information due to large numbers of qubits), and will enable organizations to take full advantage of this amazing technology.

Quantum technology in the near term is available for end users in the form of hybrid computing. To harness the full potential of existing quantum computers, players such as D-Wave and Rigetti have started providing an interface between classical and quantum computing via microprocessors. While classical components take care of communication with end users, quantum microprocessors are used in solving NP-hard problems. Quantum technology, through quantum annealers and universal quantum computers, and using technologies such as superconducting and ion trap, will be able to harness its full potential in the near future.

In the next section, let's have a look at what kind of people are needed to build quantum technology and its ecosystem.

Building a workforce for a quantum leap

Quantum technology needs a variety of people in the workforce to harness its true potential. The entire technology stack can be divided into hardware, software, and related technologies. Currently, the technology has called for scientific research and technology implementation experts. According to a survey report prepared by Forbes, a graduate must have a primary degree in STEM to understand the basic workings of quantum computers. A research-oriented mindset is essential to further investigate the development of quantum computers. To achieve scientific breakthroughs related to the development of computer hardware, a researcher must have a deep understanding of the underlying technologies such as annealing, superconducting, and ion trap. These technologies are at the forefront of the scientific breakthroughs that can be achieved with the help of a knowledgeable workforce.

In addition to building a quantum computer, it is also challenging to operate one. The current focus of software development is to write low-level programs that can interface with the memory core of the quantum computer. IBM and Google are among the companies that have developed Python-based **software development toolkits** (**SDKs**) such as Qiskit and Cirq. Programs such as IBM Summer School are good starting points for developers to get acquainted with the methodology of software interfacing with quantum memory processors. Due to the limitations of the current technology in the quantum field, a lot of emphasis is given to developing a hybrid computer. A software developer needs to know about cloud computing to operate a quantum computer. Most quantum computers are nested in big rooms at below-freezing temperatures, and can be accessed remotely using cloud computing. The algorithms written for quantum computers are also used to boost the performance of existing machine learning algorithms.

Quantum solutions also include aided technologies, making quantum technologies an exciting field to work in. Quantum sensors, annealers, and the internet are the potential applications of quantum mechanics. In addition, quantum algorithms have also shown promise in solving problems related to finance, supply chain, healthcare, and cryptography. *Figure 1.8* summarizes the discussion related to the aptitudes and qualifications related to starting a career in the field of quantum technologies:

	Research Areas	**Application**	**Potential Qualification**
Hardware	Quantum Mechanics, Theoretical Physics, Applied Physics	Superconducting Ion Traps, Quantum Dot	PhD, Master's in Quantum Physics
Software	Quantum Information Science	Quantum Algorithms, Quantum Machine Learning	Software Development, Master's in Computer Science
Quantum Business Technologies	Optimization, Simulation and Cryptography	Finance, Supply-Chain, Healthcare	Business Evangelist, Domain Expert

Figure 1.10 – List of qualifications

From *Figure 1.10*, it can be observed that a potential candidate for quantum technologies needs some background in STEM. Research aptitude and a capacity to learn, unlearn, relearn, and apply new concepts are a must to sustain in this dynamic field. Since it's a research-oriented field, companies' inclination is more toward inducting doctoral candidates from relevant fields. However, there is a significant demand for software engineers who can write code for hybrid computers to solve problems in a faster and more accurate way.

Summary

Computing paradigms, such as calculators and analog and digital computers, have evolved over the years to assist humans in making rapid strides in technological developments and reaching new knowledge frontiers. The contributions of Jon von Neumann, Alan Turing, and Graham Moore have been immense in achieving superior computing power.

The current business environment has given rise to the need to make faster and more accurate decisions based on data. Hence, there is a need for faster, optimized computers to process large amounts of data.

Digital computers cannot solve NP-hard problems, including simulation, optimization, and pattern-matching problems, thus emphasizing the need for new computing technologies to do faster and more accurate calculations.

Emerging computing paradigms, such as quantum computing and molecular computing, promise to solve large-scale problems such as portfolio optimization, protein foldings, and supply chain route optimization more effectively and efficiently.

Quantum computing is based on the underlying principles of quantum mechanics such as qubits and the quantum states, superposition, interference, entanglement, and quantum measurement.

Current quantum hardware and microprocessors are based on technologies such as superconducting, trapped ions, annealing, cold atoms, and simulators.

The quantum computing value chain is based on the innovations achieved using quantum solutions and technologies such as quantum sensors, quantum communication, and the quantum internet.

Global players across the value chain in the quantum computing domain include giants such as IBM, Microsoft, and Google, and well-funded start-ups such as Rigetti, IQM, and Quantinuum.

Aligning business strategy with quantum computing involves developing the strategy roadmap for companies based on quantum computing eras such as NISQ, broad quantum advantage, and full-scale fault tolerance.

The future quantum workforce needs to work on three dimensions, concerning the development of hardware, software, and related quantum technologies.

2

Quantum Machine Learning Algorithms and Their Ecosystem

In recent decades, many quantum computing scientists have leaned towards researching and generating quantum algorithms and their practical realization (*Cerezo et al., 2021; Montanaro, 2016*). As discussed in the previous chapter, quantum computers differ from classical computers mainly in the form of computation they employ. They can solve problems that are intractable for classical systems (*Arute et al., 2019*). In a quantum computer, instead of classical bits, **qubits** are the fundamental unit of information. The implementation of quantum algorithms is based fundamentally on the physical qualities of these qubits compared to classical bits. Still, the physical realization of quantum computers has not yet reached the level of maturity attained by their classical counterparts, where millions of transistors can be placed in a limited space without compromising their accuracy or functioning.

Noise and error control are crucial for quantum information processing, and effective strategies to deal with noise are an active area of research (as reviewed by *Fedorov et al., 2022*). In this regard, **quantum error correction** (QEC) protocols have been proposed to tame the effects of noise (*Campagne-Ibarcq et al., 2020*). Unfortunately, even with the progress made in QEC so far, we haven't yet developed fault-tolerant machines; the number of qubits required to pass from physical to logical qubits (without errors) is too substantial. Current quantum gate-based devices have a magnitude of around 100 physical qubits, and are often referred to as **Noisy Intermediate-Scale Quantum** (NISQ) devices given their imperfect operations (*Bharti et al., 2021*). In this context, one possibility for realizing fault-tolerant quantum computation is to scale up the number of qubits while ensuring they remain usable via efficient implementation and measurement operations. More detail on how we can work in this error-filled environment will be covered in *Chapter 9*.

Classical computers have not yet been dethroned, in any case. Classical computers have been used for many tasks, and realizing quantum computation and interfacing with quantum devices is essential, particularly when data is involved. Most of the data we use daily comes in bytes, so it is necessary to use classical resources for storing, preprocessing, and postprocessing, as well as describing the algorithm implementations that will run on our specialized hardware: the quantum computer.

These quantum and classical algorithms can be applied in many regimes to solve problems related to our daily activity. In particular, one area that has attracted a lot of attention is **Quantum Machine Learning (QML)**, where **Variational Quantum Algorithms (VQAs)** represent the family of algorithms that use classical computing to find the parameters of a **Parameterized Quantum Circuit (PQC)** or ansatz (as it is called in the literature). Specific implementations of the VQA family that will be explained in this chapter are the **Variational Quantum Eigensolver (VQE)**, **Variational Quantum Solver (VQS)**, **Variational Quantum Classifier (VQC)**, and **Quantum Approximate Optimization Algorithm (QAOA)**. These are the most well-known ones, but we will also examine some variations, modified versions, and different implementations related to specific **Software Development Kits (SDKs)**, code languages, platforms, and hardware (*Cerezo et al., 2021*).

One of the first tasks we must tackle when dealing with those algorithms is encoding our classical data into the quantum regime. Quantum algorithms work using quantum states; we will need to encode our data in those states to be able to take advantage of quantum algorithms. One of the first implementations that used this mapping between classical and quantum regime was kernel methods, which demonstrated the advantages of quantum encoding when tackling the challenges of supervised machine learning (*Mengoni et al., 2019*). These algorithms employ conventional machine learning models such as a **Support Vector Machine (SVM)** but benefit from classical data encoding in quantum states, allowing for better data separability. Their advantages derive from quantum computers' ability to recognize intrinsic labeling patterns in datasets that, to classical computers, appear as random noise. This recognition feature is specific to data that requires more than two or three dimensions to be properly represented for classification (nonlinear embeddings) and is often difficult to interpret.

This chapter offers a survey of the NISQ-era algorithms, focusing on the efforts to draw the highest computational potential from existing devices and develop techniques to meet the sector's long-term goals, including fault-tolerant quantum computation. In the quest to derive advantages from the current state of quantum computing, hybrid quantum-classical and quantum-inspired algorithms represent one of the best current approaches to challenges including QML, optimization, and simulations (*Gilyén et al., 2022*).

There are dozens of **quantum computing (QC)** algorithms throughout the literature, and more are under investigation. This chapter will exemplify the use cases, articles, platforms, and implementation methods in the contemporary NISQ stage. QC companies and academic groups have made efforts to make the most of the advantages of QC in the present day. For this purpose, they have implemented most of the algorithms shared in this chapter and the following pages. These will be presented in detail and from different angles for a better understanding of the libraries, code languages, cloud services, and qubit-realization approaches, highlighting the most important players of this ecosystem.

To summarize, this chapter will cover the following:

- Baseline quantum algorithms (Grover, Shor, Deutsch-Jozsa, and others)
- The main NISQ QML and optimization algorithms (variational, quantum-kernel-based, and QUBO-based)
- Technological ecosystems that use the aforementioned algorithms (code languages, libraries or SDKs, hardware, clouds, and tools)
- Technical challenges (using real-world data, analyzing business applications, and current advantages)

Technical requirements

To be able to follow this chapter, you will require the following technical skills:

- A basic level of Python
- Familiarity with Visual Studio Code or any **Integrated Development Environment** (**IDE**) that supports Jupyter Notebooks

Foundational quantum algorithms

A review of foundational quantum algorithms is necessary to understand the state-of-the-art progress in QC and its potential to overcome problems intractable for classical computation. Starting from the basic concepts, an algorithm is a series of computer-executable steps to conduct a computation or solve a problem (*Montanaro, 2016*). Consequently, an algorithm is considered quantum when it successfully performs on a quantum machine. Generally speaking, all classical algorithms could theoretically perform on such a system. Nevertheless, in a strict sense, quantum algorithms refer to those with at least one step involving quantum mechanical properties, such as superposition or entanglement. One of the main attributes of quantum computers is quantum parallelism, which allows for many existing quantum algorithms (*Álvarez et al., 2008*).

A quantum circuit often characterizes a quantum algorithm. A quantum circuit is a structure where the problem-solving stages are performed on ≥ 1 qubits that modify their quantum status; this procedure is known as a quantum gate (*Chow et al., 2012; Mitarai et al., 2018*). Quantum gates are divided into single, two-qubit, or three-qubit gates based on how many qubits they simultaneously operate on. All quantum circuits terminate with a measurement of one or more qubits.

Figure 2.1 shows how to construct a Bell state (an entangled two-qubit state) to exemplify this process. The circuit is read from left to right, starting with the basic state of all devices composed by $|0\rangle$ state qubits (two in this case). The first gate we see is the Hadamard gate, which puts the qubit in a superposition state ($|0\rangle + |1\rangle$), which ends up being all possible options from a classical bit perspective. One of the most used gates is the following blue gate entangling both qubits, the CNOT gate. This acts over the second qubits if the first one is active ($|1\rangle$). Therefore, at this stage, the quantum state looks as follows:

$$|\Phi^+\rangle = \tfrac{1}{\sqrt{2}}\left(|0\rangle_A \otimes |0\rangle_B + |1\rangle_A \otimes |1\rangle_B\right)$$

This is the canonical representation of one of the Bell states. After this, we only need to measure our quantum state into a sequence of classically read bits.

> **Note**
>
> Bell states are the simplest form of states for quantum entanglement. This means the state can't be separated into the state of each qubit. The entanglement is the result of the CNOT gate (blue gate in *Figure 2.1*).

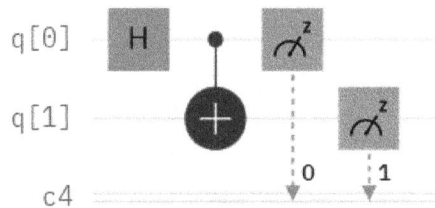

Figure 2.1 – Quantum circuit of two qubits under Hadamard and
CNOT gates. The result is a Bell state entanglement

In many instances, quantum algorithms can be more effective under the simultaneous usage of classical and quantum computers for the same task. Comparing classical and quantum means to solve a task takes the complexity order shown in *Figure 2.2*. The order of complexity a problem may belong to is often discussed in terms of whether it is solvable in **polynomial time (P)**. If not, we enter the **Nondeterministic-Polynomial time** family (**NP**), meaning we face quite a challenging task for classical computation. Portfolio optimization, for example, which will be discussed in *Chapter 5*, is known to be NP-complete (*Kellerer, 2000*). Quantum algorithms are frequently under the umbrella of a **Bounded-Error Quantum Polynomial-Time (BQP)** complexity class (*Yung, 2019*). The latter is a category of judgment problems that can be solved by quantum computers in polynomial time with a maximum error chance of ⅓.

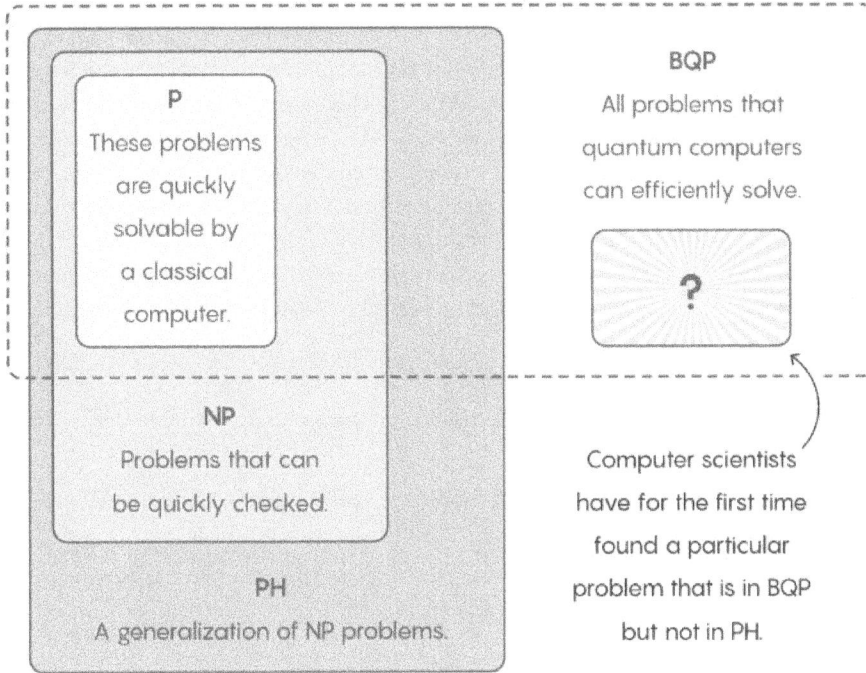

Figure 2.2 – Graphical representation of the connection between
the problems of BQP and classical P, NP, and PH

Note

Complexity theory (**CT**) primarily involves the evaluation of quantum computation. In CT, an algorithm or a family of problems is typically associated with a specific class. *Figure 2.2* illustrates the connections between several classes. **Polynomial Hierarchy** (**PH**) serves as a broader class than NP, indicating higher complexity levels.

As mentioned earlier, a broad overview of the quantum algorithms that impacted the history of this field should be conducted to better understand the current trends of QC and the foundations of contemporary algorithms.

We will now look at three foundational algorithms.

Deutsch-Jozsa algorithm

This is a quantum algorithm that solves a particular problem in linear time, for which a classical algorithm would require exponential time. Consequently, it is considered one of the first quantum algorithms to demonstrate a quantum speedup over its classical counterpart (*Z. Li et al., 2020*). It was named after David Deutsch and Richard Jozsa, who proposed the algorithm in 1992 (*Deutsch et al., 1992*). It can be used to determine whether a Boolean function is balanced or constant. If the function is constant, Deutsch's algorithm will output 0, while in the balanced case, the output will be 1. This means that the worst case in the classical regime will estimate half of the values plus one (*0.5*n+1, where n is the number of inputs*) to test the function to find whether it is constant or balanced.

Figure 2.3 shows the actual form it takes when described over quantum registers with the following steps:

1. Apply Hadamard gates so that all combinations of classically readable values (0 and 1) are considered.

2. Apply a unitary gate to encode the output for a given function in the last qubit that is initialized as $|1\rangle$ (instead of the usual $|0\rangle$ state).

3. Apply back the Hadamard gate to all qubits and measure the first N qubits used as function input.

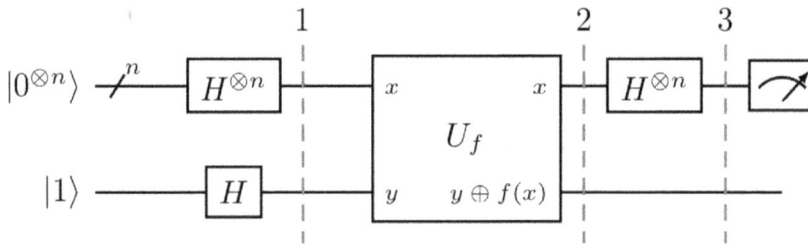

Figure 2.3 – Deutsch-Jozsa's schematic circuit

It uses what is called an oracle (black box unitary) that performs the action of a binary function $f(x):\{0,1\}^n \rightarrow \{0,1\}$ where x represents the inputs to which a Hadamard gate is applied in the preceding figure. Thanks to the action over the qubit initiated with state $|1>$ and the effect it has over the entry qubits upon the effect of the oracle, the Deutsch-Jozsa algorithm is able to establish whether a binary is balanced or constant. An oracle (black box) is a function in which the properties are unknown in advance, but that you can call with queries in order to determine them. You have inputs and outputs to evaluate the operation of the oracle.

This algorithm accelerates the search to determine whether a function possesses a particular attribute (being balanced). The algorithm saves time since it requires the function (or, more accurately, a function derivative) to be called *only once*, as opposed to the $\frac{n}{2} + 1$ times that a classical algorithm requires (*n* being the input size). When the function is extremely "expensive," for example, in terms of processing resources, it might be advantageous to compute it just once.

Grover's algorithm

In 1996, Lov Grover developed a quantum technique that locates an item four times faster than traditional search methods for unsorted databases. This search method for unstructured data is known as Grover's algorithm (*Grover, 1996*), and can alternatively be described as an oracle. As previously defined in the Deutsch-Jozsa section, the oracle will be evaluated repeatedly to determine its characteristics.

An example of such a task is searching for a specific card in a shuffled deck of N cards. Traditionally, this can only be done by sequentially examining each card, requiring N steps in the worst-case scenario using classical approaches (N evaluations for N cards). In contrast, Grover's algorithm achieves this task with just $\sqrt{N}$ oracle evaluations, resulting in a time complexity of $O(\sqrt{N})$ in the worst case. However, it is important to note that the probability of obtaining the correct answer is not guaranteed to be 100 percent due to the influence of the algorithm's phases.

Figure 2.4 shows the quantum circuit that implements Grover's algorithm. It follows a similar shape to the previous example.

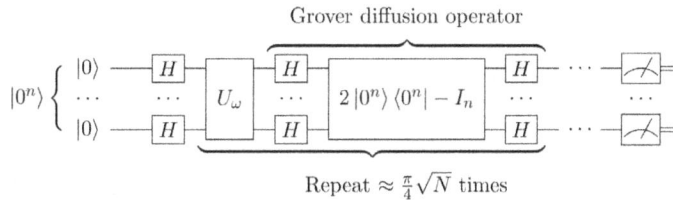

Figure 2.4 – Grover's algorithm schematic circuit

For the two-qubit case, the first set of Hadamard gates puts our initial $|00\rangle$ state, into the superposition of all potential combinations:

$$|\psi\rangle = \tfrac{1}{2}(|00\rangle + |01\rangle + |10\rangle + |11\rangle)$$

Then we apply the unitary operator U of our problem so that the solution gets tagged by a phase change by putting a minus sign in front of it.

$$|\psi\rangle = \tfrac{1}{2}(|00\rangle - |01\rangle + |10\rangle + |11\rangle)$$

Thanks to this flagging, the Grover operator can identify our candidate solution state such that we would measure $|01\rangle$ at the end of our first iteration. An illustration can be seen in *Figure 2.5*:

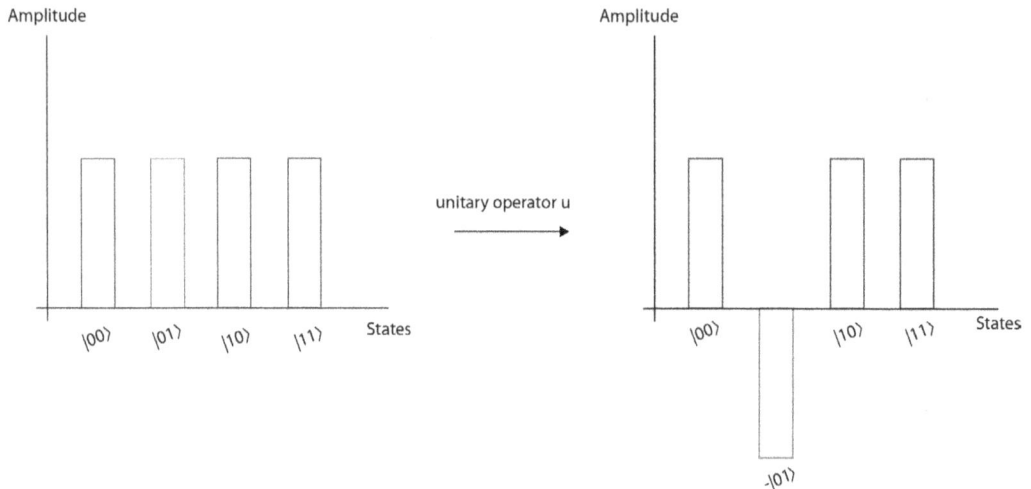

Figure 2.5 – Phase change of the flag element by Grover's algorithm during the first application

When the oracle function has N potential input values (4 in our two-qubit system), the approach requires only $O(\sqrt{N})$ evaluations. In contrast, the best classical algorithm requires $O(N)$ executions. That is why, by only applying our Grover operator one time, we were able to find the solution to our problem in the example just shown.

This could be used to efficiently search in a big search space (a needle in a haystack). We will see how to use it in *Chapter 5* to find the best portfolio from all potential combinations.

To summarize, the core of Grover's algorithm is *amplitude amplification*. This is the process that Grover's algorithm uses to speed up the search. It's all about manipulating the probability amplitudes of the quantum states involved. The process works as follows:

1. **Initial state**: At the beginning of Grover's algorithm, you start with a quantum system in an equal superposition of all possible states. This means that if you have a system of n qubits, you have 2^n possible states, and each of these states has the same probability of $1/2^n$.

2. **Oracle application**: An oracle is then applied to the system, which inverts the state sign corresponding to the solution. This means the solution state now has a negative amplitude while all other states retain their positive amplitude.

3. **Amplitude amplification**: The amplitude amplification process then amplifies the amplitude (or probability) of the correct state and decreases the amplitude of the incorrect states. It is achieved by applying the Grover diffusion operator (also called Grover iteration), which flips the state around the mean amplitude.

Steps *2* and *3* are repeated approximately $\sqrt{N}$ times to maximize the amplitude of the correct state.

The beauty of Grover's algorithm is that the amplitude of the "correct" state (the solution we're interested in) gets amplified after each iteration of the algorithm. By contrast, the amplitudes of the "incorrect" states get reduced. This leads to a high probability of measuring the correct state when the final measurement is made.

Shor's algorithm

The mathematician Peter Shor was working on the discrete log problem in 1994. Using the quantum Fourier transformation, he found a solution by using the periodicity between two numbers. He then extended his discovery to the factorization problem. Factorization can be used to find the prime numbers of an integer.

The main approach to encrypting data is the RSA protocol, which employs asymmetric encryption by generating public and private keys based on multiplying two big prime numbers. Shor's algorithm could find these two prime numbers by factoring in the key. Classically, this problem is intractable because cracking a 2,048-bit RSA key would require thousands of years with an **high-performance computing (HPC)**. Shor's can break the key in polynomial time. This algorithm can't be yet used to break the 2,048-bit RSA key due to the high number of qubits required.

Shor's method is probabilistic, as are many other algorithms. Specifically, it provides the right response with a robust degree of probability, and the likelihood of failure can decrease through repetition of the procedure.

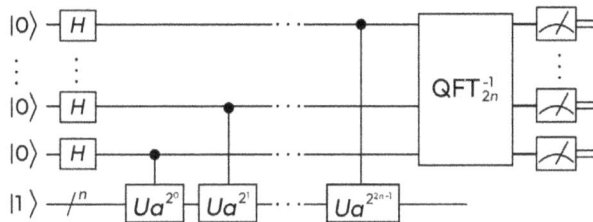

Figure 2.6 – Shor's algorithm schematic circuit

Figure 2.6 shows that the algorithm performs two main actions besides the already covered superposition by the Hadamard gates. The qubit at the bottom (1) are used as the entry point, and the remaining qubits (0) the ones used to encode our solution. The first stage applies different exponents of a given function to the qubit below, which switches phases in the qubit that applies the action. By the action of an inverse quantum Fourier transformation (QFT^{-1}), we can read the set of bit strings that encodes a numeric value encoding the phase that is used to derive the two numbers factoring our target value N.

Next, we will explore a new field that has been created from the merge of **Quantum Computing (QC)** and **Machine Learning (ML)**, called **Quantum Machine Learning (QML)** (*Martín-Guerrero et al., 2022*).

QML algorithms

This discipline combines classical machine learning with quantum capabilities to produce better solutions. Enhancing ML algorithms and/or classical training with quantum resources broadens the scope of pure ML, as happens with some classical devices such as GPUs or TPUs.

It has been extensively reported that using quantum approaches in learning algorithms could have several advantages (reviewed by *Schuld et al., 2018*). However, most of the earliest research in this framework chased a decrease in computational complexity in conjunction with a speedup. Current investigations also study methods for quantum techniques to provide unconventional learning representations that could even outperform standard ML in the future.

In recent years, the theories and techniques of QC have evolved rapidly, and the potential benefits for real-world applications have become increasingly evident (*Deb et al., 2021; Egger et al., 2021*). How QC may affect ML is a key topic of research. Recent experimentations have demonstrated that quantum computers may successfully tackle certain problems with intricate correlations between inputs that are exceptionally challenging for conventional systems.

There is a consensus that quantum computers could provide advantages in several applications. However, they are not yet a perfect substitute for classical ML. The quantum models generated by QC may be significantly more effective for particular applications, enabling faster processing time and generalization with less input. Consequently, it is crucial to ascertain whether a quantum advantage can be realized.

The following sections offer a thorough review of the most relevant QML algorithms.

Variational Quantum Classifiers

Variational Quantum Classifiers (VQCs) belong to the regime of hybrid algorithms as they require a classical interaction in order to set the free parameters of the quantum ansatz. The *Variational* part determines how the quantum circuit is iteratively trained based on some classical criteria that ensure the parameters are selected to make the circuit converge on a target objective. When this objective is a classification task between labels of a given dataset, that makes our algorithm a VQC (*W. Li et al., 2021*). *Figure 2.7* shows the canonical steps of the VQC. Data must be preprocessed and introduced in the first step to represent the classical data as a quantum state. Previously, we have shown examples where the Hadamard action set all potential combinations on the initial encoding state. We use a feature map (a specific type of quantum circuit) to encode the classical data into quantum states.

Then a set of parameterized gates are described to represent different configurations (we will cover that in detail later), and finally, a measuring step where the outcome is obtained. The key step in VQC is the measurement; the output becomes classical and is used to update the parameters of the parametrized circuit. This procedure is similar to a neural network where the output is used to compute the loss.

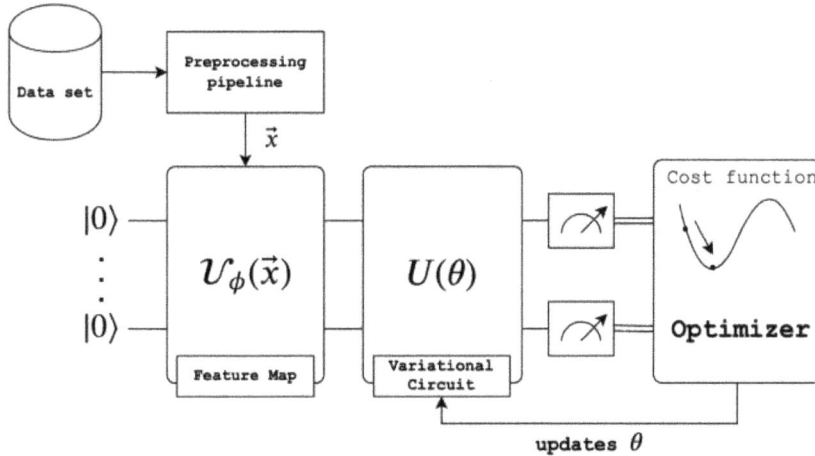

Figure 2.7 – VQC schematic circuit

Gradient- and non-gradient-based techniques can be used to train a QML model. The gradient-based approaches are known to be prone to falling into local minima of a function during the classical execution.

Quantum regimens may overcome this fact thanks to quantum tunneling, even though some problems known to classical methods are magnified in the quantum regime (vanishing gradients or barren plateaus, among others). That is why a big effort exists to design **parameterized circuits (PQC)** or ansatz and methods to deal with those issues, in the hope of surpassing classical means.

When defining those PQCs, we can also learn from classical ML and mimic what is known to be the Swiss Army knife of the field: neural networks.

Quantum neural networks

Quantum neural networks (**QNNs**) are a subtype of VQA that consist of circuits with parameterized gate operations (*Abbas et al., 2021*) as described earlier. Initially, the information is encoded into prepared quantum states that may involve a feature map. Typically, the choice of a specific feature map is made to improve the performance of the quantum model that needs to be optimized and trained. This feature map, represented as a yellow box in *Figure 2.8*, refers to the step where our data gets encoded into the circuit. After data has been encoded into a quantum state, a PQC or ansatz (the variational model in blue) with parameterized gates is applied and optimized for a specific job. The states at the output of the variational model are then measured to estimate the loss function. Then the classical parts estimate the error and propagate it to the estimations of the parameters in the PQC. This whole pass from the initialization of the qubits to the final measurement phase describes a QNN, as shown in *Figure 2.8*.

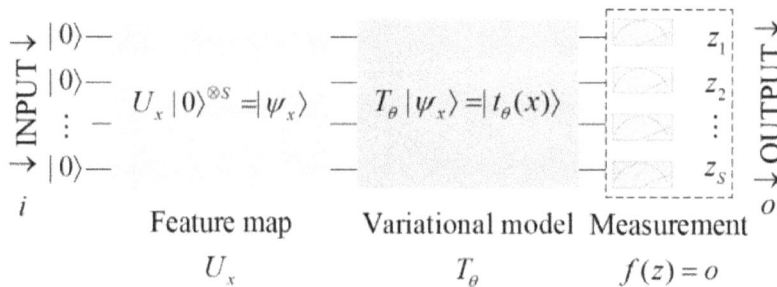

Figure 2.8 – QNN schematic circuit

QNNs are trained using the previously mentioned approaches where gradient-based optimizers are very much the ones showing good results in general. The Adam (*Carena et al., 2022*) optimizer is one of the most widely used, coming as it does from classical neural network optimization. We will see a working example in *Chapter 4* of how to train a QNN using gradient-based approaches when dealing with derivative valuation.

Quantum Support Vector Classification (QSVC)

Supervised classification systems are trained on labeled data and later used to predict the labels of unseen data points. This type of training is called supervised learning and has also made its way into QML (*Schuld et al., 2018*). Well-known classical approaches such as **Support Vector Machines** (**SVMs**) (*Meyer, 2015*) have undergone that training and have been used for various large-scale classification tasks. We can get an improved separability over the classical data by using previously discussed feature maps. This fact is exploited simply by encoding and decoding this data into a larger domain using quantum SVMs.

In supervised classification, a set of labeled data points indicates whether they are related to one particular class. The learning process establishes a dividing line or hyperplane between the groups. Kernel-based classifiers, such as SVC, rely heavily on the kernel notion (*Park et al., 2020*). A hyperplane cannot typically separate data in its original space; therefore, a common strategy is to apply a non-linear transformation function (φ), also known as a feature map, to find such a hyperplane. The feature map will project the encoded data into a new representation (more complex) to transform the data and help the separation. In this function, $\varphi : x \to F$, where F is the feature space. The output of the map on individual data points, $\varphi(x)$ for every $x \in X$, is known as a feature vector.

Another helpful tool is the kernel trick. The data will be only represented by pairwise similarity. Using a kernel trick and a high-dimensional non-linear feature map, the quantum kernel approach may be expanded to decision functions that depend on non-linear data. In this case, the data is transferred from a lower-dimensional space to a higher-dimensional nonlinear Hilbert space (H) (*Skorohod, 2012*), sometimes referred to as a feature space. After selecting an appropriate feature map, applying the SVM classifier to the mapped data in the Hilbert space is feasible. Classifying data points in this new feature space involves evaluating their proximity. For its part, the kernel is the collection of inner products between every pair of data points.

The execution of these computations is easier on a quantum computer than on a regular system. The kernel can be estimated easily using a quantum processor. After the kernel matrix has been formed, the quantum kernel information must be extracted from the quantum circuit and fed into the SVM or SVC algorithm.

Variational Quantum Eigensolver

From the previous definition of VQCs, we know that the **Variational Quantum Eigensolver** (**VQE**) is composed of both classical and quantum parts that are integreted together to achieve a specific goal. When used to find the state of minimum energy, also called the ground state, of a particular Hamiltonian, the learning algorithm takes the form of VQE (*Wang et al., 2019*). It belongs to the broader family of VQA. It follows the same steps where a classical optimization process tweaks the parameters of a given ansatz (PQC) to produce the boundary of the minimum expectation of the Hamiltonian upon measurement. The energy expectation value is the metric used to drive this training as if it were the cost function of any classical ML method.

Simply expressed, VQE refers to the usage of a quantum computer, on one hand, to assess the energy of an Hamiltonian and usage of a classical computer, and on the other hand, to enhance the parameters for energy reduction in the subsequent quantum iteration. The concept behind VQE is the implementation of a quantum computer for a single purpose: calculating the energy value of a given set of parameters. Everything else is carried out on a traditional computer. VQE is mostly utilized to predict the characteristics of molecules and materials, and is generally used for combinatorial optimization problems such as in the case of portfolio optimization.

QAOA

Quantum Approximation Optimization Algorithm (**QAOA**) is one of the most promising techniques for demonstrating quantum advantage (*Choi et al., 2019*). QAOA is an approximation method that does not provide the "best" result, but rather seeks a "good enough" outcome instead, characterized by the lower bound of the approximation ratio.

It takes inspiration from digitizing the adiabatic approach. The adiabatic theorem establishes that if we can start with a simple case where the optimal solution is known, then by making small perturbations, we change it to the problem we aim to solve. If the target state we obtain at the end of the circuit execution remains as the ground state of the problem, its readout will reveal the classical set of bits we were looking for.

This is one of the approaches quantum annealers use to solve complex problems. One of the digital implementations of this annealing procedure involves the use of alternating blocks of operations, where the initial candidates are encoded by the superposition of all possible options (the H gates at the beginning of *Figure 2.9*) and a discrete number of steps is added, alternating and enhancing our target problem the final quantum states generated is our target state.

Establishing the optimal amount of perturbation required is not trivial, and classical optimizers can be used for this to establish the best parameters that will work to solve our problem.

The entirety of this process is pictured in *Figure 2.9*, where β and γ correspond to the parameters affecting the problem Hamiltonian (C in yellow) and mixer Hamiltonian (B in green) for p levels or layers.

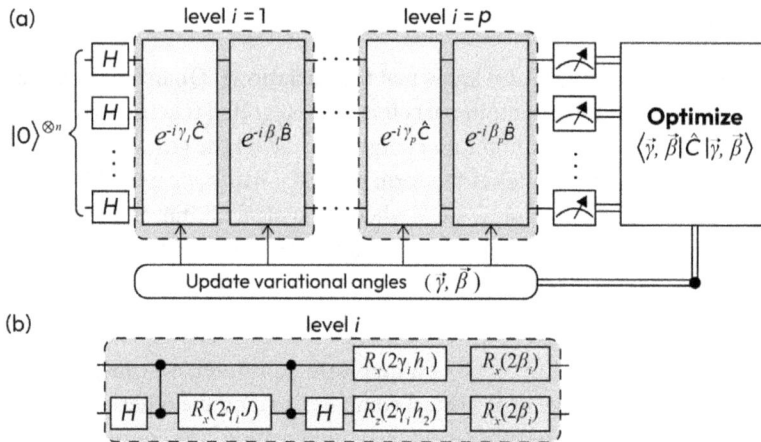

Figure 2.9 – QAOA schematic circuit

For a given NP-Hard problem (*Bittel et al., 2021*), an approximation algorithm is a polynomial-time solution that solves all instances of the problem with a quality guarantee. The merit value is the ratio between the quality of the polynomial time solution and the quality of the actual solution.

Quantum programming

In the last decade, the development of QC has accelerated. A significant example is the development of tools to offer solutions using high-level coding languages (*Chong et al., 2017; Ganguly et al., 2021*). Quantum programming languages are the basis for translating concepts into instructions for quantum computers. Nature Reviews (*Heim et al., 2020*) states that quantum programming languages are used for the following purposes:

- Examining the QC fundamentals (qubits, superposition, entanglement), then testing and validating quantum algorithms and their implementations

- Managing existing physical quantum hardware

- Forecasting the costs of quantum program execution on probable hardware

Current quantum programming languages primarily aim to optimize quantum gate-based low-level circuits. Quantum circuits are constructed from quantum gates and used for universal quantum computers. A list of the main quantum gates is provided as follows:

Operator	Gate(s)	Matrix
Pauli-X (X)	X ⊕	$\begin{bmatrix} 0 & 1 \\ 1 & 0 \end{bmatrix}$
Pauli-Y (Y)	Y	$\begin{bmatrix} 0 & -i \\ i & 0 \end{bmatrix}$
Pauli-Z (Z)	Z	$\begin{bmatrix} 1 & 0 \\ 0 & -1 \end{bmatrix}$
Hadamard (H)	H	$\frac{1}{\sqrt{2}} \begin{bmatrix} 1 & 1 \\ 1 & -1 \end{bmatrix}$
Phase (S, P)	S	$\begin{bmatrix} 1 & 0 \\ 0 & i \end{bmatrix}$
$\pi/8$ (T)	T	$\begin{bmatrix} 1 & 0 \\ 0 & e^{i\pi/4} \end{bmatrix}$ »
Controlled Not (CNOT, CX)		$\begin{bmatrix} 1 & 0 & 0 & 0 \\ 0 & 1 & 0 & 0 \\ 0 & 0 & 0 & 1 \\ 0 & 0 & 1 & 0 \end{bmatrix}$
Controlled Z (CZ)	Z	$\begin{bmatrix} 1 & 0 & 0 & 0 \\ 0 & 1 & 0 & 0 \\ 0 & 0 & 1 & 0 \\ 0 & 0 & 0 & -1 \end{bmatrix}$
SWAP	X	$\begin{bmatrix} 1 & 0 & 0 & 0 \\ 0 & 0 & 1 & 0 \\ 0 & 1 & 0 & 0 \\ 0 & 0 & 0 & 1 \end{bmatrix}$
Toffoli (CCNOT, CCX, TOFF)		$\begin{bmatrix} 1 & 0 & 0 & 0 & 0 & 0 & 0 & 0 \\ 0 & 1 & 0 & 0 & 0 & 0 & 0 & 0 \\ 0 & 0 & 1 & 0 & 0 & 0 & 0 & 0 \\ 0 & 0 & 0 & 1 & 0 & 0 & 0 & 0 \\ 0 & 0 & 0 & 0 & 1 & 0 & 0 & 0 \\ 0 & 0 & 0 & 0 & 0 & 1 & 0 & 0 \\ 0 & 0 & 0 & 0 & 0 & 0 & 0 & 1 \\ 0 & 0 & 0 & 0 & 0 & 0 & 1 & 0 \end{bmatrix}$

Figure 2.10 – Core gates for quantum computing

Quantum programming started in 1996 when E. Knill introduced the **Quantum Random Access Machine (QRAM)** model and proposed what could be recognized as the first convention of quantum pseudocode (*Knill, 1996*). Since then, numerous methods have been developed, such as the quantum programming language (QCL) by Ömer (*Ömer, 2002*), C++ quantum extensions (*McCaskey et al., 2021*), and many other acronyms that represent the different evolution stages of these languages.

The focus of this section is to specifically explore quantum **Software Development Kits (SDKs)**, which are tools for developing quantum algorithms to be used in quantum computers, simulators, and emulators (*Ablayev et al., 2020*). Microsoft, IBM, Google, Xanadu, and Rigetti are among the firms that have released open source development kits. SDKs provide the tools for software developers to solve their problems and give them access to simulators or quantum computers for the cloud-based implementation of their quantum algorithms.

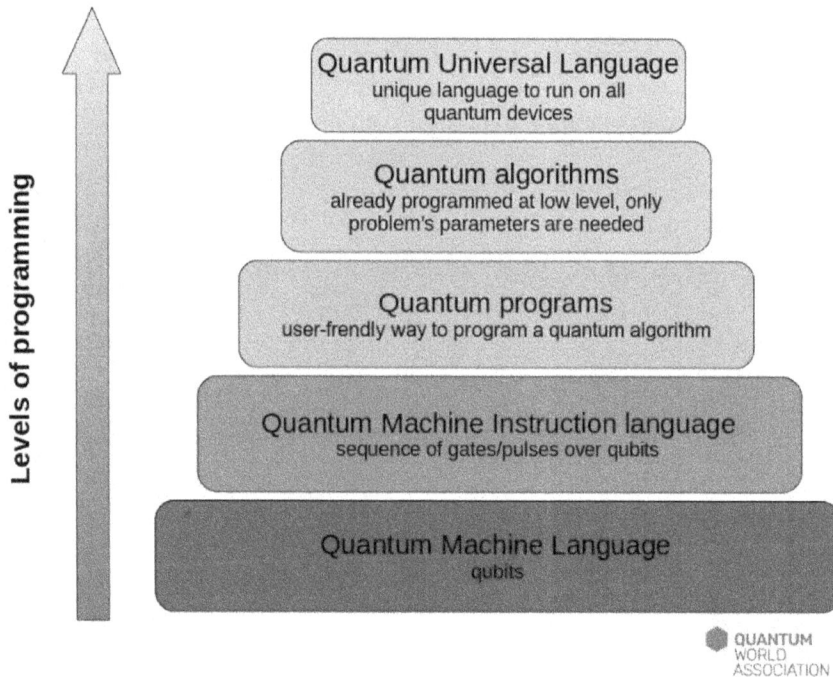

Levels of programming

Quantum Universal Language
unique language to run on all quantum devices

Quantum algorithms
already programmed at low level, only problem's parameters are needed

Quantum programs
user-frendly way to program a quantum algorithm

Quantum Machine Instruction language
sequence of gates/pulses over qubits

Quantum Machine Language
qubits

QUANTUM WORLD ASSOCIATION

Figure 2.11 – Comparison of QC programming levels

These kits frequently permit the use of traditional programming languages, such as Python, as the main interpreter over which a framework with specific functionalities are built. Others prefer to build their own versions of quantum software languages, such as Microsoft's Q#.

Even though we are not yet at the top of the ladder shown in *Figure 2.11* (`https://medium.com/@ quantum_wa/quantum-computing-languages-landscape-1bc6dedb2a35`), different frameworks specialize in particular tasks or fields where certain specific hardware implementations perform better than others.

The most prominent ecosystems of tools are the following:

- Qiskit from IBM offers high-abstraction modules for finance, among things
- PennyLane from Xanadu specializes in QML and differentiable computing
- Cirq from Google, which allows the use of Sycamore and QSVM simulators can be used
- The **Quantum Development Kit (QDK)** from Microsoft for Q# users

Other SDKs can also be found on the market, usually more specialized or specifically related to the efforts of particular companies to improve their own solutions, hardware, and infrastructure. These SDKs include the following:

- Ocean from D-Wave
- Orquestra from Zapata
- Braket SDK from **Amazon Web Services (AWS)**
- Anian from Riverlane
- Forest from Rigetti

In the following sections, the most relevant SDKs with the largest communities, documentation, and online support will be discussed. By making use of these support bases, anyone with an average knowledge of math and/or physics can start learning from scratch and interacting very quickly with real or simulated quantum devices.

Qiskit

Qiskit (originally called QISKit) is an SDK for Python released by IBM Research in 2017 (`https:// qiskit.org/`). The purpose of this package/library is to provide a bridge between quantum algorithms and physical devices so that more people can understand and interact with quantum computers. Qiskit was also created to help widen access to quantum education and expand quantum information challenges and structures.

Currently, Qiskit enables users to quickly construct experiments and applications and run them on genuine quantum computers and classical quantum simulators. Another aim is the advancement of quantum software, both at the machine-code level with OpenQASM and at the abstract level for end users without experience in quantum computing.

Since Qiskit is an open source SDK, anyone can cooperate and interact with it. It is well known for having the largest QC community in the world, featuring many people from different backgrounds and places who collaborate. In 2020, Qiskit already comprised 15,000 scientists and developers working in the field using Qiskit tools, and over 300,000 people using these resources to learn about quantum computation. In 2021, 157 research articles were published involving implementations of Qiskit. The community continues to grow today, with certified users and advocates all over the globe (https://quantumcomputingreport.com/).

The classical elements (Terra, Ignis, Aer, Metal, and Aqua) were used for naming Qiskit packages in the early days. This convention has been abandoned in favor of more descriptive titles for Qiskit packages. Terra and Aer retain their original names, while others have been deprecated and replaced. Aqua, for example, has been replaced by high-level application modules, and Ignis by Qiskit Experiments. Qiskit Metal is more related to circuit design and thus has a very specific appeal to those seeking to design quantum computing chips based on superconducting circuits.

Qiskit Terra contains the most relevant functionalities. Across the Qiskit ecosystem, Terra is the largest package with the most comprehensive set of quantum computation tools; many other packages interact with it. Considering Terra as the core of Qiskit, the most interesting part for the business sector is probably the high-level applications available, which contain four different products that formerly comprised a single bundle (Qiskit Aqua). Each application package focuses on an area where QC has the potential to significantly impact the real world, as follows:

- Qiskit Nature, with a focus on quantum simulations

- Qiskit Machine Learning, which provides tools for various applications related to QML

- Qiskit Finance, which aims to help researchers discover and expand quantum financial solutions

- Qiskit Optimization, which offers tools to explore optimization problems, such as Traveling Salesman or Knapsack

Chapters 4, 5, and *6* explore these solutions in depth, mostly focusing on Qiskit for Finance, given its interesting modules to develop some topics covered in the following chapters. Also, *Chapter 9* highlights some basic usages of Qiskit Terra and Qiskit Experiments for error mitigation. Qiskit Machine Learning will also be mentioned and referenced.

PennyLane

PennyLane presents a robust and novel method to program on quantum computers (*Bergholm et al., 2018*). It merges conventional ML libraries with quantum hardware and simulators; as a result, users can train quantum computers similarly to neural networks. This SDK for Python was released in 2018 by Xanadu and combines the most widespread QC systems with the top ML tools through a device-agnostic and open source strategy. Data scientists (including ML researchers) who use TensorFlow, PyTorch, or NumPy will quickly adapt to PennyLane's work environment.

As mentioned previously, PennyLane provides a simple Python-based user interface compatible with any gate-based QC platform (such as Qiskit), including qubit and continuous-variable designs.

The user creates a quantum function circuit coupled to a device, constituting a QNode, as illustrated in *Figure 2.12*. One of the main advantages of PennyLane and its approach is that all computations done in the device are taped, which means gradients can be directly requested with almost no computational effort. This is why it is placed alongside TensorFlow or PyTorch, given that these automatic differentiation capabilities have made them successful within the ML community.

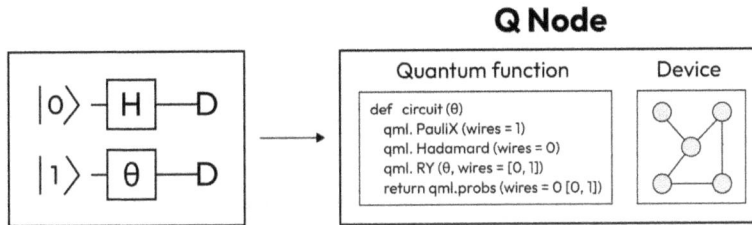

Figure 2.12 – PennyLane basic core structure

When dealing with specific needs for QML, as seen in *Chapters 4* and *6*, we will see how PennyLane can easily tackle those techniques that may sound complicated from a technical standpoint. Further, thanks to PennyLane, implementations are easier to tackle at an experimental level.

Cirq

Another Python framework is Cirq, released by Google in 2018 (`https://github.com/quantumlib/Cirq`). It can compose, execute, and evaluate quantum computer program results. It was built for quantum computers with a few hundred qubits (NISQ) and a few thousand quantum gates. At present, with over 3,000 commits since its launch, version 1.0 of Cirq is available.

A thriving community of libraries that facilitate many fields of research in QC has developed around Cirq. These libraries include the following:

- **TensorFlow Quantum**: An instrument for investigating QML.
- **OpenFermion**: An open source tool for QC, used in chemical simulations.
- **Pytket**: A Python-based optimization and manipulation tool for quantum circuits.
- **Mitiq**: An open source library for error prevention strategies. Developed by the non-profit Unitary Fund.
- **Qsim**: A high-performance state vector emulator created with AVX/FMA vectorized instructions. Includes GPU acceleration as an option. Qsimcirq is the Cirq interface for gaining access to qsim.

Additionally, Cirq is one element of the Google quantum ecosystem (*Figure 2.13*) that can be integrated with previous SDKs such as PennyLane and other cloud services such as Microsoft Azure Quantum.

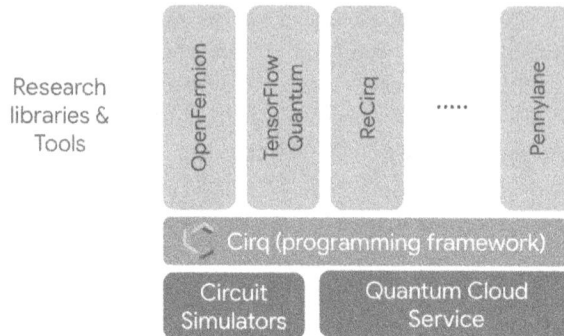

Figure 2.13 – Cirq quantum ecosystem

When no quantum processor is available, Cirq can be tested using Google Quantum Virtual Machine, a Colab laptop replicating a Google quantum processor (currently, Weber or Rainbow). If greater emulation power is required, it's simple enough to update the Google Quantum Virtual Machine to operate in Google Cloud.

Quantum Development Kit (QDK)

The QDK was launched by Microsoft in 2017 and comprises the foundational elements for getting started in quantum software development (Microsoft, 2017). These include the following:

- APIs for QC simulation utilizing .NET or Python

- A language for quantum programming by Microsoft, called Q#

- Development and simulation tools for quantum applications using command-line tools

This and the other SDKs on the market have recently converged; thus, the QDK currently allows the building and running of QC applications using Cirq and Qiskit.

This kit is intended for programmers eager to learn how to program quantum computers. No prior knowledge of quantum physics is required. The QDK is an open source structure with a suite of documentation, tutorials, libraries, example algorithms, and a community of contributors (*Figure 2.14*). As previously stated, the QDK supports various development platforms, including Windows, Linux, and macOS, as well as programming languages such as Python.

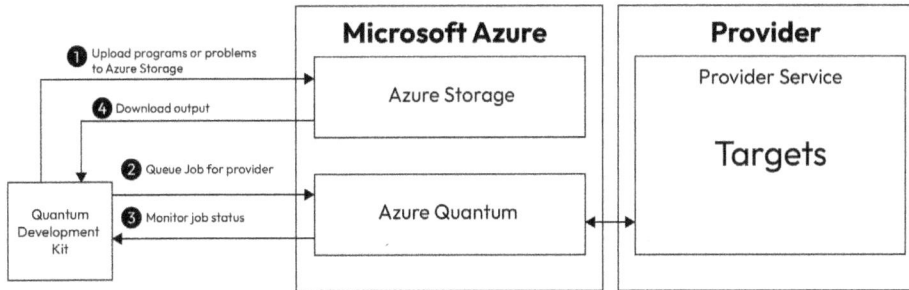

Figure 2.14 – The QDK and Microsoft Azure Quantum workflow

The ever-growing Microsoft quantum ecosystem enables problem-solvers from various fields and at different skill levels to explore the realm of quantum development to address game-changing real-world issues.

Quantum clouds

Along with programming languages, widespread research and commercial use of quantum programs requires the fundamental element of cloud access (*Gong et al., 2021*). These cloud solutions are directly linked to quantum circuits and chips for the final testing and experiments with quantum algorithms.

Cloud access has allowed institutions and individuals to advance their QC exploration. Businesses and universities can now experiment with QC on the cloud regardless of how technology evolves and becomes popular. This began back in 2016, when IBM linked a quantum computer to the cloud and enabled the development and execution of basic cloud-based quantum apps (*Castelvecchi, 2017*). By 2022, at least 13 well-known companies were offering online access to quantum computers:

- Amazon Braket (AWS)
- Leap (D-Wave)
- IBM Q Experience (IBM)
- Google Quantum AI (Google)
- Xanadu Quantum Cloud (Xanadu)
- Azure Quantum (Microsoft)
- Forest (Rigetti)
- Quantum Inspire (Qutech)
- Forge (QC Ware)
- AQT

- Quantinuum

- Alibaba Cloud

- Oxford Quantum Circuits

Quantum cloud services also enable direct connections between users, quantum emulators, and simulators. Moreover, some vendors accommodate different programming languages, tools, and documentation to help users build QC applications more efficiently.

The following sections will review in depth the most prominent services in this field and how they work and evolve.

IBM Quantum

As mentioned earlier, IBM launched its QC cloud platform in 2016. **IBM Quantum Experience** has a 5-qubit quantum processor and a simulator. Anyone can access 7-qubit and 5-qubit quantum machines and cloud simulators for free. Moreover, many features in the IBM platform, such as the IBM Quantum Composer, Qiskit examples and learning materials, and IBM Quantum Lab, allow users to create, explore, and run quantum applications through Jupyter Notebooks.

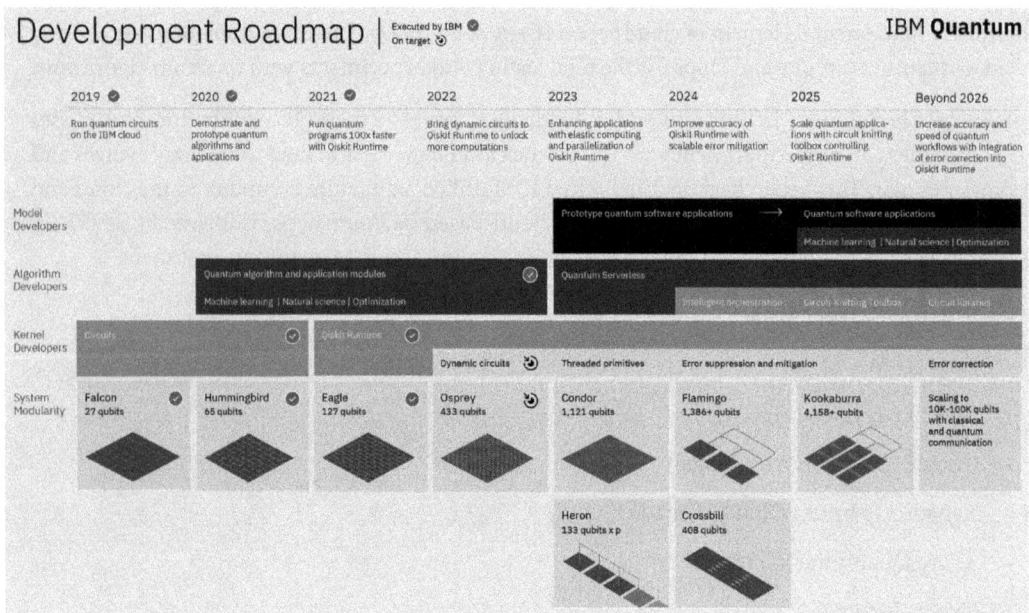

Figure 2.15 – IBM Quantum roadmap

IBM's quantum technology development roadmap may seem quite aggressive but, at the same time, it is concrete, as the company has accomplished every intended step so far. By 2025, IBM expects to have multiple QPUs interconnected on a new arrangement of a 4,158-qubit machine called Kookaburra. If a higher number of qubits is required (beyond the free tier of machines), there are also two possibilities:

- Pay-as-you-go: Access to the 27-qubit Falcon R5 processors, paying per runtime second with a credit card
- Premium plan: Access the 127-qubit Eagle processor and pay through a customized agreement as a member of the IBM Quantum Network

A further important challenge for IBM is the increment of the quantum volume of their machines. This is the maximum square circuit of random two-qubit gates that a processor can properly execute. Success is considered to be reached when the processor can compute the heavy outputs (the most probable outputs of the circuit) more than two-thirds of the time with a 2-confidence interval. If a processor can employ 8 qubits to operate a circuit with eight-time steps' worth of gates, then its quantum volume is 256 — we raise 2 to the power of the number of qubits.

Amazon Braket

Amazon Web Services (**AWS**) launched Amazon Braket in 2019 (*Patterson, 2019*). Amazon Braket is a quantum cloud **platform as a service** (**PaaS**) provided in collaboration with five hardware-based QC companies: D-Wave, IonQ, Rigetti, OQC, and Xanadu. Amazon Braket offers not only quantum annealing services through D-Wave, but also access to universal quantum computers via different types of hardware technologies; these include trapped-ion (IonQ), superconducting (Rigetti and OQC), and photonic (Xanadu) technology. Each of these technologies has its advantages and drawbacks according to five criteria: well-characterized and scalable qubits, qubit initialization, extended coherence duration, universal set of gates, and quantification of individual qubits.

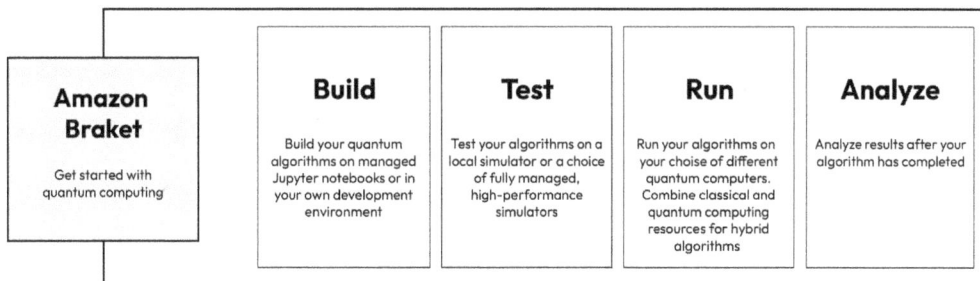

Figure 2.16 – AWS quantum roadmap

Overall, Amazon Braket offers a coherent set of services based on a Python environment to build, test, run, and analyze quantum algorithms based on a Python environment. With Braket, users can access universal quantum computers, simulators, hybrid jobs, and managed notebooks. Gate-based quantum computers may be utilized through a **quantum processing unit (QPU)** or a quantum annealer provided by D-Wave. Furthermore, users can use the available SDK to build and implement their quantum algorithms. **State Vector 1 (SV1)**, **Density Matrix 1 (DM1)**, and **Tensor Network 1 (TN1)** simulators can be employed simultaneously to run and test quantum algorithms and mitigate the effect of noise on the algorithm performance (*Figure 2.16*).

To test hybrid algorithms, AWS combines its classical EC2-based computer resources (the job instance) with Braket **quantum processing units (QPUs)** or quantum circuit simulators. Users can also access a notebook to test quantum algorithms, share code, and visualize the results (`https://aws.amazon.com/braket/pricing/`).

Amazon Braket offers access to various QC microprocessors at a reasonable price. The efficiency of a quantum algorithm can be tested on different systems and a use case then developed on the more efficient system.

Microsoft Quantum

Since 2019, Microsoft has provided researchers, businesses, and developers with cloud access to quantum computers (*Kanamori et al., 2020*). The company has created a dynamic environment for this ecosystem to thrive and sustain itself by creating spaces for enterprises, researchers, and developers to produce, test, and deploy quantum algorithms. In particular, the Azure cloud has facilitated access to multiple platforms offered by companies like (but not limited to) 1QBit, Quantinuum, QCL, and Pasqal (*Figure 2.17*).

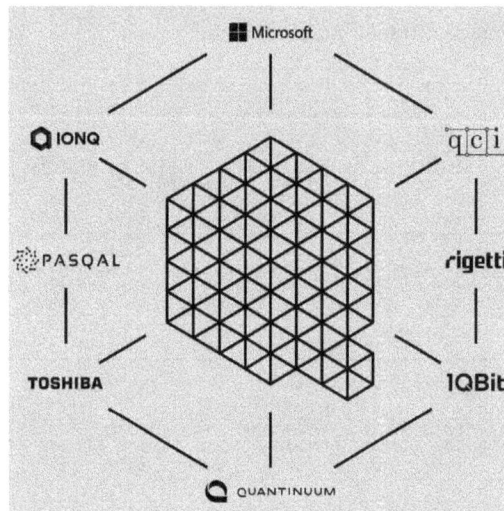

Figure 2.17 – Microsoft quantum ecosystem

Microsoft's quantum services are positioned at three levels: business, researcher, and developer. Through its enterprise acceleration program, the company provides easy access to the industry via optimization solvers and quantum hardware. Prestigious organizations including NASA and Ford have already embarked on explorations of quantum computing through the cloud to develop solutions for scheduling problems and vehicle tracking. At the same time, by having access to modules such as Cirq, Qiskit, and Q#, researchers and developers can now engage in developing new algorithms.

Summary

- The foundational quantum computing algorithms have already demonstrated the potential benefits of this new computational paradigm, provided that a specific set of hardware capable of harnessing the advantages of the physical approach is available.

- There is an interesting variety of options regarding quantum and hybrid quantum-classical algorithms for solving problems related to machine learning, optimization, and simulation. Most have documentation and open source code available to reduce the learning curve for new adopters.

- Quantum computers are a reality since anyone who needs to can access them and start the process of research and discovery toward a potential solution. Also, if there is commercial interest, multiple cloud services provide access to several quantum technologies that can be explored in parallel with high computational power to run quantum simulators.

References

- *Abbas, A., Sutter, D., Zoufal, C., Lucchi, A., Figalli, A., & Woerner, S. (2021). The power of quantum neural networks. Nature Computational Science 2021 1:6, 1(6), 403–409. doi: 10.1038/s43588-021-00084-1*

- *Ablayev, F., Ablayev, M., Huang, J. Z., Khadiev, K., Salikhova, N., & Wu, D. (2020). On quantum methods for machine learning problems part I: Quantum tools. Big Data Mining and Analytics, 3(1), 41–55. doi: 10.26599/BDMA.2019.9020016*

- *Albash, T., & Lidar, D. A. (2018). Adiabatic quantum computation. Reviews of Modern Physics, 90(1), 015002. doi: 10.1103/REVMODPHYS.90.015002/FIGURES/11/MEDIUM*

- *Álvarez, G. A., Danieli, E. P., Levstein, P. R., & Pastawski, H. M. (2008). Quantum parallelism as a tool for ensemble spin dynamics calculations. Physical Review Letters, 101(12), 120503. doi: 10.1103/PHYSREVLETT.101.120503/FIGURES/3/MEDIUM*

- *Arute, F., Arya, K., Babbush, R., Bacon, D., Bardin, J. C., Barends, R., Biswas, R., Boixo, S., Brandao, F. G. S. L., Buell, D. A., Burkett, B., Chen, Y., Chen, Z., Chiaro, B., Collins, R., Courtney, W., Dunsworth, A., Farhi, E., Foxen, B., … Martinis, J. M. (2019). Quantum supremacy using a programmable superconducting processor. Nature 2019 574:7779, 574(7779), 505–510. doi: 10.1038/s41586-019-1666-5*

- *Bayerstadler, A., Becquin, G., Binder, J., Botter, T., Ehm, H., Ehmer, T., Erdmann, M., Gaus, N., Harbach, P., Hess, M., Klepsch, J., Leib, M., Luber, S., Luckow, A., Mansky, M., Mauerer, W., Neukart, F., Niedermeier, C., Palackal, L., … Winter, F. (2021). Industry quantum computing applications. EPJ Quantum Technology, 8(1), 25. doi: 10.1140/EPJQT/S40507-021-00114-X*

- *Bergholm, V., Izaac, J., Schuld, M., Gogolin, C., Ahmed, S., Ajith, V., Alam, M. S., Alonso-Linaje, G., AkashNarayanan, B., Asadi, A., Arrazola, J. M., Azad, U., Banning, S., Blank, C., Bromley, T. R., Cordier, B. A., Ceroni, J., Delgado, A., Di Matteo, O., … Killoran, N. (2018). PennyLane: Automatic differentiation of hybrid quantum-classical computations. doi: 10.48550/arxiv.1811.04968*

- *Bharti, K., Cervera-Lierta, A., Kyaw, T. H., Haug, T., Alperin-Lea, S., Anand, A., Degroote, M., Heimonen, H., Kottmann, J. S., Menke, T., Mok, W.-K., Sim, S., Kwek, L.-C., & Aspuru-Guzik, A. (2021). Noisy intermediate-scale quantum (NISQ) algorithms. Reviews of Modern Physics, 94(1). doi: 10.1103/RevModPhys.94.015004*

- *Bittel, L., & Kliesch, M. (2021). Training Variational Quantum Algorithms Is NP-Hard. Physical Review Letters, 127(12), 120502. doi: 10.1103/PHYSREVLETT.127.120502/FIGURES/1/MEDIUM*

- *Campagne-Ibarcq, P., Eickbusch, A., Touzard, S., Zalys-Geller, E., Frattini, N. E., Sivak, V. V., Reinhold, P., Puri, S., Shankar, S., Schoelkopf, R. J., Frunzio, L., Mirrahimi, M., & Devoret, M. H. (2020). Quantum error correction of a qubit encoded in grid states of an oscillator. Nature 2020 584:7821, 584(7821), 368–372. doi: 10.1038/s41586-020-2603-3*

- *Carena, M., Lamm, H., Li, Y.-Y., & Liu, W. (2022). Improved Hamiltonians for Quantum Simulations of Gauge Theories. Physical Review Letters, 129(5), 051601. doi: 10.1103/PhysRevLett.129.051601*

- *Castelvecchi, D. (2017). IBM's quantum cloud computer goes commercial. Nature, 543(7644).*

- *Cerezo, M., Arrasmith, A., Babbush, R., Benjamin, S. C., Endo, S., Fujii, K., McClean, J. R., Mitarai, K., Yuan, X., Cincio, L., & Coles, P. J. (2021). Variational quantum algorithms. Nature Reviews Physics 2021 3:9, 3(9), 625–644. doi: 10.1038/s42254-021-00348-9*

- *Choi, J., & Kim, J. (2019). A Tutorial on Quantum Approximate Optimization Algorithm (QAOA): Fundamentals and Applications. ICTC 2019 - 10th International Conference on ICT Convergence: ICT Convergence Leading the Autonomous Future, 138–142. doi: 10.1109/ICTC46691.2019.8939749*

- *Chong, F. T., Franklin, D., & Martonosi, M. (2017). Programming languages and compiler design for realistic quantum hardware. Nature 2017 549:7671, 549(7671), 180–187. doi: 10.1038/nature23459*

- *Chow, J. M., Gambetta, J. M., Córcoles, A. D., Merkel, S. T., Smolin, J. A., Rigetti, C., Poletto, S., Keefe, G. A., Rothwell, M. B., Rozen, J. R., Ketchen, M. B., & Steffen, M. (2012). Universal quantum gate set approaching fault-tolerant thresholds with superconducting qubits. Physical Review Letters, 109(6), 060501. doi: 10.1103/PHYSREVLETT.109.060501/FIGURES/4/MEDIUM*

- *Deb, A., Dueck, G. W., & Wille, R. (2021). Exploring the Potential Benefits of Alternative Quantum Computing Architectures. IEEE Transactions on Computer-Aided Design of Integrated Circuits and Systems, 40(9), 1825–1835. doi: 10.1109/TCAD.2020.3032072*

- *Deutsch, D., & Jozsa, R. (1992). Rapid solution of problems by quantum computation. Proceedings of the Royal Society of London. Series A: Mathematical and Physical Sciences, 439(1907), 553–558. doi: 10.1098/RSPA.1992.0167*

- *Egger, D. J., Gambella, C., Marecek, J., McFaddin, S., Mevissen, M., Raymond, R., Simonetto, A., Woerner, S., & Yndurain, E. (2021). Quantum Computing for Finance: State-of-the-Art and Future Prospects. IEEE Transactions on Quantum Engineering, 1, 1–24. doi: 10.1109/TQE.2020.3030314*

- *Endo, S., Cai, Z., Benjamin, S. C., & Yuan, X. (2021). Hybrid Quantum-Classical Algorithms and Quantum Error Mitigation. Https://Doi.Org/10.7566/JPSJ.90.032001, 90(3). doi: 10.7566/JPSJ.90.032001*

- *Fedorov, A. K., Gisin, N., Beloussov, S. M., & Lvovsky, A. I. (2022). Quantum computing at the quantum advantage threshold: a down-to-business review. doi: 10.48550/arxiv.2203.17181*

- *Ganguly, S., & Cambier, T. (2021). Quantum Computing with Silq Programming: get up and running with the new high-level programming language for quantum computing. PACKT PUBLISHING LIMITED.*

- *Gilyén, A., Song, Z., & Tang, E. (2022). An improved quantum-inspired algorithm for linear regression. Quantum, 6, 754. doi: 10.22331/q-2022-06-30-754*

- *Gong, C., Dong, Z., Gani, A., & Qi, H. (2021). Quantum k-means algorithm based on trusted server in quantum cloud computing. Quantum Information Processing, 20(4), 1–22. doi: 10.1007/S11128-021-03071-7/FIGURES/16*

- *Grover, L. K. (1996). A fast quantum mechanical algorithm for database search. Proceedings of the Annual ACM Symposium on Theory of Computing, Part F129452, 212–219. doi: 10.1145/237814.237866*

- *Heim, B., Soeken, M., Marshall, S., Granade, C., Roetteler, M., Geller, A., Troyer, M., & Svore, K. (2020). Quantum programming languages. Nature Reviews Physics 2020 2:12, 2(12), 709–722. doi: 10.1038/S42254-020-00245-7*

- *Kanamori, Y., & Yoo, S.-M. (2020). Quantum Computing: Principles and Applications. Journal of International Technology and Information Management, 29(2). Retrieved from https://scholarworks.lib.csusb.edu/jitim/vol29/iss2/3*

- *Kaoudi, Z., Quiané-Ruiz, J.-A., Thirumuruganathan, S., Chawla, S., & Agrawal, D. (2017). A Cost-based Optimizer for Gradient Descent Optimization. Proceedings of the 2017 ACM International Conference on Management of Data. doi: 10.1145/3035918*

- *Kellerer, Hans et al. "Selecting Portfolios with Fixed Costs and Minimum Transaction Lots." Annals of Operations Research 99 (2000): 287-304.*

- *Knill, E. (1996). Conventions for quantum pseudocode. Retrieved from* https://www.osti.gov/biblio/366453

- *Li, W., & Deng, D. L. (2021). Recent advances for quantum classifiers. Science China Physics, Mechanics & Astronomy 2021 65:2, 65(2), 1–23. doi: 10.1007/S11433-021-1793-6*

- *Li, Z., Dai, J., Pan, S., Zhang, W., & Hu, J. (2020). Synthesis of Deutsch-Jozsa Circuits and Verification by IBM Q. International Journal of Theoretical Physics, 59(6), 1668–1678. doi: 10.1007/S10773-020-04434-Z/FIGURES/11*

- *Martín-Guerrero, J. D., & Lamata, L. (2022). Quantum Machine Learning: A tutorial. Neurocomputing, 470, 457–461. doi: 10.1016/J.NEUCOM.2021.02.102*

- *Mccaskey, A., Nguyen, T., Santana, A., Claudino, D., Kharazi, T., & Finkel, H. (2021). Extending C++ for Heterogeneous Quantum-Classical Computing. ACM Transactions on Quantum Computing, 2(2), 1–36. doi: 10.1145/3462670*

- *Mengoni, R., & Di Pierro, A. (2019). Kernel methods in Quantum Machine Learning. Quantum Machine Intelligence 2019 1:3, 1(3), 65–71. doi: 10.1007/S42484-019-00007-4*

- *Meyer, D. (2015). Support Vector Machines * The Interface to libsvm in package e1071. Retrieved from http://www.csie.ntu.edu.tw/~cjlin/papers/ijcnn.ps.gz.*

- *Microsoft. (2017). Get started with quantum development. Get Started with Quantum Development. Retrieved from https://www.microsoft.com/en-us/quantum/development-kit*

- *Milanov, E. (2009). The RSA algorithm. Retrieved from* https://sites.math.washington.edu/~morrow/336_09/papers/Yevgeny.pdf

- *Mitarai, K., Negoro, M., Kitagawa, M., & Fujii, K. (2018). Quantum circuit learning. Physical Review A, 98(3), 032309. doi: 10.1103/PHYSREVA.98.032309/FIGURES/6/MEDIUM*

- *Montanaro, A. (2016). Quantum algorithms: an overview. Npj Quantum Information 2016 2:1, 2(1), 1–8. doi: 10.1038/npjqi.2015.23*

- *Ömer, B. (2002). Procedural Quantum Programming. AIP Conference Proceedings, 627(1), 276. doi: 10.1063/1.1503695*

- *Park, D. K., Blank, C., & Petruccione, F. (2020). The theory of the quantum kernel-based binary classifier. Physics Letters A, 384(21), 126422. doi: 10.1016/J.PHYSLETA.2020.126422*

- *Patterson, S. (2019). Learn AWS serverless computing : a beginner's guide to using AWS Lambda, Amazon API Gateway, and services from Amazon Web Services. Packt Publishing.*

- *Schuld, M., & Petruccione, F. (2018). Supervised Learning with Quantum Computers. Springer International Publishing. doi: 10.1007/978-3-319-96424-9*

- *Shor, P. W. (1994). Algorithms for quantum computation: Discrete logarithms and factoring. Proceedings - Annual IEEE Symposium on Foundations of Computer Science, FOCS, 124–134. doi: 10.1109/SFCS.1994.365700*

- *Skorohod, A. V. (2012). Integration in Hilbert Space (Springer Science & …). Springer Berlin Heidelberg.*

- *Wang, D., Higgott, O., & Brierley, S. (2019). Accelerated variational quantum eigensolver. Physical Review Letters, 122(14), 140504. doi: 10.1103/PHYSREVLETT.122.140504/FIGURES/3/MEDIUM*

- *Yung, M. H. (2019). Quantum supremacy: some fundamental concepts. National Science Review, 6(1), 22–23. doi: 10.1093/NSR/NWY072*

3

Quantum Finance Landscape

Quantum computing holds great promise for addressing numerous challenges across various domains, and the financial sector is no exception. With its increased computational power, quantum computing can significantly enhance the efficiency and capabilities of stock exchanges, banks, and technical analysts by enabling more sophisticated simulation and optimization models. Many major banks are already exploring quantum technology to tackle issues such as fraud detection, credit card disbursal explainability, option pricing, and stress testing assets.

This chapter delves into the role financial services play in society and examines the key challenges they face that could potentially be addressed by quantum computing. It provides an introduction to different types of financial institutions and highlights the critical problems within the financial services sector. Additionally, the chapter outlines the necessary preparations for creating a work environment that facilitates tackling exercises related to quantum computing in finance, ensuring that technical requirements and accounts are properly established. By understanding the potential impact of quantum computing in the financial landscape, stakeholders can better prepare for a future where this technology plays a pivotal role in addressing complex challenges and driving innovation.

In this chapter, we will explore various topics essential to understanding the financial services landscape:

- Introduction to types of financial institutions
- Key problems in financial services

Additionally, this chapter will offer guidance on preparing the work environment for the practical exercises that will be presented in subsequent chapters. This includes ensuring that technical requirements are met and accounts are properly set up, enabling a seamless learning experience. By covering these essential topics, we aim to provide a comprehensive foundation for understanding the financial services sector and the potential impact of emerging technologies such as quantum computing in addressing its most pressing challenges.

Introduction to types of financial institutions

The financial industry is integral to the health and growth of a country's economy. This sector is responsible for providing essential financial services to both businesses and retail consumers. As depicted in *Figure 3.1*, the financial sector is a diverse ecosystem, encompassing banks, investment houses, insurance companies, real estate brokers, consumer financing firms, mortgage lenders, and **real estate investment trusts (REITs)**. These organizations collectively contribute to the stability and expansion of the economy.

In addition to the provision of loans and mortgages, the financial industry plays a critical role in offering insurance services to individuals and enterprises. This ensures that both personal and commercial assets are protected against unforeseen risks, fostering a sense of security and stability within the economy. Employment opportunities within the financial sector are vast, with millions of people working in various capacities across the industry. From entry-level positions to executive leadership roles, this sector offers a diverse range of career paths for individuals with varying skill sets and interests. Furthermore, the financial industry plays a pivotal role in helping individuals build and maintain their retirement funds, offering long-term financial security and peace of mind. Many of the world's most renowned banks, such as JPMorgan Chase, Bank of America, and Goldman Sachs, are key players in the financial sector, and their performance significantly influences the S&P 500 index. The success of these institutions, as well as others in the sector, is indicative of a robust and thriving economy.

Figure 3.1 – Types of financial institution

Retail banks

Retail banks act as intermediaries between depositors and borrowers. They facilitate the flow of capital, ensuring that funds are available for those in need of credit while simultaneously offering safe storage and interest for deposited funds. These banks play a crucial role in the economy, contributing to the circulation of money and supporting the growth of businesses and individuals alike. Additionally, retail banks offer various financial services, such as money transfers, credit cards, and investment products. The financial stability of retail banks is essential for maintaining a healthy economy. By diligently managing risk and adhering to regulatory requirements, they can protect their depositors' funds and maintain a reliable source of credit for borrowers. Retail banking is a fiercely competitive industry, with banks constantly vying for deposits and customers. As such, they must continually innovate and develop new products to remain attractive and relevant to their client base.

Investment banks

Investment banks play a critical role in helping companies access financial markets and raise capital. One notable method is through the facilitation of an **initial public offering** (**IPO**), which allows a company to go public and offer its shares to investors. In addition to capital-raising services, investment banks provide prime brokerage and securities financing to major institutions. These services enable large-scale clients to access the financial markets with increased efficiency and flexibility. Revenue generation for investment banks primarily stems from consulting and underwriting fees. These fees are collected as compensation for their expertise and assistance in navigating complex financial transactions. Moreover, investment banks earn income from financial market trading. By engaging in various trading activities, they capitalize on market movements and profit from the dynamic nature of the financial markets.

Investment managers

Investment managers cater to both individual and institutional clients, encompassing mutual fund, ETF, and hedge fund managers. Mutual fund and ETF managers offer preset services to retail and institutional customers, generating revenue through management fees based on total assets. Hedge funds primarily target institutions and affluent individuals, and the term "hedge fund" encompasses alternative asset management strategies, such as private equity, venture capital, and **commodities trading advisors** (**CTAs**).

Government institutions

Investment managers provide investment services to both individual and institutional clients, such as mutual fund, ETF, and hedge fund management. Mutual fund and ETF managers offer pre-packaged investment solutions catering to the needs of different types of investors. To generate revenue, mutual fund and ETF managers charge an asset-based fee calculated based on the total assets managed.

This fee compensates them for their expertise and services provided to their clients. Hedge funds, on the other hand, serve institutions and high-net-worth individuals, offering alternative asset management services, including private equity, venture capital, and commodities trading advisory. Hedge funds generate revenue through performance-based fees calculated as a percentage of the profits generated. Investment managers offer customized investment solutions tailored to the specific needs of their clients. They earn revenue through asset-based or performance-based fees, depending on the type of fund and its clients.

Exchanges/clearing houses

A stock market exchange serves as a platform for companies to trade their stocks. To be tradable, a stock must be listed on an exchange. Purchase and sell orders are compiled in an order book, and trades occur when orders match. Electronic exchanges can execute millions of deals daily, while clearing houses settle accounts and manage risks, including cash-settled derivatives transactions. In summary, stock market exchanges and clearing houses work together to provide a secure and efficient trading environment for companies and investors.

Payment processors

Payment processors are essential for facilitating secure financial transactions between parties. They serve as intermediaries, managing the exchange of funds between buyers and sellers. Payment processors employ advanced security measures to safeguard financial data and prevent fraud. They offer customized payment solutions for businesses, including mobile and international payment options. Payment processors enable global transactions, helping businesses expand and optimize their payment processes.

Insurance providers

Insurance companies provide policies such as life, health, vehicle, and home insurance to individuals, as well as maritime insurance, data breach insurance, and workers' compensation insurance to businesses. The purpose of insurance is to transfer the risk of financial loss from the policyholder to the insurance company in exchange for a premium. Insurance policies offer a sense of security and peace of mind to individuals and institutions. Life insurance supports the policyholder's beneficiaries in the event of their death, while health insurance covers medical expenses. Vehicle and home insurance protect against damages or losses related to the policyholder's property. For businesses, insurance is essential to mitigate the risk of financial loss from various events. The insurance industry continually evolves to ensure individuals and institutions have access to the necessary coverage to protect their financial interests.

The following section will discuss the challenges faced by financial institutions while serving their clients.

Key problems in financial services

Financial services can be categorized as banking, financial services, and insurance. Banks must manage customer expectations, maintain loan quality, and prevent customer churn, while financial market participants must regularly perform stress tests to avoid future troubles. Financial services must stay up to date with technological advancements to meet evolving client needs. Insurance companies must disburse claim amounts correctly and quickly to genuine customers, adhere to regulatory compliance, and invest in robust fraud detection and prevention measures. Overcoming these challenges requires ongoing investment in technology, staff training, and a commitment to providing high-quality services to clients.

Banking services provide depository and lending services to customers via commercial and investment banks. They must manage customers' expectations and arrest customer churn in this dynamic environment of interest rate fluctuations. On the other hand, providing loans to eligible customers with a good track record is essential to maintain the loan quality and avert future crises. Similarly, financial market participants must regularly perform a stress test on their assets to predict and avoid future troubles brewing due to uncertain market conditions. For the insurance industry, correct and quick disbursal of the claim amount to genuine customers has been defined as a critical parameter to success.

Banking	Financial Markets	Insurance
Monetary authorities	Commodities	Health insurance
Retail banking	Stock exchanges	Property & casualty insurance
Commercial banking	Bond markets	Life insurance & annuity
Investment banking	Money markets	Reinsurance
Non-banking financial institutions	Derivatives	

Figure 3.2 – Segments of the financial services industry

The upcoming sections will list the problems faced by financial institutions, and later in the book we will cover some cases where technology-enabled solutions such as quantum computing may provide an early-stage advantage.

Asset management

Asset management is a critical function in this process, as it involves the planning and knowledge required to minimize risks and costs associated with a set of assets. Risk is a significant driver in financial interactions, and events such as the 2008 financial crisis have highlighted the importance of stress testing banks and insurance companies to prevent systemic market crises from occurring. Investors aim to strike a balance between expected returns and risk, and diversifying their portfolios is one way to achieve this balance. However, unforeseeable events can still occur, and regulators and financial entities must remain vigilant to control risks in the financial sector. Although regulators have strengthened their interaction with financial entities to prevent such events from happening in the future, the complexity of human behavior and financial markets remains a challenge. Overall, managing assets and risks is a critical consideration in the financial sector, as it impacts the potential return on investment and the stability of the entire system. While stress testing and regulatory controls can help mitigate risks, ongoing vigilance and preparation are necessary to prevent systemic market crises from occurring.

Risk analysis

Evaluating the risks associated with assets is crucial, especially when dealing with **money market funds (MMFs)**. Factors such as short-term interest rates and sector-specific evaluations can influence the volatility of these funds. Additionally, consumer behavior and fluctuations in short-term interest rates can have a significant impact on portfolio management.

In order to conduct a thorough assessment of an MMF's health, regulatory authorities provide guidelines outlining the extreme scenarios and risks to be considered. This ensures a strong foundation for understanding the global status of these funds. For instance, Article 28(7) of the **Money Market Funds Regulation (MMFR)** mandates that stress-test guidelines be provided by the **European Securities and Markets Authority (ESMA)**, establishing homogeneity in the scenarios considered by all MMFs. Examining the latest ESMA report reveals a clear set of risks highlighted during stress tests, including the effects on liquidity levels, credit and interest rate risks, redemption levels, and macro-economic shocks.

$$\textbf{Asset liquidity risk impact } (\%) = \frac{\textbf{Reporting NAV} - \textbf{Stressed NAV}}{\textbf{Reporting NAV}}$$

Figure 3.3 – Asset liquidity risk impact formulation taken from the ESMA stress testing guidelines

The primary driver for evaluating these factors is the **net asset value** (**NAV**), defined as the net value of an investment fund's assets, minus its liabilities, divided by the number of shares remaining. By projecting the NAV into various potential future scenarios, authorities can assess, for instance, the liquidity risk impact on investment fund assets. This process demands a comprehensive range of metrics, which inevitably places stress on the technology required to traverse the full spectrum of necessary scenarios and deliver detailed reports to regulators.

While regulators provide calibration conditions for simulating stressed NAV, the actual methods for producing accurate simulations are largely left to practitioners. They must determine how to evaluate potential value fluctuations based on specific parametrization for their assets. One approach involves the statistical evaluation of historical data to identify future trends and fluctuation regimes, considering past crises and sudden events as potential, albeit less plausible, options. Exploring all these future scenarios necessitates the use of methods such as Monte Carlo simulation, a widely adopted technique in this context.

In the forthcoming *Chapter 4*, we will delve into the simulation of these scenarios and the parametrization and calibration processes required for regulatory reporting. Moreover, we will investigate how quantum computers could potentially enhance the evaluation of future NAV distribution and establish efficiency frontiers across scenarios. By leveraging their capacity to superpose different options and simultaneously evaluate multiple scenarios, quantum computers could substantially expedite the parallelism needed for these intensive stress tests, thus proving invaluable for financial risk management.

Investment and portfolios

Financial services are tasked with managing portfolios to maximize revenue for both the entity and its clients without compromising the risk involved. This delicate balance necessitates specialized expertise in portfolio optimization, which consumes a significant portion of IT resources for these institutions. Beyond stress testing, generating a set of options that balance expected return and tolerated risk involves evaluating a potentially infinite number of choices, a complex and demanding endeavor. Pricing assets is critical not only for stress testing and regulatory reporting but also for anticipating potential market scenarios and making informed investment decisions. While Monte Carlo simulations have been widely utilized, the availability of historical data and advancements in forecasting and multivariate time series have led to a surge in **machine learning** (**ML**) applications for generating and evaluating future scenarios for sets of correlated values in specific markets.

The financial sector encompasses various types of banks and banking activities, including investment banks, which are considered a specialized subset of commercial banks. Investment banks primarily serve entities rather than individuals, managing a diverse array of assets with varying degrees of complexity. Their income is generated primarily from profits on managed activities, distinguishing them from the core services of commercial and retail banks, which focus on deposits, loans, and credit generation for the general public and large institutions. Traditionally, investment bankers relied on experience and market exposure to determine transaction prices. However, the availability of data and technology has allowed investment to take place on a much larger scale, with more statistically sound and less human-biased outcomes. Consequently, investment banking has been an early adopter of technological advancements in recent years, embracing new information paradigms, cloud transitions, big data storage and processing, and cutting-edge technologies such as **artificial intelligence** (**AI**) and ML for business process refinement and better insight generation.

A critical task for investors is identifying the most effective configuration of assets to invest in, maximizing the expected return within a given budget. The uncertainty of future trends and potential negative returns (losses) in some scenarios necessitates managing these possibilities under the concept of risk. In *Chapter 5*, we will examine how this is systematically addressed, but it is vital to understand that two main concepts drive asset selection: return and risk. The expertise of investment professionals plays a significant role in navigating the trade-offs between these factors. Assessing risk, also referred to as asset volatility, is essential to optimizing asset portfolios. Numerous complex techniques exist for determining risk, but traversing the potential scenarios an entity may face can be both time-consuming and computationally intensive. AI and ML can provide heuristic approaches to approximate solutions within this complex potential portfolio landscape. Techniques such as unsupervised learning enable the segmentation of generated portfolios based on different profitability schemes, offering a rapid approach to portfolio analysis.

The use of supervised learning techniques, such as those employed by DeepMind, has gained traction due to the ability to derive successful strategies from data, even self-generated data, and produce actionable recommendations for a given task. This automation allows for high-frequency trading capable of capturing micro-changes in the market, potentially outperforming human-driven activities. However, this technology comes with its own risks, as highly automated systems could cause global crises within milliseconds if left unchecked. This underscores the critical balance between harnessing the power of technology and understanding its potential consequences.

Profiling and data-driven services

The emergence of extensive datasets and evolving interaction channels between users and institutions has revolutionized the banking industry, paving the way for improved profiling and personalization of those interactions. Both human behavior and business processes have been transformed by digitized interactions, offering enhanced curation and customization. Investment banks, for example, are crucial in assisting firms with capital requirements, functioning as intermediaries between companies and investors. They help clients determine the issue volume and timing of bond offerings, as well as gauging market demand.

ML offers promising advancements for investment banks, enabling them to augment customer experiences by providing data-driven options and valuable market insights. ML assists clients in maximizing the value of transactions while minimizing potential financial losses. The combination of machines and humans proves to be more powerful than either alone, with the advantages and potential pitfalls of computer-aided assistance over traditional methods already becoming evident. According to Deloitte, AI can be employed throughout the **merger and acquisition** (**M&A**) life cycle, offering in-depth due diligence, aiding negotiation, and facilitating post-merger integration.

Credit card evaluation processes within banks also frequently utilize AI and ML models. In retail and corporate banking, customizing user experiences is crucial in reducing churn and providing valuable product and service recommendations to customers. AI/ML models enable detailed profiling based on data, allowing for the targeted delivery of information.

As financial institutions increasingly adopt technology, it is essential to consider the opportunities and limitations when making strategic decisions. Key questions include whether investment banks should rely more on data than experience or regulatory understanding and whether technology companies and banks should share their data to benefit from ML in an information-based economy. The potential for biased ML models to result in inadequate credit card due diligence and discriminatory lending practices must also be addressed.

Companies utilizing data-driven decision-making must ensure they are held accountable for automated outcomes and that appropriate controls are in place to guarantee unbiased and ethical decisions throughout the process. Inadequate or biased decisions can harm not only the business processes in which these intelligences are implemented but also the reputation of the institutions that fail to exercise sufficient oversight of their customer-facing interactions.

Technology is advancing to provide tools for fairness and bias evaluation, moving from explainable AI toward ethical AI. This is a complex issue, as ethical standards can vary between countries, cultural regions, or even among individuals with different religious backgrounds. Quantum ML is one area being explored by the scientific community to offer improved methods for population segmentation and information complexity reduction without introducing bias. Techniques such as probabilistic quantum clustering and quantum feature selection are emerging to enhance the ML toolbox for processing large, high-dimensional datasets efficiently and fairly.

Customer identification and customer retention

Traditional banks face ongoing competition from innovative start-ups and FinTech companies that leverage AI and ML to deliver efficient, rapid solutions. These new players are known for their inventive and transparent products and services, transforming the financial landscape. Conventional banks grapple with strict regulations, discerning customers, and a lack of product differentiation, which hinder their profitability. To succeed in this evolving market, banks must prioritize building and maintaining customer trust. Customer service is essential for retaining clients, yet traditional banks often struggle to provide exceptional service through physical infrastructure and customer service professionals. AI offers the potential to significantly improve customer service in the banking sector by providing scalability, personalization, quality, a unified experience, and access to extensive information. AI can deliver these benefits at a lower operational cost, delighting customers while increasing the margin between expenditure and product revenue.

Trust is a critical component of the financial industry, and many financial institutions are still grappling with the aftermath of the 2008 financial crisis, which was driven by widespread mistrust. This lack of trust hampers financial firms' ability to acquire new clients and can lead to increased acquisition costs. A strong relationship between a customer and a financial services provider is crucial for long-term success. The concept of **customer lifetime value (CLV)** is central to this relationship. The longer a customer remains with a financial institution, the higher their CLV will be. When customers have negative experiences, they are more likely to leave, reducing their CLV and resulting in lost acquisition costs. However, excellent customer service can increase customer retention, discourage clients from exploring alternatives, and ultimately raise CLV. Happy customers are more likely to refer others to their financial service provider, lowering client acquisition costs and boosting profits.

Balancing customer retention with the ability to accurately identify valuable customers is vital for financial institutions in the digital age. Profiling and targeting strategies must be implemented to engage the majority of the customer base. However, executing these strategies systematically can present challenges that banks must be prepared to address. In conclusion, the digitization of the financial sector offers both opportunities and challenges for traditional banks as they strive to adapt to the ever-changing landscape. By leveraging AI and ML, banks can improve customer service, build trust, and enhance the customer experience. However, they must also navigate the potential pitfalls of customer profiling and targeting to ensure fair, unbiased, and effective strategies for customer retention and acquisition.

Information gap

An institution operates as a complex system with multiple layers interacting between the customer and the core banking processes. It is a common experience for customers to encounter delays when reaching out to an organization's contact center, as representatives take time to gather relevant information about the customer and their products or services. The intricacies of customer interactions, their satisfaction levels, their complaint history, and the overall strategy based on CLV, credit scoring, or general bank policies can be challenging for a call agent to synthesize during a fluid conversation. In fact, less empathetic and interactive call agents may contribute to customer dissatisfaction with their banking institution.

The ongoing digital revolution has enabled customers to directly access and manage their services through digital channels, such as websites, apps, and home assistants. This digitization of channels and customer interactions has transformed the way banking processes are conducted and facilitated more intelligent decision-making. Natural-language interaction and understanding of individual needs and inquiries have become possible, as well as the ability to gauge customer satisfaction levels through behavioral analytics. With the increased use of AI and ML technologies, banks can now offer personalized and efficient customer experiences. These technologies not only enhance customer interactions but also provide valuable insights for bank executives. A comprehensive 360-degree customer view enables decision-makers to evaluate specific customers or cohorts, ensuring well-informed decisions that prioritize customer needs and satisfaction.

Moreover, the digital transformation of the banking industry has expanded the potential for cross-selling and up-selling opportunities. By analyzing customer data and preferences, banks can now provide tailored product and service recommendations, thereby strengthening customer relationships and increasing overall revenue. Despite the benefits of digitization, it is crucial for financial institutions to maintain a human touch in their customer interactions. As technology advances, banks must strike a balance between leveraging digital channels and maintaining empathetic, personal connections with their clients. Ensuring that customers feel valued and understood should remain a top priority, even as institutions embrace innovative solutions.

The digitization of banking processes and customer interactions has revolutionized the industry, providing opportunities for more intelligent decision-making, personalized experiences, and improved customer satisfaction. As financial institutions continue to adopt these digital technologies, they must also prioritize maintaining strong, empathetic connections with their clients to ensure long-term success and trust in the banking relationship.

Customization

The personalization of services is essential for delighting customers in today's competitive market. Recognizing that every individual is unique, standardized methods and procedures fall short of providing tailored solutions. AI tools, capable of handling various processes and operations, offer a means to deliver customized experiences without sacrificing efficiency. Consequently, AI strikes a balance between scalability, personalization, and cost-effectiveness, making it an ideal solution for large organizations seeking to maintain a competitive edge.

Customer acquisition necessitates high sales volume and numerous touchpoints, often requiring increased infrastructure and human resources. Expanding physical locations and hiring additional customer service representatives can be costly, while also potentially leading to the inconsistent application of company policies across different locations. However, localized expertise and personalized interactions remain crucial components of customer satisfaction. Overly generalized AI systems can disrupt the delicate balance between cost-effective automation and customer satisfaction, highlighting the need for tailored solutions.

Developing and implementing AI or ML solutions within the banking sector requires considerable effort to ensure seamless integration with existing processes. A multitude of transactions, customer interactions, product life cycles, and fast-paced market activities must be analyzed to identify patterns and fully leverage these advanced techniques. Furthermore, it is vital to incorporate methods for fair and unbiased model delivery when curating and distilling knowledge from these systems.

One example of an AI application is the use of facial recognition technology to streamline the customer onboarding and identification process. This technology gained popularity during the smart banking trend, but several cases of bias emerged when dealing with individuals with darker skin tones. Such discriminatory practices can significantly damage a financial institution's reputation, making it crucial to address potential biases in AI systems.

Personalization is key to meeting customer expectations and maintaining a competitive edge in the banking industry. AI offers a powerful solution for delivering tailored experiences while maintaining efficiency and cost-effectiveness. However, financial institutions must carefully consider the potential pitfalls of AI implementation, such as bias and the inconsistent application of company policies, to ensure successful integration with existing banking processes. As the financial sector continues to embrace AI and ML technologies, it is essential to prioritize both the benefits and potential risks associated with these advanced tools. By striking a balance between personalization, scalability, and fairness, banks can leverage AI to deliver exceptional customer experiences, build trust, and ensure long-term success in an ever-evolving market.

Fraud detection

Beyond the effect of customization in CLV, one key issue many entities face is the ability to identify and set countermeasures for fraud within their customer base. It is a critical issue as it damages the activity of the entity, introducing risk where customers should be an asset to the entity's activity.

Given the ability to segment and profile the customer base, it is evident AI or ML techniques can be used for said purpose. It can identify fraudsters, forecast patterns for existing customers that have not yet shown that behavior, and limit the harm those potential future actions could cause to the entity's business activity.

It is also a matter of sensibility as there exists a chance our models may flag a customer as a fraud committer when this is just a prediction associated with a probability of it happening. This requires best practices while training and evaluating fraud detection models as the sensibility and specificity of it will need to be tuned for proper usage. Luckily, defaulters are a minority in the general case, but this also means less evidence is found in the data the entity may have available when evaluating this condition within its customer base.

Having gone over some best practices and critical points on performing said evaluations, we will see in *Chapter 6* how QML models may help in broadening the scope of the models available for performing this task and, in some cases, thanks to the expressivity quantum neural networks have shown in the literature, we may have an advantage over the classical methods that, even if minimal, may pose a substantial impact on the business.

Summary

Financial institutions, which encompass a broad spectrum from retail and investment banks to insurance providers, play an indispensable role in facilitating transactions and risk management. Asset management, a critical function, often employs stress testing and regulatory controls to evaluate and mitigate risks associated with assets such as money market funds, a process that may be expedited and enhanced by quantum computing in the future. Portfolio optimization, another foundational aspect of financial services, balances anticipated returns against associated risks, increasingly utilizing advanced technologies such as artificial intelligence (AI) and machine learning (ML). As these technologies become integral to the investment landscape, it is crucial to thoroughly comprehend the implications of such automation. The adoption of AI and ML by financial institutions aims not only to enhance customer experiences and optimize business operations but also to maintain ethical standards and accountability. This technological evolution also presents challenges from FinTech start-ups that leverage these technologies, thus underlining the need for traditional banks to continuously build customer trust and improve service delivery. The ongoing digital transformation of customer interaction channels fosters intelligent decision-making and enables natural-language interaction with banking processes, thereby improving customer satisfaction. Concurrently, the application of AI and ML models must emphasize fairness and unbiasedness alongside the pursuit of personalization and efficiency to safeguard institutional reputation. Lastly, AI and ML can serve as effective tools for detecting potential fraud within the customer base and devising appropriate countermeasures, which necessitates adherence to best practices and careful evaluation.

In the next chapter, classical and quantum algorithms used to determine derivatives pricing have been used.

Further reading

Some of the topics that were briefly explained in this chapter have extensive literature behind them. Financial services have been around for a while and many resources can be found for those new to the field and willing to learn more details about the topics that we covered in this specialized material on financial quantum computing.

Problems and techniques around derivative pricing, portfolio optimization, and fraud detection will have some specific literature referenced in their corresponding chapters. Additionally, the next chapter will provide in-depth coverage of the techniques employed in computational finance.

For those wanting to better understand the complex ecosystem of the banking sector and how it operates, some interesting references on financial markets are the publications by Pagano (1993) and Bond et al. (2012).

Those interested in ethical and fairness terms relating to the financial market may find the paper by Sherfin & Statman (1993) helpful. If your interest is related to ethical challenges in the domain of AI and ML, and is applied by companies worldwide, you may find the work of Jobin et al. (2019) interesting.

For guidelines for risk assessment, stress testing guidelines, and a general overview, we highly encourage browsing ESMA's website (https://www.esma.europa.eu/) as well as the US Government Accountability Office website (https://www.gao.gov/). The guidelines and recommendations are quite general and given the size of the markets they regulate, it might be of general use, but it is recommended to also query your local authorities.

From the topics mentioned previously that may not be covered in this book but may be of interest to you, we would like to highlight the relevance of high-frequency trading systems and recommender systems, which allow for further automation in many financial institutions nowadays. Both are highly active topics, but we would like to point out two recommendations for those interested in these topics.

Zibriczky (2016) offers a gentle introduction that presents a review of relevant examples of the application of different types of recommender systems for financial use cases presented in this chapter. Many references can be found on high-frequency trading due to its popularity, but Cartea et al. (2015) present a nice compendium to introduce and understand the fundamentals of these techniques.

Some of these techniques, even though they might be relevant to the sector and interesting, still do not offer a good counterpart to the classical ones in the quantum domain. Nevertheless, quantum computing brings new ideas and applications daily, and hardware providers are continuously improving their offerings, adding more capacity for applications, so it is important to remain aware of the advancements in the field.

References

Bond, P., Edmans, A., & Goldstein, I. (2012). The real effects of financial markets. Annu. Rev. Financ. Econ., 4(1), 339-360.

Cartea, Á., Jaimungal, S., & Penalva, J. (2015). Algorithmic and High-Frequency Trading. Cambridge University Press.

Jobin, A., Ienca, M., & Vayena, E. (2019). The global landscape of AI ethics guidelines. Nature Machine Intelligence, 1(9), 389-399.

Pagano, M. (1993). Financial markets and growth: An overview. European economic review, 37(2-3), 613-622.

Shefrin, H. & Statman, M. (1993). Ethics, fairness, and efficiency in financial markets. Financial Analysts Journal, 49(6), 21-29.

Zibriczky, D. (2016). Recommender systems meet finance: a literature review. In Proc. 2nd Int. Workshop Personalization Recommender Syst (pp. 1-10).

Part 2:
Advanced Applications of
Quantum Computing in Finance

This section explores the role of **Quantum Machine Learning** (**QML**) in diverse financial domains. First, it unpacks how QML eases the complex task of derivatives valuation. Next, it investigates the potential of QML in redefining portfolio management, a process involving prudent financial decision-making. The analysis then moves to credit risk, where QML could help identify potential defaulters more accurately. Finally, it emphasizes the significance of the practical implementation of these quantum technologies in real-world environments.

This part has the following chapters:

- *Chapter 4, Derivatives Valuation*
- *Chapter 5, Portfolio Valuations*
- *Chapter 6, Credit Risk Analytics*
- *Chapter 7, Implementation in Quantum Clouds*

4
Derivative Valuation

Derivatives pricing is one of the most crucial aspects of quantitative finance. The gross market value of derivatives contracts stood at $12.4 trillion (*OTC derivatives statistics at end-December 2021 – bis.org*), making it one of the most lucrative and challenging problems to simulate and optimize. Although many aspects of derivative pricing can be computed using classical computing, gate-based quantum computers can be an efficient resource when multiple computations are required, due to their ability to parallelize and handle multiple assets. This chapter looks into the theoretical aspects of derivatives pricing and examines its real-time applications through classical computing and gate-based quantum computers.

This chapter addresses the need to explain option pricing from a layman's point of view. Various aspects of option pricing will be described in an easy-to-understand manner. Different case studies and anecdotes will be incorporated to make the explanation more comprehensive and detailed. The first part covers the theoretical aspects of derivatives pricing, while the practical aspects of transitioning to more complicated **Quantum Machine Learning** (**QML**) models are also introduced.

In subsequent sections, we will see a demo example of implementing options pricing using classical and quantum computing. The valuation of a plain vanilla option will be derived using the classical Monte Carlo simulation method. Afterward, a comprehensive case study with code snippets will help you understand the implementation of mathematical modeling of derivatives pricing on quantum computing.

The following topics will be covered in this chapter:

- Derivatives pricing – the theoretical aspects
- Classical implementation of the Monte Carlo simulation for derivatives valuation
- A quantum computing algorithm for derivatives valuation

Derivatives pricing – the theoretical aspects

Learning the factors that go into setting derivatives pricing is crucial. An in-depth knowledge of financial product pricing is essential to make sound investing decisions, whether you're on the buying or selling side of the market. After all, knowing how a product's attributes interact to produce value is necessary to decide what to offer or bid for a financial product. It is crucial to comprehend the price of financial assets. The capital asset pricing model and its variants, based on discounted cash flow, help establish values for financial assets. However, unlike traditional assets such as stocks and bonds, derivatives have their challenges, but they also have several unexpectedly straightforward properties. In the next section, we will discuss the important concept of money's time value, which forms the basis for securities pricing.

The time value of money

The value of money fluctuates over time. What does this imply in detail? If you had the choice between getting $100 now or $100 a year from now, which would you choose? The majority would probably get the $100 as quickly as feasible (today). The further a cash flow is in the future, the less valuable it becomes. A similar approach may be extended to compare the values of cash flows at various times. Let's say we want to get $100 one year instead of two years from now. Mathematically, a risk-free interest rate is to blame for the temporal variation in the value of money. The quicker funds are received, the quicker interest may be collected. Calculating the present value of the cash flows and comparing them makes it possible to compare various amounts of money at different dates.

Case study one

The time value of money is a key concept in finance that refers to the idea that money today is worth more than the same amount in the future, due to its earning potential. This concept is important in many financial decisions, including investments, loans, and other transactions. In this essay, we will explore an example of the time value of money in the context of a future discounted price, with a $450 cash flow for three years at a 10% discount rate.

Assuming a discount rate of 10%, the present value of a $450 cash flow in three years can be calculated using the following formula:

$$PV = \frac{FV}{(1 + r)^n}$$

where r represents the discount rate, n refers to the number of periods, and PV and FV represent the present and future values respectively.

Using this formula, we can calculate the present value of a $450 cash flow in three years as follows:

$$PV = \frac{\$450}{(1 + 0.1)^3}$$
$$PV = \$300.30$$

This means that the present value of a $450 cash flow in three years at a 10% discount rate is $300.30. In other words, if we were to receive $450 in three years and wanted to know how much that cash flow is worth today, we would discount it back to its present value of $300.30.

The time value of money can also be applied to investments. For example, let's say we can invest $1,000 today in a fund that promises to pay a 10% annual return for three years. Using the formula to calculate the future value of a lump sum investment, we can calculate the future value of this investment as follows:

$$FV = PV \times (1 + r)^n$$

$$FV = \$1,000 \times (1 + 0.1)^3$$

$$FV = \$1,331$$

If we were to invest $1,000 today at a 10% annual return for three years, the investment would be worth $1,331 at the end of the third year.

Hence, the time value of money is a fundamental concept in finance that plays a crucial role in many financial decisions. Whether calculating the present value of future cash flows or the future value of investments, understanding the time value of money is essential to make informed financial decisions and manage risk effectively. By applying the formulas and concepts discussed in this essay, investors can make better financial decisions and achieve their financial goals. The following passage will discuss a fundamental concept of securities pricing.

Securities pricing

Securities pricing refers to determining the value of financial instruments such as stocks, bonds, options, and other investment products. The price of a security reflects the supply and demand for that security in the market, which is affected by a wide range of factors, including company performance, economic conditions, and investor sentiment.

In general, the price of a security is determined through the interaction of buyers and sellers in the market. When there are more buyers than sellers, the security price goes up, and when there are more sellers than buyers, the price goes down.

There are several methods used to determine the price of securities, including the following:

- **Market-based pricing**: This is the most common method of pricing securities, where the price of a security is determined based on its current market value. Market-based pricing is often used for publicly traded securities, where prices are determined through bidding and trading on an exchange.

- **Fundamental analysis**: This method involves analyzing a company's financial statements and other relevant information to determine its intrinsic value. Fundamental analysis considers revenue, earnings, assets, liabilities, and growth potential to determine whether a security is undervalued or overvalued.

- **Technical analysis**: This method involves analyzing price and volume data to identify patterns and trends that can be used to predict future price movements. Technical analysis is often used with fundamental analysis to make investment decisions.

- **Options pricing models**: These models use mathematical formulas to determine the fair value of options contracts, based on factors such as the underlying asset price, the time to expiration, and the underlying asset's volatility.

In addition to these methods, market participants also consider other factors, such as interest rates, inflation, geopolitical events, and market sentiment when determining the price of securities.

Case study two

Securities pricing values financial assets such as stocks, bonds, and other securities. Market demand, economic conditions, and company performance influence securities pricing. Let's consider an example of securities pricing for a company, ABC, that issued a bond with a face value of $1,000 and a coupon rate of 5%, payable annually for ten years.

Step one – determine the market interest rate

The market interest rate is the rate of return that investors expect to earn on similar securities. Let's assume that the market interest rate for bonds with similar characteristics as ABC's bond is 6%.

Step two – calculate the present value of the bond

Using the market interest rate of 6%, we can calculate the present value of the bond using the following formula:

$$PV = \frac{C}{(1+r)^n} + \frac{FV}{(1+r)^n}$$

For ABC's bond, the annual coupon payment is $50 (5% of $1,000 at face value), and the bond matures in 10 years. Using these values and the market interest rate of 6%, we can calculate the present value of the bond as follows:

$$PV = \frac{\$50}{(1+0.06)^1} + \frac{\$50}{(1+0.06)^2} + \dots + \frac{\$50}{(1+0.06)^{10}} + \frac{\$1,000}{(1+0.06)^{10}}$$

$$PV = \frac{\$50}{1.06} + \frac{\$50}{1.236} + \dots + \frac{\$50}{1.791} + \$385.54$$

$$PV = \$850.31$$

Step three – determine the market price of the bond

The bond's market price is the present value of the expected cash flows from the bond. In this case, the market price of ABC's bond is $850.31, which is the present value of the annual coupon payments and the face value discounted at the market interest rate of 6%.

Step four – compare the market price with the face value

If the market price is lower than the face value, the bond sells at a discount, and if the market price is higher than the face value, the bond sells at a premium. In this case, the market price of ABC's bond is lower than the face value of $1,000, which means the bond sells at a discount.

Thus, securities pricing is a complex process, involving analyzing various factors that influence the value of financial assets. By understanding the principles of securities pricing and using the appropriate valuation methods, investors can make informed decisions about buying and selling securities to maximize their returns and manage risk. The following section will discuss the process and methodology involving derivatives pricing.

Derivatives pricing

Derivatives pricing is a vital aspect of financial portfolio management. Within the vast realm of financial instruments, derivatives, as their name suggests, derive value from the asset they are represented by. These assets or securities may be represented by stocks, bonds, commodities, or currencies. Derivatives pricing involves determining the fair value of these instruments, which can be used for trading, hedging, or speculation purposes.

Factors that affect derivatives pricing

Several factors may affect the price of a given derivative. Relevant drivers are the price of the underlying asset, the time to expiration, the volatility of the underlying asset, and the interest rate. For example, if the price of the underlying asset increases, the price of a call option on that asset will also increase, while the price of a put option will decrease. Similarly, if the time to expiration increases, the price of an option will also increase. The underlying asset's volatility is also a significant factor in pricing derivatives, as higher volatility implies a greater chance of the asset moving in the desired direction. Finally, the interest rate can affect the price of a derivative, as it can influence the cost of borrowing and the opportunity cost of holding the underlying asset.

The methods of derivatives pricing

There are several types of pricing derivatives, including the Black-Scholes model, the binomial option pricing model, and the Monte Carlo simulation. The Black-Scholes model is a mathematical model used to price European-style options, which assumes that an underlying asset's price follows a lognormal distribution. The binomial option pricing model is a discrete-time model that uses a tree structure to represent the possible outcomes of the underlying asset's price. The Monte Carlo simulation is a stochastic model that uses random sampling to simulate the underlying asset's price path and calculate the derivative's expected value.

The risks involved in derivatives pricing

Derivatives pricing involves several risks, including market, credit, and operational risks. Market risk arises from changes in an underlying asset's price, which can affect the value of the derivative. Credit risk arises when one party fails to fulfill its obligation to the other party, which can lead to default. Operational risk arises from errors in the trading, settlement, or accounting of derivatives, which can result in financial losses.

Derivatives pricing is a crucial aspect of financial portfolio management, as it allows investors to hedge their risks, speculate on market movements, and create customized investment strategies. There are several methods to calculate the price of derivatives, including the Black-Scholes model, the binomial option pricing model, and the Monte Carlo simulation. However, derivatives pricing also involves several risks, including market, credit, and operational risks. Therefore, it is essential to thoroughly understand these risks and use appropriate risk management strategies to minimize their impact on financial portfolios.

Case study three

One example of securities pricing is the pricing of a stock option. A stock option is a derivative that, without the obligation for it, gives the holder the right to buy or sell a specific number of shares of a stock. This is done at a contract-binding price (known as the strike price) within a specific time frame. The price of a stock, as mentioned, may be affected by a number of factors.

For example, let's consider a call option for 100 shares of XYZ Corporation, with a strike price of $50 and an expiration date of three months from now. If the current market price of XYZ Corporation's stock is $55, the option would have an intrinsic value of $5 per share (the difference between the market price and the strike price). However, the option's price would also be influenced by factors such as the time to expiration, the volatility of the stock, and the interest rate.

Suppose the stock's volatility is high, indicating a higher likelihood of significant price swings, and the interest rate is low, making it cheaper to borrow money. In that case, the option's price would be higher, due to the increased likelihood of the stock price moving in the desired direction, making the option more valuable. Conversely, if the stock's volatility is low and the interest rate is high, the option's price would be lower, since the likelihood of the stock price moving in the desired direction is lower.

The cost of borrowing money is higher. Overall, pricing securities, such as options, involves assessing multiple factors and using various pricing models to determine a fair value. The pricing process helps investors make informed investment decisions and manage risk effectively.

The process of securities pricing involves several steps, including the following:

1. **Identifying the security**: The first step in pricing securities is to identify the specific security being priced. This could be a stock, bond, option, or another financial instrument.

2. **Gathering information**: Gather all relevant information about the security, including its current market price, historical price trends, any news or events that may affect its value, and any associated risks.

3. **Determining pricing factors**: The price of a security is influenced by several factors, including supply and demand, interest rates, economic conditions, and market sentiment. Identify the most relevant factors likely to affect the security's price.

4. **Choosing a pricing model**: There are several pricing models used to determine the fair value of securities, including the **discounted cash flow (DCF)** model, the **dividend discount model (DDM)**, and the Black-Scholes model for options. Choose the most appropriate model, based on the type of security being priced and the available information.

5. **Calculating the price**: Once the pricing model is chosen, calculate the security's fair value, using the relevant pricing factors and any assumptions required by the model. This may involve complex mathematical calculations, especially for options and other derivatives.

6. **Evaluating the results**: Evaluate the results of the pricing model and ensure that the calculated price is reasonable and consistent with market conditions and other available information.

7. **Updating pricing regularly**: Securities pricing is an ongoing process, and prices can change rapidly based on new information and market conditions. Regularly update the pricing model, and recalculate the security's price as needed to ensure that the investment portfolio is up to date and accurately reflects the value of the securities.

This shows that securities pricing is a complex process that involves multiple steps, including identifying the security, gathering information, determining pricing factors, choosing a pricing model, calculating the price, evaluating the results, and updating pricing regularly. By following these steps, investors can make informed investment decisions and manage risk effectively.

Derivatives pricing – theory

The Black-Scholes model is widely used for pricing derivatives such as options. Fischer Black and Myron Scholes came up with this formalism in 1973, which has since become a cornerstone of modern finance. The model considers various factors that influence the value of an option, including the underlying asset price, the option's strike price, the time to expiration, volatility, and the risk-free interest rate. Let's consider an example of the Black-Scholes model when setting the price a call option could pose on a stock.

Let's assume that a call option on the XYZ stock with a strike price of $50 is set to expire in six months. The current stock price is $52, and the volatility of the stock is 20%, while the risk-free interest rate is 3%.

Step one – calculate the d_1 and d_2 values

$$d_1 = \frac{[\ln \frac{S}{K} + (r + \frac{\sigma^2}{2})t]}{(\sigma \sqrt{t})}$$

$$d_2 = d_1 - \sigma \sqrt{t}$$

where S is the current stock price, K is the option's strike price, r is the risk-free interest rate, σ is the volatility of the stock, and t is the time to expire in years.

Using the given values, we can calculate d_1 and d_2 as follows:

$$d_1 = \frac{[\ln \frac{52}{50} + (0.03 + \frac{0.2^2}{2})0.5]}{(0.2 \sqrt{0.5})} = 0.$$

$$d_2 = 0.5601 - 0.2\sqrt{0.5} = 0.4187$$

Step two – calculate the option price

Using the following formula, we can calculate the theoretical price of the call option:

$$C = S \times N(d_1) - Ke^{-rt}N(d_2)$$

Where C is the theoretical price of the call option, S is the current stock price, K is the option's strike price, r is the risk-free interest rate, t is the time to expiration in years, N() is the cumulative distribution function of the standard normal distribution.

Using the given values, we can calculate the theoretical price of the call option as follows:

$$C = 52 \times N(0.5601) - 50\,e^{-0.03*0.5}N(0.4187) = \$4.42$$

Step three – analyze the results

The calculated theoretical price of the call option is $4.42, which means that an investor can purchase the option for $4.42 and has the right to buy the XYZ stock for $50 before the expiration date in six months. If the stock price goes above $54.42 (the strike price plus the option price), the investor can exercise the option and make a profit. On the other hand, if the stock price stays below the strike price, the investor can let the option expire and only lose the premium paid for the option.

Thus, the Black-Scholes model is an important tool for pricing derivatives such as options. By taking into account various factors that influence the value of an option, investors can make informed decisions about buying and selling options to manage risk and maximize returns. However, it's important to note that the model has some limitations and assumptions, such as constant volatility and no transaction costs, which may only sometimes be true in real-world situations.

The Black-Scholes-Merton (BSM) model

The BSM model is widely regarded as one of the most important breakthroughs in modern finance, and its widespread use has made options trading more efficient and accessible to investors.

The BSM model uses six variables to determine the fair value of an option. These variables include volatility, the type, the stock price, the strike price, time, and the risk-free rate. Volatility refers to the degree of fluctuation in the underlying asset's price. In contrast, the type refers to whether the option is a call or a put option. A call option refers to the buying action as opposed to a put option, which refers to the selling right. The stock price and strike price refer to the current market price and the predetermined price at which the underlying asset can be bought or sold. Time refers to the length of time until the option expires. The risk-free rate is the theoretical rate of return on a risk-free investment, such as a government bond.

The BSM model is often used to determine the fair value of options based on these six variables. To illustrate the BSM model, let us consider an example of an investor who holds a call option with a strike price of $100, which will expire in six months. We will assume that the current market price of the underlying asset is $110, the risk-free rate is 3%, and the underlying asset's volatility is 20%.

Using the BSM model, we can calculate the fair value of the call option. The formula to calculate the fair value of a call option using the BSM model is:

$$C = S \times N(d_1) - Ke^{-rt}N(d_2)$$

where C is the fair value of the call option, S is the current market price of the underlying asset, K is the strike price of the option, r is the risk-free rate, t is the time until expiration, and $N(d_1)$ and $N(d_2)$ are cumulative standard normal distribution functions.

Applying the formula to the given example, we have:

$$d_1 = \frac{[\ln\frac{110}{100} + (0.03 + \frac{0.2^2}{2})0.5]}{(0.2\sqrt{0.5})} = 0.9568$$

$$d_2 = 0.9568 - 0.2\sqrt{0.5} = 0.8154$$

$$N(d_1) = 0.831$$

$$N(d_2) = 0.7926$$

$$C = 110 \times 0.831 - 100 \times e^{-0.03\times0.5} \times 0.7926 = \$13.29$$

Therefore, the fair value of the call option is $13.29. This means that if the investor were to sell the option at this price, it would be a fair price based on the BSM model.

The BSM model is a widely used formula that allows investors to determine the fair value of options based on six variables – volatility, type, the stock price, the strike price, time, and the risk-free rate. The model has revolutionized the options market by making pricing more efficient and transparent. The example presented here illustrates the application of the BSM model and highlights its importance in modern finance.

Assumptions

The BSM model is a widely used options pricing model that assumes several factors. These assumptions are critical in determining the fair value of an underlying asset for either of the two options – put or call. Here are some of the significant assumptions of the BSM model:

- **Efficient markets**: The model assumes that markets are efficient, meaning all available information is immediately reflected in the asset's price

- **No dividends**: The model assumes that the underlying asset does not pay dividends during the option's life

- **No transaction costs**: The model assumes no transaction costs are associated with buying or selling the underlying asset or option

- **No arbitrage**: The model assumes that there are no arbitrage opportunities, which means it is impossible to make a riskless profit by simultaneously buying and selling the underlying asset and option

- **Lognormal distribution**: The model assumes that the underlying asset's price follows a lognormal distribution, which means that the price changes are proportional to the current price and a random variable

- **Constant volatility**: The model assumes that the underlying asset's volatility is constant over the option's life

These assumptions may be false, but they provide a useful framework to understand the factors influencing price options.

Limitations

The BSM model is one of the most widely used models for options pricing. However, despite its popularity, the model has several limitations that make it less suitable for certain options and market conditions. Some of the limitations of the BSM model include the following:

- **An assumption of continuous trading**: The BSM model assumes that trading in the underlying asset is continuous, which means that the stock price can change by an infinite number of small amounts. In reality, trading is not continuous, and stock prices can experience sudden and large changes due to news events, market shocks, and other factors.

- **No consideration of market frictions**: The BSM model assumes that no transaction costs, taxes, or other market frictions affect the price of the underlying asset. In reality, these frictions can significantly impact the value of options.

- **An assumption of constant volatility**: The BSM model assumes that volatility is constant over the option's life. In reality, volatility can be highly variable and change significantly over short periods.

- **Limited applicability to specific options**: The BSM model is most suitable for pricing European options, which can only be exercised at expiration. The model is less suitable for pricing American options, which can be exercised before expiration, and other exotic options.

- **Limited applicability to specific market conditions**: The BSM assumes specific behavior distribution on both the asset and markets. This limits the normal case where they can show all types of distributions, ranging from skewed to normal distributions as observed in reality.

- **Use of the risk-neutral approach**: The BSM model uses a risk-neutral approach to pricing options, which assumes that investors are indifferent to the risk and that the expected return on the option is equal to the risk-free rate. This assumption may not apply, especially for highly risky or illiquid options.

Despite these limitations, the BSM model remains a valuable tool for options pricing and has been used extensively by traders, investors, and academics since its introduction in 1973. However, it is essential to recognize the model's limitations and use it appropriately in the context of specific market conditions and types of options. These limitations can be overcome with the help of computational modeling.

Computational models

The BSM model is a popular mathematical formula used to calculate the price of European-style options. However, the traditional BSM model has limitations, such as the assumption of constant volatility and risk-neutral pricing, which can lead to inaccurate pricing predictions. In recent years, machine learning algorithms have been applied to enhance the BSM model and improve its predictive power. In this subsection, we will explore the implementation of the BSM model using machine learning algorithms, its benefits, and its limitations.

The BSM assumes the following:

- The price of an underlying asset exhibits a random behavior characterized by a stochastic process known as Geometric Brownian motion

- The volatility of the asset's returns is constant over the option's life

- The risk-free rate is known and constant

- The option can only be exercised at the expiration date

To implement the BSM model using machine learning algorithms, you can use historical data to train the model and learn from past market behavior. The model can then use this learned information to predict future prices. Machine learning algorithms, such as neural networks and decision trees, can help overcome the limitations of the traditional BSM model by doing the following:

- Accounting for non-constant volatility in asset returns

- Incorporating new market data in real time to update pricing predictions

- Considering non-normal distributions of asset returns and incorporating skewness and kurtosis into pricing calculations

Using machine learning algorithms to enhance the BSM model has several benefits, such as the following:

- Improved accuracy in predicting option prices

- Increased flexibility in modeling complex financial instruments

- Faster pricing calculations, allowing for more timely trading decisions

However, there are also limitations to using machine learning algorithms in conjunction with the BSM model, such as the following:

- Increased complexity and the need for specialized technical expertise

- The potential to overfit the model with historical data, leading to inaccurate pricing predictions

- A large amount of high-quality data is needed to train the model effectively

Despite these limitations, implementing the BSM model using machine learning algorithms represents a promising approach to pricing financial instruments. Incorporating new market data in real time and accounting for non-constant volatility can improve accuracy, helping traders to make more informed decisions. Implementing the BSM model using machine learning algorithms significantly advances financial modeling. By incorporating new data and accounting for non-constant volatility, this approach can improve the accuracy of pricing predictions and allow for more informed trading decisions. However, it is essential to recognize this approach's limitations and use it with other financial models and analysis techniques.

Machine learning

Machine learning in derivative pricing employs complex algorithms to predict future derivative prices, drawing from a vast dataset of historical trading data. By modeling market dynamics and identifying patterns, it provides more accurate price forecasts than traditional models. This not only reduces financial risk but also optimizes trading strategies. Furthermore, it provides insights into market behavior, assisting in the development of more resilient financial systems.

Geometric Brownian motion

We must model the underlying equities before estimating the price of derivative instruments based on their value. The **geometric Brownian motion (GBM)**, also called the Wiener process, is the method often uses to model the stochastic process of a Brownian motion, driving the future values of an asset. It helps create trajectories that the asset price of the underlying stock may take in the future.

A stochastic or random process, here defined as the time-dependent function S(t), is said to follow GBM if it can be expressed as the following SDE:

$$dS_t = \mu S_t dt + \sigma S_t dW_t$$

where:

- S_t – the stock price at time t
- dS_t – the change in stock price from time t
- μ – the drift term
- σ – the volatility term
- d_t – the change in time
- dW_t – the Brownian motion

Wt notation belongs to the Wiener process or Brownian motion, μ is the percentage drift, and σ is the percentage volatility. Itô's lemma (reference), the following analytical solution can be derived:

$$S(t) = S_0 \exp\left(\left(r - \frac{1}{2}\sigma^2\right)t + \sigma\sqrt{t}\,z\right)$$

Where S_0 is the initial stock index level, t the time to maturity when the stock will be acted on, r a constant representing the risk-less short rate, σ the constant volatility (often computed as the standard deviation of the stock), and z a normally distributed random variable. Thus, S(t) can easily be estimated for a given stock at time t.

One key feature of GBM is that the projected distribution of the asset follows a log-normal distribution. This is convenient given that, as we saw before, we expect certain skewness for the value to be lower.

By setting I random numbers for z_i $i \in 1, ..., I$, and computing the associated $S_i(t)$ for each sample, we can generate said future price distribution. Let's create a hypothetical case to prove that:

```python
import numpy as np
from scipy.stats import norm
t = 1.0 # year
K = 105 # Strike price
r = 0.05 # Riskless short rate
sigma = 0.25 # Volatility (stdev)
S0 = 100 # Present price
```

With those parameters set, we can simply code our St for future stock prices at the projected time t:

```python
I = 1000 # Samples
z = np.random.standard_normal(I) # z_i values
ST = S0 * np.exp((r - 0.5 * sigma ** 2) * t + sigma * np.sqrt(t) * z)
```

It is interesting to plot the trajectories behind those numbers so that we know where they come from. We will place the trajectories for the future by one year:

```
months = 12 # months in a year
dt = t/months

S = np.zeros((months+1, I))
S[0] = S0
for ti in range(1, months+1):
    Z = np.random.normal(size=I)
    S[ti] = S[ti-1]*np.exp((r-0.5*sigma**2)*dt+sigma*np.sqrt(dt)*Z)
```

This iterative process will create sufficient samples of future scenarios projecting to our target time T, based on each time step preceding the value (t-1). The final code is the coded representation of the formulation described previously for the stochastic process:

```
import matplotlib as mpl
import matplotlib.pyplot as plt

mpl.style.use('seaborn-v0_8')

plt.figure(figsize=(10, 6))
for si in S.T:
    plt.plot(range(len(si)), si)

plt.xlabel("Months", fontsize=14)
plt.ylabel("Option price", fontsize=14)
plt.grid()

plt.title(f"{I} trajectories", fontsize=16)
plt.show()
```

This should yield a graph like the following one:

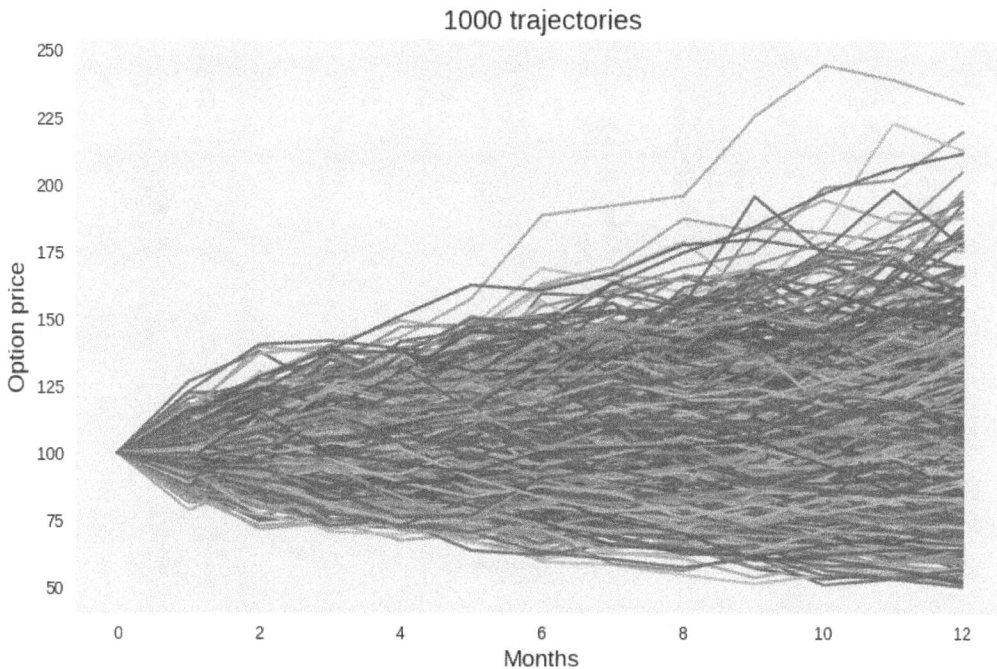

Figure 4.1 – GBM trajectories generated for a given asset price and 12 month projection (image generated by the preceding code)

It may look chaotic but it is, in fact, the representation of the underlying stochastic process we described before. We can see how all trajectories start from the same point (the price today) and evolve in different directions, according to previously described equations, broadening the range as we move forward in time. If we plot the distribution at time T (one year in our case), we can see that the potential evolution meets the criteria previously explained, and by showcasing the price distribution, we are able to make assumptions about the likelihood of some of those specific trajectories, some of which are more plausible than others:

```
plt.figure(figsize=(10, 6))
plt.hist(S[-1], 100, density=True, facecolor='b', alpha=0.75)
plt.xlabel("Option price at time t", fontsize=14)
plt.ylabel("Probabilities", fontsize=14)
plt.grid()
plt.title(f"Price distribution at time t", fontsize=16)
plt.show()
```

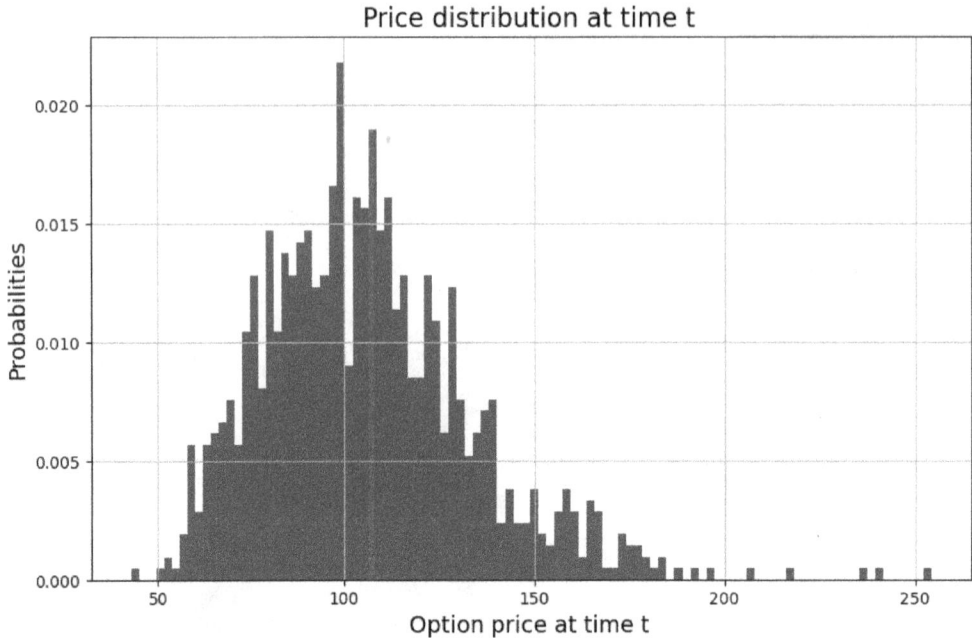

Figure 4.2 – Distribution of the price

This distribution is one that will drive all our calculations associated with the call and put prices of a stock option. Also, it is skewed toward a lower-value bet than the high valuations, which are plausible but less probable.

Quantum computing

As we saw in the previous section, in order to estimate the future price of an equity, many iterations over potential future prices need to be run. However, what if we could establish a way to load those potential distributions into quantum states and evaluate them using quantum devices? The following subsection will dig into different ways to load those future price distributions into quantum states using existing solutions for direct loading, such as Qiskit functionalities and adversarial training using PennyLane, which might be better suited for ML tasks due to its differentiable programming approach (similar to TensorFlow or PyTorch in the classical ML domain).

Implementation in Qiskit

As discussed in *Chapter 2*, Qiskit is one of the most mature quantum computing frameworks available and counts with higher-level modules so that specific applications can be easily translated to the quantum regime. This is the case with Qiskit Finance, which we will explore in detail while translating previous exercises to a quantum approach.

As we already know, classical data must be converted into a quantum state to work with it on a quantum device. In the case of price valuation, that means representing our target distribution as a quantum state. Therefore, we should build a quantum state like the following:

$$\left|\psi\right\rangle_n = \sum_0^{2^n-1} \sqrt{p_i} \left|i\right\rangle_n,$$

where p_i is the probability associated with the truncated distribution, and i is the mapping between our discrete bins, representing each value range of our target distribution.

Quantum hardware may face some challenges, which is one of the first to affect us. We need to truncate our distribution into discrete bins, as possible prices can fall into infinite bins, depending on the numerical precision we want to achieve. Thus, $\left|i\right\rangle$ will be associated with a range of values sufficiently precise to encode a probability associated with that range. The truncation for i qubits is placed as follows:

$$\{0,...,2^n-1\} \in i \longrightarrow \frac{high-low}{2^n-1} \times i + low$$

By setting the number of qubits of our algorithm, we also limit the response resolution:

```
n       qubits = 5
```

Then, we need to embed our target distribution into the quantum state explained before:

```
# Price scaling
scale = 100
S = 0.067077 * scale # initial spot price (scaled)

import numpy as np

# parameters for considered random distribution
vol = 0.6  # volatility of 60%
r = 0.02   # annual interest rate of 2%
T = 40 /  365  # 40 days to maturity

# resulting parameters for log-normal distribution
mu = (r - 0.5 * vol**2) * T + np.log(S)
sigma = vol * np.sqrt(T)
mean = np.exp(mu + sigma**2 / 2)
variance = (np.exp(sigma**2) - 1) * np.exp(2 * mu + sigma**2)
stddev = np.sqrt(variance)

# lowest and highest value considered for the spot price; in between,
an equidistant discretization is considered.
low = np.maximum(0, mean - 3 * stddev)
high = scale
```

Now that the truncated target distribution is ready, we must generate a circuit encoding the quantum state. It is a manageable task and can take time to learn how to do it properly. Luckily for us, Qiskit Finance is here to help. It already provides this functionality:

```
from qiskit_finance.circuit.library import LogNormalDistribution
dist_circ = LogNormalDistribution(num_qubits, mu=mu, sigma=stddev**2,
bounds=(low, high))
```

This circuit we just created encodes the distribution of our assets. We can print it if we like, but it will look like a big box at our working level:

```
dist_circ.draw('mpl', fold=120)
```

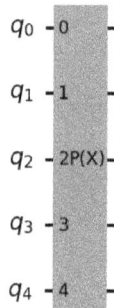

Figure 4.3 – Logical circuit generated by the code above encapsulating
the target distribution into a quantum state

However, if we look at the distribution it encodes, we can check whether it fits our expectations:

```
import matplotlib.pyplot as plt

# plot probability distribution
x = dist_circ.values / scale
y = dist_circ.probabilities

plt.bar(x, y, width=0.2)
plt.xticks(x, rotation=90)
plt.xlabel("Option price at time $t$", size=15)
plt.ylabel("Probability ($\%$)", size=15)
plt.show()
```

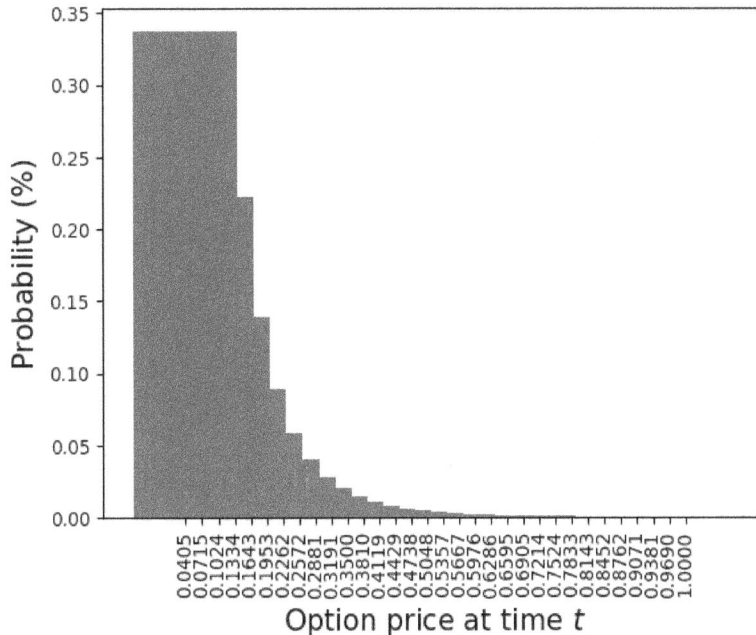

Figure 4.4 – Discretized distribution generated by the previous circuit in Figure 4.3

This target distribution shows an additional limitation we will face when encoding the problem into quantum states. Given that they encode the bin representation of our probability distribution, the truncation we might decide on could cut some of the values at each end. Therefore, an important initial assessment needs to be done in order to properly characterize the distribution we aim to fit into our quantum states.

Now that our target distribution is loaded, it is just a matter of evaluating the call and put options within the quantum regime. For that, we might need to encode a linear piecewise function that will do this price calculation according to the probability, encoded as state amplitudes of our $|i>$. It is able to estimate these prices for each of our bins, simultaneously leveraging the parallelism that quantum states provide:

$$F|x\rangle|0\rangle = \sqrt{1 - f(x)}\,|x\rangle|0\rangle + \sqrt{f(x)}\,|x\rangle|1\rangle$$

for a function $f:\{0,\ldots,2^{\wedge}n\text{-}1\} \rightarrow [0,1]$ mapping the option function and x being a n qubit state mapping the option price bin. This encoded function will flag price buckets in the distribution, with the positive probability amplitude associated with their likelihood:

```
from qiskit.circuit.library import LinearAmplitudeFunction
# set the strike price (low << strike << high)
strike = S*1.05
# and function parameters
```

```
slopes = [0, 1]
offsets = [0, 0]
```

This will be our call objective function:

```
call_option = LinearAmplitudeFunction(
    nqubits,
    slopes,
    offsets,
    domain=(low, high),
    image=(0, high - strike),
    breakpoints=[low, strike],
    rescaling_factor=0.05)
```

We can compose a European call circuit by adding this amplitude estimation block to our previous circuit. This is mostly provided by Qiskit, thanks to its high-level module:

```
from qiskit import QuantumCircuit
total_qubits = call_option      .num_qubits
european_call = QuantumCircuit(total_qubits)
european_call.append(dist_circ, range(num_qubits))
european_call.append(call_option      , range(total_qubits))
# draw the circuit
european_call.draw('mpl')
```

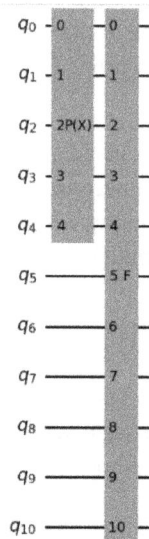

Figure 4.5 – Probability distribution generation block (P) followed by linear amplitude function block (f)

First, block (P) will add the price distribution we loaded into quantum states as the second block (F), as shown in the preceding diagram, evaluates their potential outcome. Given that amplitudes have been encoded already after the F block in the preceding figure, the last step is to extract from the quantum state into classical values the probabilities for our equity to fall into different bins of future pricing. Different methods exist for **Quantum Amplitude Estimation (QAE)**; this technique allows you to extract the amplitudes on a given quantum state. Formally, we would pose it as the ability to estimate amplitude a for state ψ, defined as:

$$a = |\langle \psi | \psi \rangle|^2$$

It is often used as the quantum counterpart of the classical Monte Carlo simulation. We will here use an iterative QAE variant that has proven better error rates compared to other approaches:

```
from qiskit import Aer
from qiskit.utils import QuantumInstance
from qiskit.algorithms import IterativeAmplitudeEstimation,
EstimationProblem
# set target precision and confidence level
epsilon = 0.01
alpha = 0.05
qi = QuantumInstance(Aer.get_backend("aer_simulator"), shots=100)

problem = EstimationProblem(
    state_preparation=european_call,
    objective_qubits=[num_qubits],
    post_processing=call_option    .post_processing,
)
# construct amplitude estimation
ae = IterativeAmplitudeEstimation(epsilon, alpha=alpha, quantum_
instance=qi)
result = ae.estimate(problem)
conf_int = np.array(result.confidence_interval_processed)
print("Estimated value:    \t%.4f" % (result.estimation_processed /
scale))
print("Confidence interval:\t[%.4f, %.4f]" % tuple(conf_int/scale))

We would obtain the following prompt then:
Estimated value:    0.0714
Confidence interval: [-0.0267, 0.1695]
```

Given that the whole process is quite systematic, Qiskit already provides all these steps in a single piece of code, so we do not have to worry about each specific step:

```
from qiskit_finance.applications.estimation import EuropeanCallPricing
european_call_pricing = EuropeanCallPricing(
    num_state_qubits=num_qubits,
    strike_price=strike       ,
    rescaling_factor=0.05,
    bounds=(low, high),
    uncertainty_model=dist_circ)
```

Using qGANs for price distribution loading

So far, we have encoded the uncertainty model of a given stock based on previously discussed statistical models, but could we exploit empirical knowledge from data instead of using statistical knowledge? We have retrieved information from Binance to get the market behaviors. We want our model to exploit the fact that each option does not behave in an isolated environment but depends on the evolutions of the rest of the stocks.

When data is available, ML techniques can have a field day, particularly generative models. Models that are once trained can create samples from a distribution.

In our particular case, we are interested in obtaining a generator model G such that:

$$G_\theta \left| \psi \right\rangle_n = \sum_0^{2^n-1} \sqrt{p_i} \left| i \right\rangle_n,$$

where the square root of p_i represents the probability amplitude of the $\left| i \right\rangle$ quantum bin to be measured. In this case, the same quantum state we have been manually loading, the state that encodes future prices as discretized probable values, will be created, based on data samples extracted from our market data through a learning process that will iterate, making G map the preceding equation.

Generative Adversarial Networks (GANs) have been successful in realistic image and video generation, as you may be aware of, due to the success in the media of deepfakes. However, GANs can be exploited in many other regimes, from tabular data to time series data, which is quite a common case in the financial sector. Their quantum version was proposed by Zoufal et al. in 2019. It is based on opposing two models, one quantum generator and one classical discriminator (a classical neural network), that are trained with opposing objectives so that we end up in a Nash equilibrium.

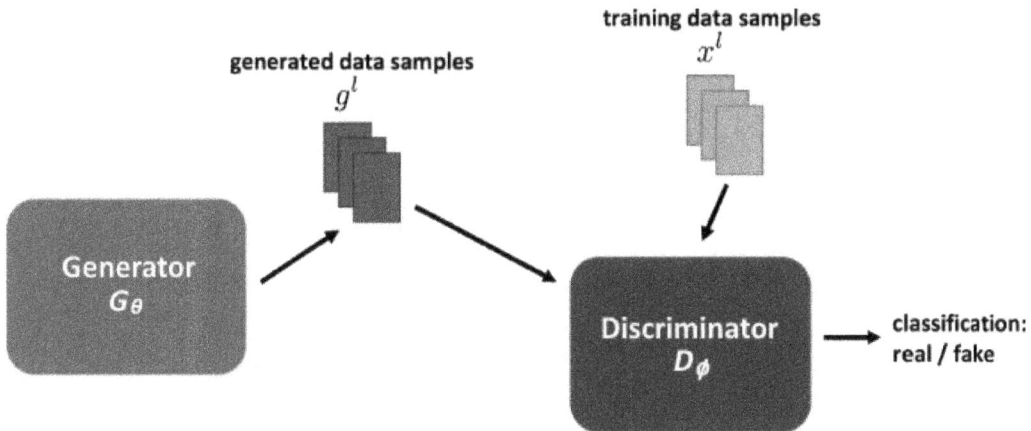

Figure 4.6 – A pictorial representation of the two models used in qGAN, the quantum
generator G and classical discriminator D, as presented by Zoufal et al.

From a dataset loaded from Binance, where we can select the stocks to be used, we can select a subset:

```
import pandas as pd
dataset = pd.read_csv("../../data/binance_data.csv")
# Lets pivot so that the date is the index and each assets presents
its closing price
pivoted = dataset.pivot(index="Closing time", columns="Asset",
values="Close")
assets = ["BNBBTC","ETHBTC","LTCBTC"]
```

As we already know, a discretized and truncated version of the data must be delivered to the quantum device to fit our data into the quantum regime:

```
    import numpy as np
# We convert the Dataframe into a numpy array
training_data = pivoted[assets].to_numpy()
# Define minimal and maximal values for the training data
bounds_min = np.percentile(training_data, 5, axis=0)
bounds_max = np.percentile(training_data, 95, axis=0)

bounds = []
for i, _ in enumerate(bounds_min):
    bounds.append([bounds_min[i], bounds_max[i]])
```

We need to map our samples to discrete values. This means depending on the qubit resolution we choose. Each sample will need to be placed in a discrete bin as before. Choosing a 3-qubit representation means our data should fit into $2^3 = 8$ bins. This is something that needs to be considered, as it affects the resolution of our model:

```
from qiskit_machine_learning.datasets.dataset_helper import
discretize_and_truncate
data_dim = [3, 3, 3]
# Pre-processing, i.e., discretization of the data (gridding)
(training_data, grid_data, grid_elements, prob_data) = discretize_and_
truncate(
    training_data,
    np.asarray(bounds),
    data_dim,
    return_data_grid_elements=True,
    return_prob=True,
    prob_non_zero=True,
)
```

We can plot our discrete distribution for the three assets to learn which distributions we can effectively encode in our quantum resource:

```
import matplotlib.pyplot as plt
fig, (ax1, ax2, ax3) = plt.subplots(1, 3, figsize=(18, 6))
ax1.hist(training_data[:, 0], bins=20)
ax1.set_title(f"BNBBTC")
ax1.set_xlabel("Values")
ax1.set_ylabel("Counts")
ax2.hist(training_data[:, 1], bins=20)
ax2.set_title("ETHBTC")
ax2.set_xlabel("Values")
ax2.set_ylabel("Counts")
ax3.hist(training_data[:, 2], bins=20)
ax3.set_title("LTCBTC")
ax3.set_xlabel("Values")
ax3.set_ylabel("Counts")
```

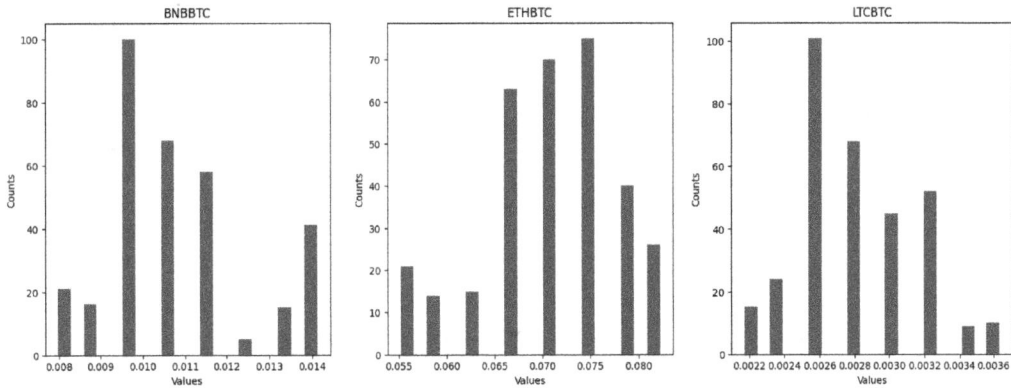

Figure 4.7 – Discretized distribution of three targeted stocks

The original paper by Zoufal et al. proposed a specific parameterized quantum circuit as the generator circuit, using a sequence of Y rotations parameterized per qubit and a cycle of CZ gates circularly entangling all qubits (called an entangling block). We will try to mimic a similar approach in PennyLane:

```
import pennylane as qml
def generator(weights, wires, repetitions):
    # Initial superposition for all possible states
    for i in range(wires):
        qml.Hadamard(wires=i)
    k = 0 # carrying index
    for i in range(wires):
        qml.RY(weights[k], wires=i)
        k += 1
    # Repetition blocks
    for _ in range(repetitions):
        # Entangling block
        for i in range(wires-1):
            qml.CZ(wires=[i, i+1])
        # Last CZ turning to zero
        qml.CZ(wires=[wires-1, 0])
        # RY rotations
        for i in range(wires):
            qml.RY(weights[k], wires=i)
            k += 1
    return qml.probs(wires=range(qubits))
```

That way we can easily use this setup for different repetitions and data dimensions we might be looking for:

```
import torch
qubits = np.sum(data_dim)
dev = qml.device("default.qubit", wires=qubits)
# Also some parameters
layers = 1
params = [np.random.uniform(np.pi) for i in range(qubits +
layers*qubits)]
gen_circuit = qml.QNode(generator, dev, interface='torch', diff_
method='best')
drawer = qml.draw_mpl(gen_circuit)
print(drawer(params, qubits, layers))
```

The output circuit should look like the one in *Figure 4.8*. Even though it does not show a detailed view in the ansatz, this circuit is parameterized by the weights or parameters provided to the generator function. To know which parameters will output our expected distribution, we need to find them by following the techniques described in *Chapter 2* for ansatz training. GANs offer a different approach to how these parameters are adapted, opposing the discriminator as the cost function for the training of the generator.

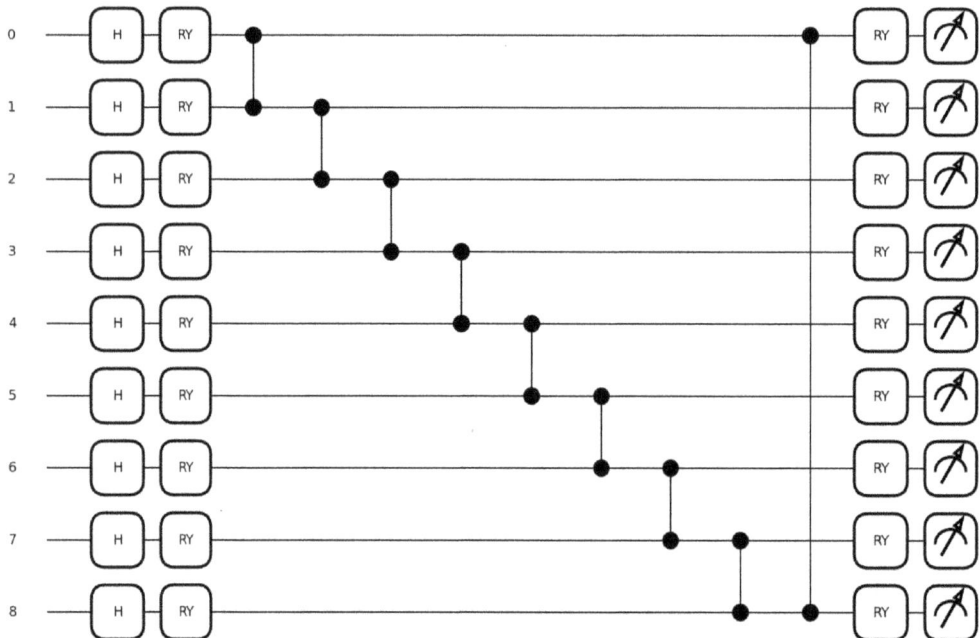

Figure 4.8 – The generator ansatz composed of Hadamard gates, the parameterized
Y rotations, and the CZ gate cycle by the nearest neighbor coupling

GANs need a counterpart for the discriminator trying to assess whether samples come from the real dataset or the data faked by the generator, as depicted in *Figure 4.8*. For this discriminator, a simple neural network will be defined, whose binary output should establish the sample source:

```
import torch.nn as nn
class Discriminator(nn.Module):
    def __init__(self, input_size):
        super(Discriminator, self).__init__()
        self.linear_input = nn.Linear(input_size, 20)
        self.leaky_relu = nn.LeakyReLU(0.2)
        self.linear20 = nn.Linear(20, 1)
        self.sigmoid = nn.Sigmoid()
    def forward(self, input: torch.Tensor) -> torch.Tensor:
        x = self.linear_input(input)
        x = self.leaky_relu(x)
        x = self.linear20(x)
        x = self.sigmoid(x)
        return x
```

This choice for the classical discriminator and its architecture of layers can be as complex as you want, and a big effort has been made by the community to identify the best-performing quantum and classical model designs for specific tasks.

The key now resides in opposing the loss functions associated with training both models, quantum and classical. The loss is opposed, so you can see how variations on the parameters associated with our generator (G) are also considered in the discriminators' loss function.

$$L_G(\phi, \theta) = -\frac{1}{m} \sum_{i=1}^{m} log D_\psi(g_i)$$

$$L_D(\phi, \theta) = -\frac{1}{m} \sum_{i=1}^{m} log D_\psi(x_i) + log\left(1 - D_\psi(g_i)\right)$$

In both cases, the Adam optimization method (*Kingma et al., 2014*) will be used to train the model. This is enabled due to the fact that both frameworks, PennyLane for the quantum model and PyTorch for the classical one, provide this method:

```
# Generator loss function
gen_loss_fun = nn.BCELoss()
# Discriminator loss function
disc_loss_fun = nn.BCELoss()
# Initialize generator and discriminator
discriminator = Discriminator(len(data_dim))

lr = 0.01  # learning rate
b1 = 0.9  # first momentum parameter
```

```
b2 = 0.999  # second momentum parameter
num_epochs = 50  # number of training epochs


    from torch.optim import Adam
# optimizer for the generator
optimizer_gen = qml.AdamOptimizer(stepsize=lr, beta1=b1, beta2=b2)
# optimizer for the discriminator
optimizer_disc = Adam(discriminator.parameters(), lr=lr, betas=(b1,
b2))
from torch.utils.data import DataLoader
# Define the training batch size
batch_size = 300
dataloader = DataLoader(training_data, batch_size=batch_size,
shuffle=True, drop_last=True)
# Generator loss list
generator_loss_values = []
# Discriminator loss list
discriminator_loss_values = []
```

Once all pieces are set, it is just a matter of iteration, looking for the Nash equilibrium between the G and D models:

```
for epoch in range(num_epochs):
    generator_loss_epoch = []
    discriminator_loss_epoch = []
    theta = torch.tensor(params, dtype=torch.float32)
    for i, data in enumerate(dataloader):
        # Adversarial ground truths
        valid = torch.ones(data.size(0), 1)
        fake = torch.zeros(data.size(0), 1)
        # Generate a batch of data points
        fake_samples = []
        for _ in range(len(data)):
            probabilities = gen_circuit(theta, qubits, layers)
            gen_data = grid_elements[torch.argmax(probabilities)]
            fake_samples.append(gen_data)
        # Train Discriminator
        optimizer_disc.zero_grad()
        # Loss measures discriminator's ability to distinguish real
from generated samples
        inputs = data.to(torch.float32)
        real_out = discriminator(inputs)
        real_loss = disc_loss_fun(real_out, valid)
```

```
        fake_input = torch.tensor(fake_samples, dtype=torch.float32)
        fake_out = discriminator(fake_input)
        fake_loss = disc_loss_fun(fake_out, fake)
        discriminator_loss = (real_loss + fake_loss) / 2
        discriminator_loss.backward(retain_graph=True)
        optimizer_disc.step()

        # Loss measures generator's ability to prepare good data
samples
        fake_input = torch.tensor(fake_samples, dtype=torch.float32)
        fake_out = discriminator(fake_input)
        generator_loss = gen_loss_fun(fake_out, valid)
        returns, prev_cost = optimizer_gen.step_and_cost(gen_circuit,
params, qubits, layers)
        params = returns[0]

        generator_loss_epoch.append(generator_loss.item())
        discriminator_loss_epoch.append(discriminator_loss.item())

    generator_loss_values.append(np.mean(generator_loss_epoch))
    discriminator_loss_values.append(np.mean(discriminator_loss_
epoch))
```

By plotting the evolution of both loss functions (appended to `generator_loss_values` and `discriminator_loss_values` arrays), we can see how both models try to adapt to one another so that the generator will ultimately be the best version of a synthetic data generator we can achieve.

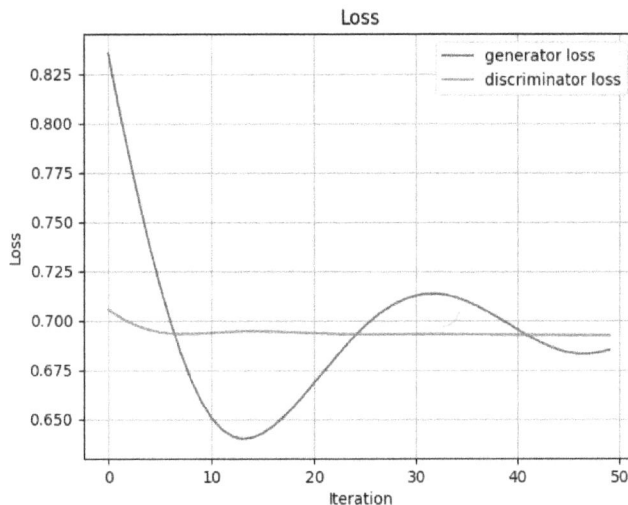

Figure 4.9 – Loss evolution while training both models reaching
the equilibrium point at the end of the iterations

With this, we obtain a P block, as shown when manually loading the distribution using Qiskit, but trained to mimic the price distribution, as seen in the historic dataset we used to train the generator in our qGAN. Therefore, by adding this trained generator as the probability and appending the linear amplitude function and QAE blocks a purely data-driven quantum approach for the pricing of our stocks would be created. It would take quite a big block of code with different frameworks to perform such a task, so the technical complexity to implement this may be too high, but we definitely recommend going through the three blocks to understand how these interfaces between different frameworks can be achieved (PennyLane for a trainable parameterized quantum circuit and Qiskit Finance to avoid implementing the already available functionalities).

Summary

In this chapter, we explored a complex use case to forecast the future, the future of how markets will evolve, how stock prices will evolve, and so on a non-trivial task indeed. We showed how classical statistics extensively used in the field can be used in a quantum regime. This brings some benefits but also, given its current status and the limitations of the devices themselves, poses other impediments we would need to work around.

Encoding a probability distribution on a gate-based quantum device entails some resolution loss. Probability distributions may need to be truncated, and value ranges will be rendered as the same discrete bin that the future price of an option may be placed. This limitation will probably change when bigger devices are made available so that larger distributions can be encoded. However, it is indeed a limitation we should have present in our minds when adopting these techniques.

Of course, there are benefits, as quantum devices are capable of native parallelization of many calculations, which are done sequentially or require large classical setups to perform fast enough. Thanks to QML setups and qGANs in particular, we can even compose a piece of machinery that does this distribution encoding, based on an asset's past evolution, which might not be entirely accurate but at least is based on evidence. So far, simulators have been used in this section to ease the complexity of using real devices, as we will explain in the following chapters. Dealing with device specifics could be quite challenging as well and add more complexity to the already complex procedure we showed here. Even though we will cover use cases that better fit the current status of quantum devices, being the growing field that it is and with its relevance in the financial sector, we must keep an eye on advances toward better price forecasting in the literature. There are really relevant research initiatives that could give us a breakthrough not far from now.

Further reading

A quintessential part of what we have discussed in this chapter relates to some of the foundational algorithms in quantum computing. Grover's algorithm (Jozsa 1999) and QAE (Rao et al. 2020) are not only key contenders for financial use cases but also for numerous applications pertaining to quantum algorithms.

More and more, QML is gaining relevance, as it allows the exploitation of existing data to create those embeddings or dynamics that quantum algorithms often require. *Chapter 6* will examine in more detail these techniques. However, for those already knowledgeable about classical generative models such as GANs, variational autoencoders, and neural networks in general, there is plenty of literature that can be found to help their adaptation to the Quantum regime (Lloyd and Weedbrook, 2018). New ways that QNNs can be exploited for financial applications (Tapia et al. 2022) or different perspectives on how a price projection can be tackled constantly appear in the literature (Singh 2021).

On a more practical note, even though understanding the basics of how these algorithms are designed and implemented can be crucial at this stage, higher and higher abstraction enablers such as Qiskit Finance or ML will boost your ability to try and test some of the cutting-edge discoveries, offering a faster-paced transition from research to corporate innovation (Moguel et al. 2020).

References

- *Glasserman, P. (2004). Monte Carlo methods in financial engineering (Vol. 53, pp. xiv+-596). New York: Springer.*

- *Jozsa, R. (1999). Searching in Grover's algorithm. arXiv preprint quant-ph/9901021.*

- *Kingma, D. P., & Ba, J. (2014). Adam: A method for stochastic optimization. arXiv preprint arXiv:1412.6980.*

- *Lloyd, S., & Weedbrook, C. (2018). Quantum generative adversarial learning. Physical review letters, 121(4), 040502.*

- *MacBeth, J. D., & Merville, L. J. (1979). An empirical examination of the Black-Scholes call option pricing model. The journal of finance, 34(5), 1173-1186.*

- *Moguel, E., Berrocal, J., García-Alonso, J., & Murillo, J. M. (2020, October). A Roadmap for Quantum Software Engineering: Applying the Lessons Learned from the Classics. In Q-SET@ QCE (pp. 5-13).*

- *Singh, P. (2021). FQTSFM: A fuzzy-quantum time series forecasting model. Information Sciences, 566, 57-79.*

- *Stojkoski, V., Sandev, T., Basnarkov, L., Kocarev, L., & Metzler, R. (2020). Generalised geometric Brownian motion: Theory and applications to option pricing. Entropy, 22(12), 1432.*

- *Tapia, E. P., Scarpa, G., & Pozas-Kerstjens, A. (2022). Fraud detection with a single-qubit quantum neural network. arXiv preprint arXiv:2211.13191.*

- *Rao, P., Yu, K., Lim, H., Jin, D., & Choi, D. (2020, August). Quantum amplitude estimation algorithms on IBM quantum devices. In Quantum Communications and Quantum Imaging XVIII (Vol. 11507, pp. 49-60). SPIE.*

- *Ross, S. M., Kelly, J. J., Sullivan, R. J., Perry, W. J., Mercer, D., Davis, R. M., ... & Bristow, V. L. (1996). Stochastic processes (Vol. 2). New York: Wiley.*

- *Zoufal, C., Lucchi, A., & Woerner, S. (2019). Quantum generative adversarial networks for learning and loading random distributions. npj Quantum Information, 5(1), 103.*

5
Portfolio Management

According to the **Global Industry Classification Standard** (**GICS**), the global asset management industry's total **assets under management** (**AUM**) value at the end of 2020 was approximately $91.7 trillion, managed across 84,000 firms. This consists of the AUM managed by investment firms, pension funds, insurance companies, and other international financial institutions. Frequently, asset managers utilize portfolio management techniques to manage these assets. Investopedia defines portfolio management as follows:

> *Portfolio management is the art and science of selecting and supervising a portfolio to achieve a specific investment goal for the investor's benefit.*

This chapter will explore the art of portfolio management using machine learning techniques and quantum algorithms. It is divided into five sections:

- Financial portfolio management

- Financial portfolio diversification

- Financial portfolio simulation

- Portfolio management using traditional machine learning algorithms

- Quantum algorithm portfolio management implementation

Let us begin by understanding the need for portfolio management by defining a financial portfolio.

Financial portfolio management

A financial portfolio refers to a collection of assets, including stocks, bonds, and other securities, that an individual or entity invests in to generate a return on investment. Creating a diversified financial portfolio is crucial for investors to minimize risk and maximize returns. A financial portfolio requires careful analysis, market research, and risk assessment.

One of the essential aspects of creating a financial portfolio is diversification. Diversification refers to investing in different types of securities to spread the risk. This strategy aims to reduce the impact of any negative events on the portfolio's overall performance. For example, a portfolio entirely invested in a single stock or industry may suffer significantly if the company or industry faces challenges. However, a diversified portfolio that includes stocks, bonds, and other securities can help mitigate such risks. Another important factor to consider when building a financial portfolio is risk tolerance. Risk tolerance refers to an individual's ability to handle market volatility and risk. It is critical to assess your risk tolerance before investing in securities. A high-risk investment may offer higher returns but only suit investors who can tolerate potential losses.

Investors should also consider their investment objectives when creating a financial portfolio. An investment objective refers to the goal that an investor wishes to achieve through their investments, such as long-term growth, income generation, or capital preservation. An investor's investment objectives will influence the type of securities they choose for their portfolio. Asset allocation is another essential aspect of building a financial portfolio. Asset allocation refers to dividing your investment portfolio among asset classes, such as stocks, bonds, and cash. This process aims to balance the risk and rewards of different investments. For instance, stocks may offer high returns but come with higher risks, while bonds may offer lower returns but lower risks.

Moreover, investors need to review and rebalance their portfolios regularly. Investment profit objectives and tolerated risk force us to check the configuration of our investments regularly to ensure their alignment. A portfolio that is not reviewed regularly may become unbalanced over time, leading to higher risks or lower returns. Building a financial portfolio is essential for investors who wish to generate returns on their investments. Diversification, risk tolerance, investment objectives, asset allocation, and portfolio review are critical aspects that investors need to consider when building a financial portfolio. By paying attention to these factors, investors can create a diversified portfolio that aligns with their investment objectives and risk tolerance.

Financial portfolio diversification

Financial portfolio diversification is crucial for investors who want to minimize risk and maximize returns. Diversification involves investing in various assets, including stocks, bonds, and other securities, to spread the risk across different markets, sectors, and asset classes. One of the main benefits of financial portfolio diversification is risk reduction. By investing in various assets, investors can avoid the risk of putting all their eggs in one basket. If one asset class or sector performs poorly, other asset classes may perform well, helping to offset losses. For example, if a portfolio is heavily invested in stocks and the stock market crashes, the portfolio's value may decline significantly. However, if the portfolio also includes bonds, commodities, and real estate, the stock value decline may be offset by gains in other asset classes.

Another benefit of financial portfolio diversification is potential returns. Investing in a range of assets offers the benefit of potential returns from different markets and sectors. For instance, stocks may offer higher returns but have higher risks. On the other hand, bonds may offer lower returns, but they come with lower risks. By diversifying their portfolio, investors can capture the potential returns of different asset classes while mitigating the risks.

When diversifying a financial portfolio, investors should consider several factors, including their investment objectives, risk tolerance, and time horizon. Investment objectives refer to the goals an investor wishes to achieve through their investments, such as long-term growth, income generation, or capital preservation. Risk tolerance refers to the level of risk an investor is comfortable with. Time horizon refers to the time an investor plans to hold their investments. Investors can create a diversified portfolio that aligns with their goals, risk tolerance, and time horizon by considering these factors.

By allocating their investments across different asset classes, investors can reduce the overall risk of their portfolio while still capturing potential returns. Financial portfolio diversification is a critical strategy for investors who want to minimize risk and maximize returns. Diversifying a portfolio involves investing in various assets, including stocks, bonds, and other securities, to spread the risk across different markets, sectors, and asset classes. Investors can create a diversified portfolio that aligns with their goals and reduces overall risk by considering their investment objectives, risk tolerance, time horizon, and asset allocation. The next subsection discusses asset allocation and its need and importance.

Financial asset allocation

Financial asset allocation is a key component of portfolio management that involves dividing investments among different asset classes to achieve a desired level of risk and return. Asset allocation is an important strategy for investors who want to build a diversified portfolio and minimize risk. One of the key benefits of financial asset allocation is risk reduction. By diversifying investments across different asset classes, investors can reduce the risk associated with any particular asset class or investment. For example, if an investor invested all their money in one stock, they would be subject to the risks of that stock alone. However, investing in a mix of stocks, bonds, and other assets can spread their risk across different asset classes, reducing the potential for significant losses.

Another benefit of financial asset allocation is the potential for higher returns. Different asset classes have different levels of risk and return potential. Stocks, for example, offer higher potential returns than bonds but come with higher levels of risk. By allocating investments across different asset classes, investors can benefit from the potential returns of multiple asset classes while minimizing risk.

When allocating assets in a financial portfolio, investors must consider their investment goals, time horizon, and risk tolerance. Investment goals may vary from one investor to another and include goals such as generating income, growing capital, or preserving wealth. Time horizon refers to the time an investor intends to hold an investment. Generally, longer time horizons allow for greater risk tolerance and potentially higher returns. Risk tolerance refers to an investor's willingness to accept risk in pursuit of higher returns.

There are several different asset classes to which investors can allocate their investments, including stocks, bonds, cash, and alternative investments. Stocks represent ownership in a company and offer the potential for capital appreciation and dividends. Bonds, on the other hand, represent debt and offer fixed-income payments. Cash is a low-risk, low-return asset that can provide liquidity and stability in a portfolio. Alternative investments include real estate, commodities, and private equity.

The optimal asset allocation for a portfolio will depend on the investor's goals, time horizon, and risk tolerance. Younger investors with a longer time horizon may be more willing to accept higher levels of risk and allocate a larger portion of their portfolio to stocks. Older investors with a shorter time horizon and a greater need for income and capital preservation may allocate a larger portion of their portfolio to bonds and cash. Thus, financial asset allocation is a critical component of portfolio management that allows investors to diversify their investments across different asset classes and minimize risk, while potentially increasing returns. When determining the optimal asset allocation, investors must consider their investment goals, time horizon, and risk tolerance. By allocating investments to a mix of stocks, bonds, cash, and alternative investments, investors can build a well-diversified portfolio that aligns with their goals and helps them achieve financial success. The subsequent subsection discusses the importance of financial risk tolerance in financial portfolio optimization.

Financial risk tolerance

Financial risk tolerance refers to an investor's willingness to take on risk in pursuit of potential returns. It is an important concept for anyone wanting to invest their money. Several factors influence an individual's financial risk tolerance. Age, income, net worth, and investment goals are all important considerations. Generally, younger investors may be more willing to take on risk, as they have a longer time horizon to recover from losses. Higher-income and net-worth individuals may also have a higher risk tolerance, as they have more resources to absorb potential losses. Investment goals are also a key factor in determining risk tolerance. Investors with long-term goals, such as retirement, may be more willing to take on risks in pursuit of higher returns. In contrast, investors with short-term goals, such as saving for a down payment on a house, may prioritize capital preservation over potential returns.

Understanding your financial risk tolerance is important because it can help investors make informed investment decisions. Investors who take on too much risk may experience significant losses that could impact their financial well-being. On the other hand, investors who are too risk-averse may miss out on potential returns that could help them achieve their financial goals. There are several strategies that investors can use to manage their risk and align their investments with their risk tolerance. Diversification is one of the most important strategies. By spreading investments across different asset classes, investors can reduce the risk of any particular investment. These types of investments offer exposure to a diversified portfolio of stocks or bonds and can help reduce risk. Another strategy is to use asset allocation to manage risk. Asset allocation involves dividing investments among different asset classes to achieve a desired level of risk and return. By allocating investments to a mix of stocks, bonds, and other assets, investors can benefit from the potential returns of multiple asset classes while minimizing risk.

Finally, it is important for investors to regularly review their asset selection to make sure that it fulfills their requirements. As an investor's circumstances change, their risk tolerance may also change. Regular portfolio reviews can help ensure that an investor's portfolio remains aligned with their risk tolerance and investment goals. Financial risk tolerance is an important concept for investors to understand. Age, income, net worth, and investment goals can influence an individual's risk tolerance. Investors need to understand their risk tolerance to make informed investment decisions. Strategies such as diversification, low-cost index funds, asset allocation, and regular portfolio reviews can help investors manage risk and align their investments with risk tolerance and goals. Hence, the following subsection talks about optimizing a financial portfolio to align risk tolerance and investment goals.

Financial portfolio optimization

Financial portfolio optimization maximizes an investor's returns while minimizing risk by selecting an optimal mix of investments. This process involves the identification of the investor's investment objectives, risk tolerance, and constraints, followed by developing an investment strategy optimized to meet these objectives. This subsection will discuss the key principles of financial portfolio optimization, its benefits to investors, and the tools used to optimize financial portfolios.

One of the key principles of financial portfolio optimization is diversification. By spreading investments across different asset classes, investors can reduce the risk associated with any one particular investment. This is because different asset classes have different risk-return characteristics. For example, equities are generally considered to be riskier than bonds, but they also offer the potential for higher returns. By diversifying investments across asset classes with different risk-return characteristics, investors can achieve a more efficient investment so that risk gets minimized while potential returns are maximized. Another principle of financial portfolio optimization is asset allocation. Asset allocation involves dividing investments among different asset classes to achieve a desired level of risk and return. By allocating investments to a mix of stocks, bonds, and other assets, investors can benefit from the potential returns of multiple asset classes while minimizing risk. Asset allocation aims to achieve an optimal portfolio that maximizes returns while minimizing risk.

There are several benefits to financial portfolio optimization. First, it allows investors to achieve their investment objectives while minimizing risk. This is important because investment risk can significantly impact an investor's financial well-being. By optimizing their portfolio, investors can achieve their investment objectives while minimizing the risk of significant losses. Second, financial portfolio optimization can help investors achieve higher returns than they would be able to achieve through a more traditional investment approach. This is because optimization allows investors to take advantage of the potential returns of multiple asset classes while minimizing risk.

There are several tools used to optimize financial portfolios. One of the most common tools is **modern portfolio theory** (**MPT**). MPT is a mathematical framework that uses statistical analysis to optimize portfolios. The framework assumes that investors are risk-averse and seek to maximize returns for a given level of risk. MPT considers the correlations between different asset classes and the expected returns and volatilities of each asset class. Another tool used to optimize financial portfolios is the Monte Carlo simulation. The Monte Carlo simulation involves statistical modeling to simulate the potential outcomes of different investment strategies. This allows investors to test different investment scenarios and identify the optimal portfolio for their investment objectives, risk tolerance, and constraints.

Financial portfolio optimization is important for investors who want to achieve their investment objectives while minimizing risk. It involves the identification of an investor's investment objectives, risk tolerance, and constraints, followed by developing an investment strategy optimized to meet these objectives. The key principles of financial portfolio optimization include diversification and asset allocation. The benefits of financial portfolio optimization include achieving investment objectives while minimizing risk and the potential for higher returns. Finally, several tools are used to optimize financial portfolios, including modern portfolio theory and the Monte Carlo simulation. The following subpart discusses MPT, used to optimize financial portfolios.

MPT

MPT is a framework that helps investors build efficient portfolios to maximize expected returns for a given level of risk. Developed by Harry Markowitz in the 1950s, MPT revolutionized the field of finance by introducing the concept of diversification and the efficient frontier. At the heart of MPT is the idea that diversification is essential to build a well-constructed investment portfolio. According to MPT, investors should not put all their eggs in one basket, as the performance of a single asset or security is subject to fluctuations that can lead to significant losses. With this balance on a diverse set of assets to invest in, you try to guarantee that no latent driver will zero out an investment.

One key concept in MPT is the efficient frontier. Levels of risk and profit will reveal more than one configuration option for our investment selection. The frontier draws a line in the risk-return trade-off that each potential portfolio selection poses, as shown in a 2D plot in *Figure 5.1*. By balancing and weighing assets in different ways, an avid investor will be able to spot that frontier so that the combinations that make up this trade-off will be visible, and a decision can be made based on those.

Therefore, understanding the efficiency frontier is a key concept to understanding the maximal capacity for a given set of assets, as their configurations will find a profit limit based on the framework established by the MPT.

The efficient frontier

The efficient frontier, as we mentioned previously, is a representation that allows us to understand the maximal capacity of a set of assets, given an expected return and the diversification risk tolerance associated with those assets.

If you plotted all potential configurations on a 2D plot, where the expected return of each portfolio is on the *y* axis and the standard deviation (a measure of risk) is on the *x* axis, you can observe that a specific shape appears instead of a potential randomly distributed plot. An efficiency limit appears where, at the extreme, you find the asset selections that balance the risk minimization while maximizing the return.

Portfolios that lie on the efficient frontier are said to be "efficient" because they yield the highest profit. Portfolios that lie to the right-hand side of the efficient frontier are considered "inefficient," given there are better options that show a lower level of risk with the same amount of expected profit. Therefore, these are selections that can be improved as opposed to the efficient ones.

Here is an example of how the efficient frontier might look when plotted on a graph:

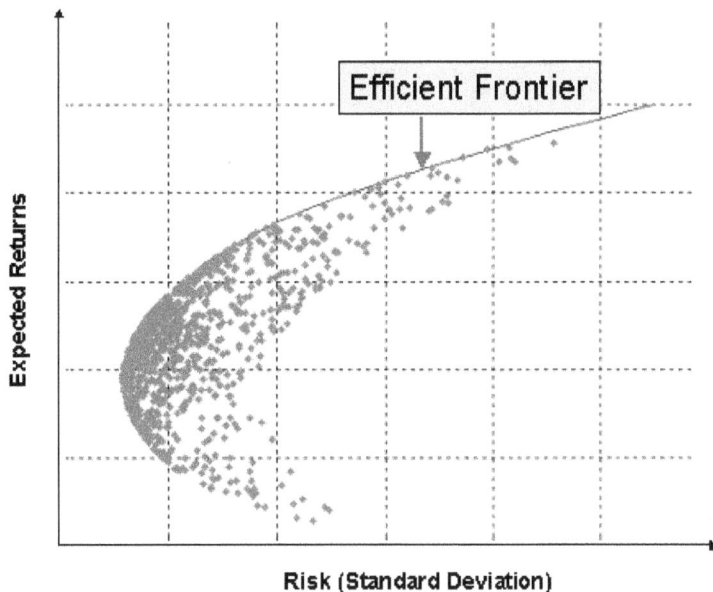

Figure 5.1 – The efficient frontier

As shown in *Figure 5.1*, the efficient frontier is a curve that slopes upward from left to right, with the portfolios plotted as red dots on it. Efficient portfolios, according to the previous definition, will be then found on the edge of the curve, drawn by the blue line where no option beyond exists.

Example

Here is an example of how MPT can be used to construct a portfolio.

Let's suppose an investor has $100,000 to invest and considers two assets – stocks and bonds. The expected return for stocks is 10% per year, and the expected return for bonds is 5% per year. The investor is also given the following information about the assets' standard deviations:

- **Stocks**: 20%

- **Bonds**: 8%

The investor wants to construct a portfolio that offers the maximum profit for an acceptable risk level. According to MPT, the investor should diversify the portfolio by investing in stocks and bonds. The optimal balance of risk and return can be determined by constructing an efficient frontier.

To do this, the investor can plot each asset's expected return and standard deviation on a graph. The investor can then plot the efficient frontier by combining different proportions of the two assets and calculating each combination's expected return and standard deviation. The efficiency frontier will then yield the asset selections the investor can bet on with a high chance of meeting the requirements initially set.

For example, if the investor were to invest 50% in stocks and 50% in bonds, the expected return of the portfolio would be 7.5% (halfway between the expected returns of the two assets), and the standard deviation would be 14% (a weighted average of the standard deviations of the two assets). This portfolio would lie on the efficient frontier.

The investor can then decide on the optimal portfolio by selecting the point on the efficient frontier that corresponds to their desired risk level. For example, if the investor is willing to take on more risk, they might choose a portfolio with a higher expected return and a higher standard deviation. On the other hand, if the investor is risk-averse, they might choose a portfolio with a lower expected return and a lower standard deviation. The following section illustrates the implementation of MPT through a case study.

Case study

Let's suppose that an investor named Sarah is considering two potential investments – a stock and a bond. The stock has a higher expected return but also a higher level of risk, while the bond has a lower expected return but also a lower level of risk. Sarah tries to decide how to allocate her money between the two investments to maximize her return while minimizing her risk.

Sarah decides to use MPT to help her optimize her portfolio. She starts by constructing a grid that shows the expected return and standard deviation (a measure of risk) for each possible combination of the two investments. The grid looks like this:

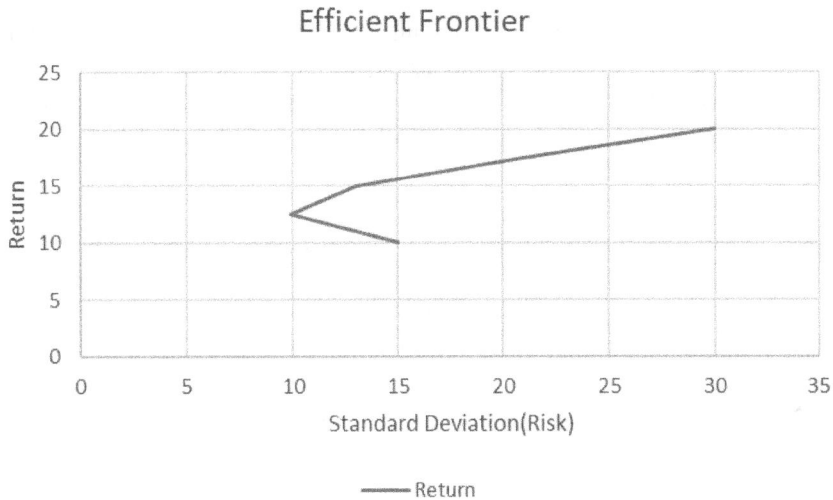

Figure 5.2 – The efficient frontier

Based on the grid shown in *Figure 5.2*, Sarah can see that the portfolio with the highest expected return is the one that is 100% invested in the stock, but it also has the highest level of risk. On the other hand, the portfolio with the lowest risk level is 100% invested in the bond, but it also has the lowest expected return.

Sarah decides to use the efficient frontier to help her identify the optimal balance between risk and return. She plots the expected return and standard deviation of each portfolio on a graph, and the efficient frontier shows Sarah that, based on the efficient frontier, the optimal portfolio is the one that is about 60% invested in the stock and 40% invested in the bond.

Sarah decides to allocate her money in this way, and she periodically rebalances her portfolio to ensure that it aligns with her investment criteria. Using MPT and the efficient frontier, Sarah can optimize her portfolio and achieve the best balance between risk and return. The subsequent subsection discusses the role of financial portfolio simulation in implementing portfolio optimization.

Financial portfolio simulation

A financial portfolio simulation is a tool investors use to assess their portfolio's performance, predict its behavior in the future, and make informed investment decisions. It involves creating a model of an investor's portfolio and testing different scenarios to determine the best investment strategy. In recent years, portfolio simulation has become increasingly popular because it provides a cost-effective way for investors to assess their risk tolerance and maximize returns. This subsection will examine the concept of financial portfolio simulation, its benefits, and how it can be used to optimize investment decisions.

One of the significant benefits of financial portfolio simulation is its ability to provide investors with a clear understanding of their risk tolerance. By simulating different scenarios, investors can determine their portfolio's sensitivity to market fluctuations and adjust their investment strategy accordingly. David McEwen, the director of investments at a leading investment firm, had the following to say about risk tolerance:

Investors who don't understand their risk tolerance could be taking on more or less risk than they can handle, which could have negative consequences for their portfolio.

Therefore, financial portfolio simulation is a valuable tool to help investors make informed investment decisions based on risk tolerance. Another benefit of financial portfolio simulation is its ability to predict how an investor's portfolio will perform in different market conditions. This is particularly useful during periods of market volatility when investors may be tempted to make hasty investment decisions. By simulating different scenarios, investors can see how their portfolios will perform under different market conditions, giving them confidence in their investment decisions.

Investors must understand their investment objectives and risk tolerance to optimize investment decisions, using financial portfolio simulation. This involves identifying their investment goals, the time horizon to achieve these goals, and the level of risk they are willing to take on. Once these factors have been established, investors can use portfolio simulation to test different investment scenarios and determine an optimal investment strategy. For example, an investor with a long-term investment horizon may be willing to take on more risk in their portfolio than an investor with a short-term investment horizon. By simulating different scenarios, the investor can determine the optimal asset allocation for their portfolio to achieve their investment objectives, while minimizing risk.

Therefore, financial portfolio simulation is a valuable tool investors can use to optimize their investment decisions. It provides investors with a clear understanding of their risk tolerance, predicts how their portfolio will perform in different market conditions, and enables them to make informed investment decisions based on their investment objectives. Using portfolio simulation to test different investment scenarios, investors can determine the optimal asset allocation for their portfolio, ensuring they achieve their investment objectives while minimizing risk. As financial markets evolve, financial portfolio simulation will remain essential for investors seeking to maximize returns and manage risk. The following passage talks about the techniques used in financial portfolio simulation techniques.

Financial portfolio simulation techniques

A financial portfolio simulation is an important tool for investors to evaluate and manage risks associated with their investment portfolio. Using different techniques, investors can simulate various scenarios to determine the potential impact of market fluctuations and make informed investment decisions. In this essay, we will discuss three popular techniques used in financial portfolio simulation – the Monte Carlo simulation, stress testing, and sensitivity analysis.

The Monte Carlo simulation is a statistical technique used to model and analyze the behavior of complex systems, such as financial portfolios. It involves running multiple simulations with different inputs to generate various potential outcomes. These inputs can include variables such as interest rates, inflation rates, and market returns. A Monte Carlo simulation outputs a probability distribution of potential investment returns, which can help investors make informed decisions about risk and reward. As expert investor Ray Dalio once said:

> *If you can simulate a situation a thousand times, you probably have a pretty good idea of what's going to happen.*

Stress testing is another technique used in financial portfolio simulation. It involves simulating extreme scenarios, such as a recession or a market crash, to determine the potential impact on a portfolio. By running stress tests, investors can identify potential portfolio weaknesses and adjust to mitigate risks. Portfolio manager John Rekenthaler had this to say about stress testing:

> *Stress testing is essential because it shows you where your portfolio is vulnerable. It's like running fire drills to prepare you in an emergency.*

Sensitivity analysis is a technique used to determine how changes in specific variables can impact the performance of a portfolio. It involves identifying key variables, such as interest rates or inflation rates, and analyzing how changes in these variables can impact the portfolio's performance. By conducting sensitivity analysis, investors can identify which variables impact the portfolio's performance the most and adjust their investment strategy accordingly. Financial advisor Lisa Kirchenbauer noted the following:

> *Sensitivity analysis can help investors understand how different variables interact with each other and how changes in one variable can impact the overall portfolio.*

Financial portfolio simulation is critical for investors to manage risks and make informed investment decisions. Using techniques such as the Monte Carlo simulation, stress testing, and sensitivity analysis, investors can simulate various scenarios and identify potential weaknesses in their portfolios. As a result, investors can make informed decisions to optimize their portfolio's performance and minimize risks. The following subsection discusses the concepts and methods involved in implementing stress testing.

Stress testing

Stress testing is a process used to evaluate the resilience of financial institutions, systems, or portfolios to potential adverse events or shocks. It involves simulating extreme scenarios and measuring the impact on a portfolio, system, or institution's financial health. Stress testing is an essential tool in risk management, allowing financial institutions to identify potential weaknesses and prepare for potential risks. The purpose of stress testing is to evaluate the impact of unexpected events on a portfolio, institution, or system. For example, a stress test may simulate the impact of a significant economic downturn, a large market sell-off, or a geopolitical crisis. The scenarios are designed to be severe enough to test the resilience of the portfolio, institution, or system but also realistic enough to provide meaningful insights.

Stress testing involves a range of techniques, including the following:

Scenario analysis: This technique involves identifying potential scenarios and simulating the impact on a portfolio, institution, or system. The scenarios are designed to be extreme and may involve a range of adverse events, such as a sharp increase in interest rates or a large drop in asset prices.

Sensitivity analysis: This technique involves varying one or more input parameters to evaluate the impact on the output. For example, sensitivity analysis may involve increasing interest rates by a specific percentage and evaluating the impact on the portfolio's returns.

Reverse stress testing: This technique involves identifying the level of stress that would cause significant losses or a severe impact on an institution, system, or portfolio. Reverse stress testing can help identify the key vulnerabilities and allow for the development of appropriate risk mitigation strategies.

A report by the International Monetary Fund had the following to say about stress testing:

> *Stress testing has become an increasingly important tool in the toolkit of regulators and supervisors for assessing the resilience of financial systems and individual institutions. It has proved invaluable for identifying potential vulnerabilities, quantifying risk, and testing the effectiveness of mitigation strategies.*

Hence, stress testing is a vital tool in risk management, allowing financial institutions to identify potential vulnerabilities and prepare for potential risks. The use of scenario analysis, sensitivity analysis, and reverse stress testing provides insights into the impact of unexpected events on the financial health of a portfolio, institution, or system. As the financial landscape continues to evolve, stress testing will remain an essential tool to ensure a financial system's stability. The following techniques used in a financial portfolio simulation are discussed in next section.

The Monte Carlo simulation

The Monte Carlo simulation is a popular technique used in financial portfolio simulation to model the behavior of financial assets and estimate a portfolio's potential risks and returns. This technique involves generating multiple random scenarios of market behavior, which are used to simulate the performance of a portfolio over a given time horizon. In this subsection, we will explore the various aspects of the Monte Carlo simulation as a tool for a financial portfolio simulation.

One of the key benefits of the Monte Carlo simulation is that it enables investors to generate a range of possible outcomes for their portfolio rather than just relying on a single prediction. By running multiple simulations, investors can better understand the risks associated with their portfolio and adjust their investment strategy accordingly. This is particularly important when dealing with complex portfolios that involve a wide range of assets.

The Monte Carlo simulation technique involves the following steps:

1. **Defining the portfolio**: The first step in the Monte Carlo simulation is defining the analyzed portfolio. This involves specifying the individual assets, their expected returns, and the correlations between them.

2. **Defining the probability distributions**: The next step is to define the probability distributions for each asset in the portfolio. This involves specifying the mean and standard deviation of returns for each asset and any other relevant statistical parameters.

3. **Generating random scenarios**: Once the portfolio and probability distributions have been defined, the Monte Carlo simulation generates many random scenarios of market behavior. These scenarios are generated based on the probability distributions specified in the previous step.

4. **Simulating portfolio performance**: For each random scenario, the Monte Carlo simulation calculates the returns for the portfolio based on the asset weights and correlations specified in the first step. This generates a distribution of possible portfolio returns.

5. **Analyzing results**: Finally, the Monte Carlo simulation provides a range of statistics that can be used to analyze the simulation results, such as the expected value of the portfolio, the standard deviation of returns, and the probability of achieving a certain level of return.

The Monte Carlo simulation is a powerful tool for financial portfolio simulation, providing investors with a range of possible outcomes and allowing them to better understand the risks associated with their investments. This technique allows investors to make more informed decisions and adjust their investment strategy to maximize their returns, while minimizing their risk exposure.

Let's suppose an investor wants to evaluate the risk and return of a particular portfolio containing a mix of stocks, bonds, and cash. The portfolio comprises 60% stocks, 30% bonds, and 10% cash. To evaluate the performance of this portfolio, the investor can use the Monte Carlo simulation, which involves the following steps:

Identify the historical returns and volatility of each asset class in the portfolio. For example, let's say that historical data shows the annual returns and volatility of stocks are 10% and 20%, respectively. In comparison, bonds have an annual return of 5% and a volatility of 10%, and cash has a return of 2% with no volatility.

Generate random numbers to simulate the future performance of each asset class in the portfolio. The Monte Carlo simulation randomly generates a set of possible future outcomes based on historical data.

Calculate the overall portfolio returns based on the simulated outcomes of each asset class. For example, if the simulation generates a return of 12% for stocks, 4% for bonds, and 2% for cash, the overall portfolio return would be 8.4%.

Repeat the simulation multiple times to generate a range of possible outcomes. The Monte Carlo simulation allows an investor to model a range of possible outcomes and assess the probability of each outcome.

Evaluate the risk and return of the portfolio based on the range of possible outcomes. This step involves calculating the portfolio's expected return and standard deviation based on the simulated outcomes. An investor can then use this information to make informed decisions about their investment strategy.

David Booth, the founder and executive chairman of a prominent investment firm, notes the following:

> *Monte Carlo simulation can help investors better understand the potential outcomes of their investment strategy and make more informed decisions. It allows investors to assess the impact of various factors on their portfolio performance and better prepare for unexpected market conditions.*

The Monte Carlo simulation is a valuable tool in financial portfolio simulation that can help investors optimize their investment strategy and mitigate risk.

Financial modeling for portfolio optimization

Computer algorithms and models have become increasingly important in a financial portfolio simulation, and the Monte Carlo simulation is a popular technique used by these algorithms and models. Here is an example of how the Monte Carlo simulation can be used in a financial portfolio simulation by computer algorithms and models:

The algorithm or model generates many scenarios that could impact a portfolio, based on historical data and assumptions about future market conditions.

For each scenario, the algorithm or model calculates the expected returns and risks for the portfolio, based on the assets it contains and their historical correlations.

The algorithm or model uses these expected returns and risks to calculate the portfolio's expected value, volatility, and the probability of various outcomes, such as gains or losses.

By repeating this process thousands or even millions of times, the algorithm or model creates a distribution of potential portfolio outcomes, which can be used to estimate the portfolio's risk and return characteristics under various market conditions.

This distribution can then be analyzed to identify potential weaknesses or opportunities in the portfolio and optimize the portfolio's asset allocation or risk management strategies.

According to Professor David Ruppert, a renowned expert in the field, the Monte Carlo simulation is a powerful tool for modeling complex systems, including financial portfolios:

> *Monte Carlo simulation allows us to deal with very high-dimensional, very complex models that we couldn't otherwise solve analytically. And it allows us to do sensitivity analyses, to see how the model output changes when we change inputs so that we can identify the most important variables and the sources of risk.*

Using the Monte Carlo simulation and other advanced techniques, computer algorithms and models can help investors make more informed decisions and manage their portfolios more effectively in a complex and rapidly changing financial landscape.

Optimization algorithms

Optimization algorithms are used in financial portfolio optimization to select the most appropriate investment mix for a given investor's preferences and constraints. Here are some commonly used optimization algorithms:

- **Linear programming**: A mathematical technique to optimize a linear objective function, subject to linear constraints. Linear programming is used in portfolio optimization to determine the optimal portfolio allocation.

- **Quadratic programming**: A mathematical technique to optimize a quadratic objective function subject to linear constraints. Quadratic programming is used in portfolio optimization to determine an optimal portfolio, considering higher-order moments of the return distribution, such as volatility and skewness.

- **Genetic algorithm**: A heuristic optimization technique inspired by natural selection. Genetic algorithms use a population of candidate solutions, apply genetic operators such as mutation and crossover to create new candidate solutions, and select the fittest candidates based on a fitness function.

According to Dr. Harry Markowitz, Nobel laureate and father of modern portfolio theory,

> *The appropriate mathematical technique for optimizing portfolios depends on the investor's objectives, constraints, and preferences, as well as the characteristics of the securities being considered.*

Therefore, the choice of optimization algorithm should be made based on the investor's specific requirements, and the portfolio should be optimized.

Portfolio management using traditional machine learning algorithms

Classical implementation

Portfolio optimization is a problem related to the financial services and banking industry that emerged with Markovitz's seminal paper in 1952 (https://onlinelibrary.wiley.com/doi/full/10.1111/j.1540-6261.1952.tb01525.x). The model describes a set of assets $x_i \in X$ from which a subset needs to be picked to maximize the revenue, while minimizing the risk at t future time steps. For a given period, each asset has an expected return linked to it, and the covariance between assets sets the risk amount in terms of diversification (for the sake of simplicity). The idea behind this diversification is that if we only invest in the assets with the highest revenue, the risk of them being driven by the same factors if our investment fails is bigger than if we diversify our portfolio. We will focus on a single-time-step process, assuming that local optima are part of the longer-time-step trajectory toward the global optima of our portfolio.

Let's consider, then, a single-time step optimization for the sake of simplicity. The investment comes at a cost. A budget (B) is associated with the investment in a portfolio configuration. It is described by the summation cost of investing in each asset as b_i, where i is the index of the particular asset. Ideally, our recommendation should not surpass this condition ($\Sigma b_i < B$). Hence, this classical optimization problem is often posed as:

$$\sum_{i=1}^{n} x_i e_i - \theta \sum_{i,j=1}^{n} x_i x_j c_{ij}$$

$$s.t. \sum_{i=1}^{n} x_i b_i \leq B$$

where $x_i \in \{0,1\}$ is the mask associated with the selection of our set of assets and θ is a Lagrangian operator modulating the amount of risk we want to assume. We have binarized this selection, as it simplifies the calculation. Still, more compelled portfolio investments can be considered to tackle those three aspects of the model (revenue, risk, and budget).

We minimize that very same model, as it will fit better the technical approach we will follow. Thus, the final model would look like this:

$$-\sum_{i=1}^{n} x_i e_i + \theta \sum_{i,j=1}^{n} x_i x_j c_{ij}$$

$$s.t. \sum_{i=1}^{n} x_i b_i \leq B$$

First, we will load our data to build the optimization problem:

```
import json
data = None
with open("binance-data.json", "r") as jsonfile:
    data = json.load(jsonfile)
```

From the loaded data, we can store calculated returns, covariance, and costs of assets in respective variables. We will also set up the budget at 50%:

```
import numpy as np
returns = data['mu']
covar = data['sigma']
assets = []
costs = []
for row in data['assets']:
    assets.append(row["Asset"])
    costs.append(float(row["Open"]))

# Half the money
budget = np.sum(costs)/0.5
```

Next, let's plot the bar chart for returns:

```
import seaborn as sns
import matplotlib.pyplot as plt
sns.barplot(y=returns, x = assets)
plt.show()
```

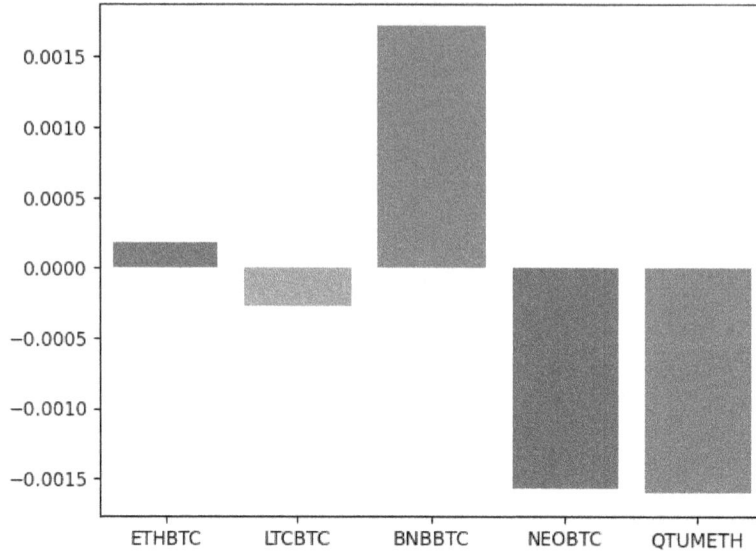

Figure 5.3 – Returns by asset

Here, we can observe that only BNBBTC and ETHBTC give positive returns, whereas LTCBTC, NEOBTC, and QTUETH give negative returns.

We already have covariance calculated in our data file. Let's create the covariance plot as well:

```
f, ax = plt.subplots(figsize=(10, 8))
sns.heatmap(covar, mask=np.zeros_like(covar, dtype=bool), annot=True,
            square=True, ax=ax, xticklabels=assets,
yticklabels=assets)
plt.title("Covariance between Equities")
plt.show()
```

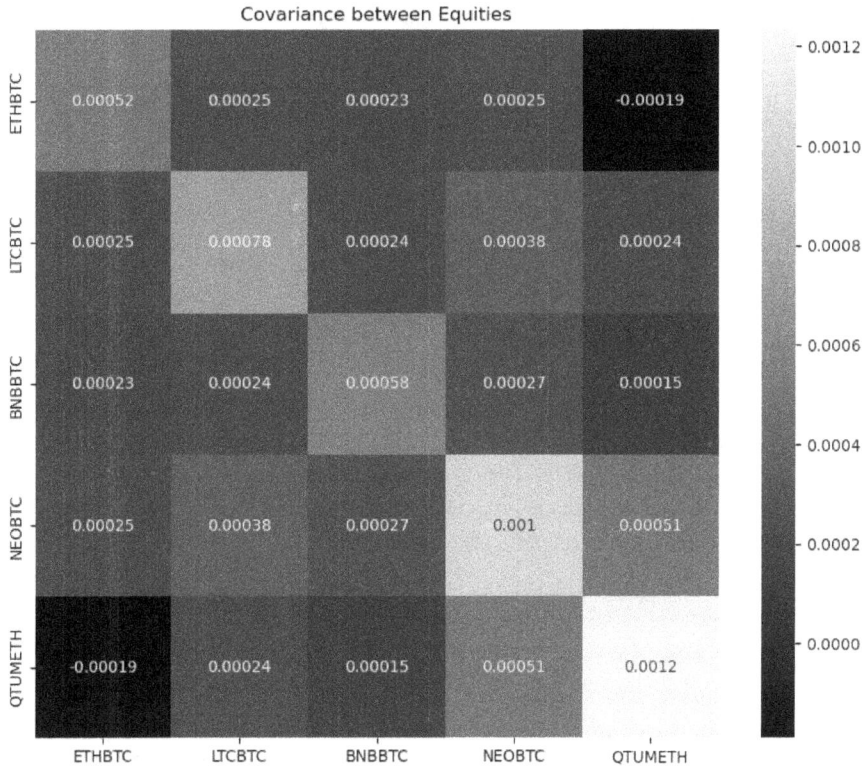

Figure 5.4 – The correlation matrix

The preceding covariance matrix shows how different joint variability is between equities. This way, we can identify equities whose variance may be driven by the same factors and be aware of the risk of investing in both as part of the same portfolio. These values will be introduced into our equation as c_{ij} coefficients.

A popular choice to solve optimization problems such as the one posed previously is the usage of optimization libraries, such as CVX and its Python implementation (cvxpy), with a mixed integer optimization approach, as our problem is restricted by the Boolean values that our x variables can take. The convexity of our problem is a major assumption at this point, which would be a requirement to be checked before the solver selection in our case, but for the number of equities involved, this option would exemplify how to use a classical solver without doing much coding:

```
import cvxpy as cp
# Our solution variable
x_val = cp.Variable(len(returns), boolean=True)
theta = cp.Parameter(nonneg=True)
ret = np.array(returns)@x_val
```

```
risk = cp.quad_form(x_val, covar)
e_costs = np.array(costs)@x_val

# Constraints
cons = [cp.sum(x_val) >= 0, cp.sum(e_costs) <= budget, x_val >= 0]

# Objective function
obj = cp.Minimize(- ret + theta*risk)

# Problem
prob = cp.Problem(obj, cons)
```

We have used 0.03 as the risk penalty for the Lagrange multiplier. CVXPY interfaces with a wide range of solvers; the algorithms used by these solvers have arguments related to stopping criteria and strategies from improving solution quality. There is no one choice of argument that is perfect for every problem. If you don't get satisfactory results from a solver, you can try changing its arguments. The exact way this is done depends on the specific solver.

We have used the 'ECOS_BB' solver in our code:

```
theta.value = 0.03 # This is related to the risk penalty lagrangian
prob.solve(solver='ECOS_BB')
for i, val in enumerate(np.round(x_val.value,1)):
    if val == 1:
        print(f"Asset {assets[i]} was selected")
    else:
        print(f"Asset {assets[i]} was not selected")
```

The optimal value for the problem we get is '-0.0018521365020072623'. The following is a snippet of the assets selected and not selected.

```
Asset ETHBTC was selected
Asset LTCBTC was not selected
Asset BNBBTC was selected
Asset NEOBTC was not selected
Asset QTUMETH was not selected
```

Figure 5.5 – The asset selection

We can see here that ETHBTC and BNBBTC were selected, and from the historical return, these two assets gave positive returns, while other assets were not selected.

Let's move toward quantum implementation now. We will look at an annealing-based implementation using the D-Wave SDK and a gate-based implementation using Qiskit.

Quantum algorithm portfolio management implementation

Quantum annealers

Quantum annealers are specialized machines capable of finding the minimum energy solution to a given problem, following the adiabatic principle. We talked about some of these machines in *Chapter 2*, but we will now cover in detail how they can be used to solve a problem such as portfolio optimization.

Quantum annealers require a target problem, set in its matrix form, to place variables as a mask. In our portfolio example, solutions will be encoded as binary decisions if the asset *n* will be included in our final portfolio. Therefore, our problem matrix should reflect the effect of including an asset or not in a solution.

For this, often in the literature, it is found that problems need to be placed on their QUBO (or Ising) form. **QUBO** stands for **Quadratic Unconstrained Binary Optimization**, which means binary variables are considered (0 or 1), only two-way multiplications are represented ($X_i \times X_j$), and all the information is contained within the objective function.

Therefore, a canonical shape for our QUBO problem would look like this:

$$x^T Q x$$

Where Q is the matrix containing all the information.

To shape our portfolio like this, we would need to construct our objective function so that the asset selection return, diversification risk, and budget constraints are included in a single equation, like the following:

$$-\sum_{i=1}^{n} x_i e_i + \theta_1 \sum_{i,j=1}^{n} x_i x_j c_{ij} + \theta_2 \left(\sum_{i=1}^{n} x_i b_i - B \right)^2$$

Here, e_i represents the expected return if the i asset is selected within the portfolio. c_{ij} represents the risk of selecting two assets simultaneously, as they could be driven by the same underlying process, increasing our risk. b_i is associated with the cost of acquiring the i asset, and the sum of all assets should not exceed the available budget (B). Two θ values represent the relevance of that term, meaning we could surpass our initial budget if we allow it or consider high-risk portfolios if we decrease the value of θ_1. We can modulate the result, as it needs to be unconstrained (the U in QUBO), but it can be modulated according to our priorities each time.

Once the problem is set into this canonical form, you can easily take it to a quantum annealing machine to obtain the results.

D-Wave implementation

D-Wave is not only one of those machines but also one of the first market-ready quantum computers, appearing almost 10 years ago. Its devices can be accessed as a cloud service and be freely used (at least for some minutes per month). Its online service is called Leap (`https://cloud.dwavesys.com/leap/login`), and after registering, the welcome page will let you know your remaining computing time, as shown in the following figure.

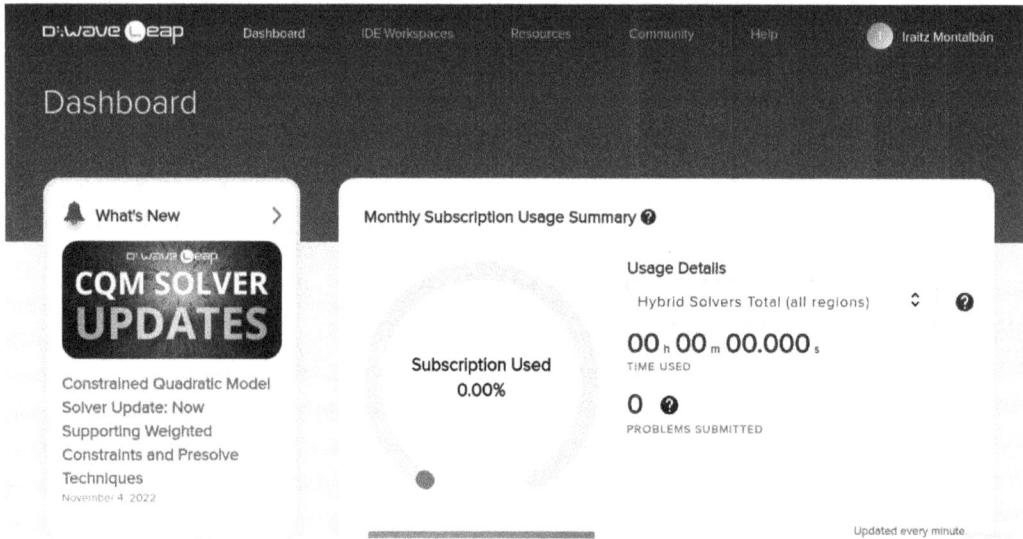

Figure 5.6 – The Leap dashboard

This is where the access token can be retrieved, which will be used to connect to the service once your local environment is ready.

Let's proceed and start building our portfolio problem to solve it using the D-Waves platform. First, we must load our previous data, based on the information retrieved from Binance:

```
import json
import numpy as np

data = None
with open("binance-data.json", "r") as jsonfile:
    data = json.load(jsonfile)

returns = data['mu']
covar = data['sigma']
```

Returns and covariances will be used to compose our target problem. Also, a budget needs to be defined to restrict the amounts of assets we want to select. In this case, this will be imposed as 50% of the total amounts our assets would add up to:

```
assets = []
costs = []
for row in data['assets']:
    assets.append(row["Asset"])
    costs.append(float(row["Open"]))


# Half the money
budget = np.sum(costs)/0.5
```

Thanks to the PyQUBO library, our previous formulation can easily translate into an encoding problem into D-Wave's chip:

```
from pyqubo import Array, Placeholder, Constraint

num_assets = len(assets)
x = Array.create('x', shape=num_assets, vartype='BINARY')

# Profit generated by each asset individually
H_linear_profit = 0.0
for i in range(num_assets):
    H_linear_profit += Constraint(
        returns[i] * x[i], label='profit({})'.format(i)
    )

# Risk obtained from the covariance matrix
H_quadratic = 0.0
for i in range(num_assets):
    for j in range(i + 1, num_assets):
        H_quadratic += Constraint(
            covar[i][j] * x[i] * x[j], label='risk({}, {})'.format(i,
j)
        )

# Constraint (budget)
H_linear_budget = 0.0
for i in range(num_assets):
    H_linear_budget += Constraint(costs[i]*x[i], label='slot({})'.
format(i))

# Final shape of the problem
theta1 = Placeholder('theta1')
```

```
theta2 = Placeholder('theta2')
H = - H_linear_profit + theta1 * H_quadratic + theta2 * (H_linear_
budget - budget)**2
model = H.compile()
```

This model serves different objectives, as we can play with theta parameters to make budget or diversification terms more or less strict:

```
# Set the Lagrange multipliers
theta1=0.5
theta2=0.3
feed_dict = {'theta1': theta1, 'theta2' : theta2}

# Transform to QUBO.
qubo, offset = model.to_qubo(feed_dict=feed_dict)
qubo

{('x[4]', 'x[0]'): -8.656820265502894e-06,
 ('x[0]', 'x[0]'): -0.003196217986409817,
 ('x[3]', 'x[1]'): 0.00019183405443636594,
 ...
 ('x[1]', 'x[1]'): 9.405658442868104e-05,
 ('x[2]', 'x[1]'): 0.00014597087707179864,
 ('x[1]', 'x[0]'): 0.00023358187881969354,
 ('x[2]', 'x[0]'): 0.000694880363473856}
```

This is the actual Q matrix, as expected in the preceding equation 1. Up to this point, it is a matter of formulating our target problem so that D-Wave's annealing machine can process it. The following steps will take this model to the annealer, so we must instantiate it:

```
from dwave.system.samplers import DWaveSampler
from dwave.system.composites import FixedEmbeddingComposite
import minorminer
import dimod

# Instanciate Sampler
dwave_sampler = DWaveSampler()
```

Apart from D-Wave's libraries, additional libraries are required to embed the problem in our target chip architecture. This will be discussed more in detail in *Chapter 9*, but the chip architecture requires us to find a suitable embedding for our problem. Thanks to the minorminer library, this only requires a few lines of code:

```
# Construct a problem
bqm = dimod.BinaryQuadraticModel(qubo, dimod.BINARY)
```

```
# Get the edge list
target_edgelist = dwave_sampler.edgelist

# And source edge list on the BQM quadratic model
source_edgelist = list(bqm.quadratic)

# Find the embeding
embedding = minorminer.find_embedding(source_edgelist, target_
edgelist)
sampler = FixedEmbeddingComposite(dwave_sampler, embedding)
```

Once the problem counts with a suitable embedding, we are set to send it to the quantum machine. We can invoke the sampler to obtain the end results after our problem has spent an amount of time, called annealing time, in D-Wave's chip:

```
ta = 10 # microseconds
num_reads = 10
response = sampler.sample_qubo(qubo, num_reads=num_reads, annealing_
time=ta)
response.first


Sample(sample={'x[0]': 1, 'x[1]': 0, 'x[2]': 1, 'x[3]': 0, 'x[4]':
0}, energy=-0.005097396148791738, num_occurrences=10, chain_break_
fraction=0.0)
```

This is the minimum energy solution found after 10 runs, with 10 microseconds of annealing time. This encoding reveals that our best portfolio would comprise the first and third assets, given the order in which we have encoded their information (ETHBTC in our BNBBTC example).

Also, it is relevant that all then runs have revealed this as the optimal solution after annealing time (num_ocurrences=10). This can be sometimes the case, as the solution may have a lower success probability. This will be more relevant when solving these problems using gate-based quantum devices.

Qiskit implementation

Qiskit is the framework we will use to try to solve the same problem, but we will use gate-based quantum devices. Gate-based devices allow more universal settings to solve annealing problems, but any other component is also allowed. There are devices you would work on when trying to solve using QML techniques or gate-based algorithms, as in the case of Shor's, Grover, and so on, as discussed in *Chapter 2*.

In this case, Qiskit already provides high abstraction level libraries for finance so that our coding requirements can be minimized, instead of doing it from scratch. For example, composing our quadratic problem based on Binance data would have the following lines:

```
from qiskit_finance.applications.optimization import
PortfolioOptimization

q = 0.5  # set risk factor
budget = len(assets) // 2  # set budget

portfolio = PortfolioOptimization(
    expected_returns=returns, covariances=covar, risk_factor=q,
budget=budget
)
qp = portfolio.to_quadratic_program()
```

The latest equation represents this quadratic program, and Qiskit already provides the means to solve it, using classical NumPy-based solvers:

```
from qiskit_optimization.converters import QuadraticProgramToQubo
from qiskit_optimization.algorithms import MinimumEigenOptimizer
from qiskit.algorithms import NumPyMinimumEigensolver

def index_to_selection(i, num_assets):
...

def print_result(result):
...

exact_mes = NumPyMinimumEigensolver()
exact_eigensolver = MinimumEigenOptimizer(exact_mes)
result = exact_eigensolver.solve(qp)
print_result(result)

Optimal: selection [1. 0. 1. 0. 0.], value -0.0011

----------------- Full result ---------------------
selection   value     probability
-----------------------------------------------------
[1 0 1 0 0]  -0.0011  1.0000
[1 1 1 1 1]   9.0971  0.0000
[0 1 1 1 1]   4.0459  0.0000
[1 0 0 0 0]   1.0102  0.0000
[0 1 0 0 0]   1.0108  0.0000
[1 1 0 0 0]   0.0010  0.0000
```

```
[0 0 1 0 0]   1.0087     0.0000
[0 1 1 0 0]  -0.0005   0.0000
[1 1 1 0 0]   1.0102     0.0000
[0 0 0 1 0]   1.0122     0.0000
[1 0 0 1 0]   0.0024     0.0000
[0 1 0 1 0]   0.0031     0.0000
[1 1 0 1 0]   1.0138     0.0000
```

Even though this shows the solution to our problem as expected, the process can be expensive when scaling to larger portfolio configurations, as it explores the whole landscape of potential solutions.

Ideally, variational approaches should be more efficient in exploring these large solution spaces, given the nature of quantum computing. When dealing with all those options simultaneously and evolving them, highlighting the one that minimizes our objective is where these techniques shine. Two main steps are needed to transfer our quadratic problem to a quantum setup:

- A **Parameterized Quantum Circuit** (**PQC**) or ansatz
- An optimization procedure that will adjust and find the appropriate parameters for our PQC

For the first example, the **Quantum Approximate Optimization Algorithm** (**QAOA**) will be our candidate algorithm to solve our problem. It is a method that is directly inherited from how annealers deal with this type of problem, setting alternating Hamiltonians for the target problem and the Mixer Hamiltonian.

The PQC has a fixed shape for a given problem, and only repetitions of it are required for selection. By varying the number of repetitions, we should be able to increase the success probability of our target state, the solution to our problem. Then, variationally, we want to find the appropriate set of parameters that maximize this success probability. In this case, COBYLA will be our chosen optimizer, given its fast performance. Other options should also be tried:

```
from qiskit.algorithms import QAOA
from qiskit.algorithms.optimizers import COBYLA

layers = 2

cobyla = COBYLA()
cobyla.set_options(maxiter=500)

qaoa_mes = QAOA(optimizer=cobyla, reps=layers, quantum_
instance=quantum_instance)
qaoa = MinimumEigenOptimizer(qaoa_mes)
result = qaoa.solve(qp)

Optimal: selection [1. 0. 1. 0. 0.], value -0.0011
```

```
----------------- Full result --------------------
selection  value    probability
----------------------------------------------------

[0 0 0 1 1]   0.0048      0.0783
[0 1 0 1 0]   0.0031      0.0777
[0 1 0 0 1]   0.0031      0.0777
[1 0 0 1 0]   0.0024      0.0775
[1 0 0 0 1]   0.0021      0.0773
[0 0 1 1 0]   0.0009      0.0770
[1 1 0 0 0]   0.0010      0.0770
[0 0 1 0 1]   0.0009      0.0770
[0 1 1 0 0]  -0.0005      0.0765
[1 0 1 0 0]  -0.0011      0.0763
...
```

Well, for our first attempt, even though we found the best solution, it competes against other solutions under the same quantum state. We must remember that the result of all the operations we perform on a quantum device will generate a quantum state that should, ideally, have our candidate solution among the states composing it. If it also has a bigger probability amplitude, it will be more likely to succeed when it collapses to one of those classical states upon measurement. Therefore, we want to find a result whose probability is bigger than the one shown here.

We could try out a different number of layers or repetitions between the problem and the mixer Hamiltonian:

```
from qiskit.algorithms import QAOA

layers = 5
qaoa_mes = QAOA(optimizer=cobyla, reps=layers, quantum_
instance=quantum_instance)
qaoa = MinimumEigenOptimizer(qaoa_mes)
result = qaoa.solve(qp)
Optimal: selection [1. 0. 1. 0. 0.], value -0.0011

----------------- Full result --------------------
selection  value    probability
----------------------------------------------------

[0 0 0 1 1]   0.0048      0.0666
[0 1 0 1 0]   0.0031      0.0663
[0 1 0 0 1]   0.0031      0.0661
[1 0 0 1 0]   0.0024      0.0659
[1 0 0 0 1]   0.0021      0.0659
[0 0 1 1 0]   0.0009      0.0656
```

```
[0 0 1 0 1]    0.0009    0.0654
[1 1 0 0 0]    0.0010    0.0654
[0 1 1 0 0]   -0.0005    0.0651
[1 0 1 0 0]   -0.0011    0.0647
...
```

If this approach does not seem right, we can try varying the optimization method of the approach in general, looking for a different ansatz composition.

Variational Quantum Eignesolver (**VQE**) allows for more generic approaches to ansatz description. For example, the TwoLocal PQC implementation is used in the following example. The TwoLocal circuit can hold several repetitions of the same scheme, containing different, arbitrarily chosen operations:

```
from qiskit.circuit.library import TwoLocal

ansatz = TwoLocal(num_assets, "ry", "cz", reps=3, entanglement="full")
ansatz.decompose().draw('mpl', fold=150)
```

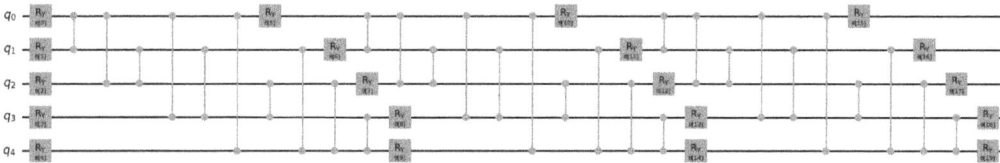

Figure 5.7 – A circuit of three repetitions of the RY rotations and CZ
two-qubit gates produced by the preceding code

We need to find the theta parameters to solve our problem. This is where a variational approach comes into play – in this case, using the COBYLA solver again to find those ideal parameters:

```
from qiskit import Aer
from qiskit.algorithms import VQE
from qiskit.algorithms.optimizers import COBYLA
from qiskit.utils import QuantumInstance
from qiskit.utils import algorithm_globals

algorithm_globals.random_seed = 1234
backend = Aer.get_backend("statevector_simulator")

cobyla = COBYLA()
cobyla.set_options(maxiter=500)

quantum_instance = QuantumInstance(backend=backend, seed_
simulator=1234, seed_transpiler=1234)
```

```
vqe_mes = VQE(ansatz, optimizer=cobyla, quantum_instance=quantum_
instance)
vqe = MinimumEigenOptimizer(vqe_mes)
result = vqe.solve(qp)
```

As shown in the preceding code, the VQE requires an ansatz or PQC, an optimizer, and a quantum instance, the device in which the evaluations of the quantum circuit will take place. In this case, a local simulation will be used, but we will see in *Chapter 8* how this evaluation can use cloud-based resources, as in the case of D-Wave. After some iterations (a maximum of 500), we can print the results for our portfolio problem:

```
print_result(result)

Optimal: selection [1. 0. 1. 0. 0.], value -0.0011

---------------- Full result --------------------
selection    value      probability
-----------------------------------------------------
[1 1 0 0 0]  0.0010     0.3613
[1 0 0 1 0]  0.0024     0.3463
[0 0 1 1 0]  0.0009     0.1285
...
[1 0 1 0 0]  -0.0011    0.0000
```

The found solution matches the optimal solution in our previous examples, but the success probability of finding it is not 1.0 but almost 0. This means if only one shot of the circuit is allowed with those parameters and we measure the classical bit string at the end of the process, it is improbable that this state will be chosen. It can be complicated to understand from the classical certainty. However, dealing with quantum states may lead to these sorts of cases, where the best solution is a composition of the optimal with suboptimal options on different mixture levels.

The work of the quantum scientist will involve finding a good approach to maximize these odds by changing the PQC, optimization method, or global procedure.

For example, by extending the number of repetitions on TwoLocal ansatz, we can see how these odds vary:

```
ansatz = TwoLocal(num_assets, "ry", "cz", reps=6, entanglement="full")
vqe_mes = VQE(ansatz, optimizer=cobyla, quantum_instance=quantum_
instance)
vqe = MinimumEigenOptimizer(vqe_mes)
result = vqe.solve(qp)

Optimal: selection [1. 0. 1. 0. 0.], value -0.0011
```

```
---------------- Full result ---------------------
selection  value      probability
---------------------------------------------------
[0 1 0 0 1]  0.0031    0.6130
[1 0 1 0 0]  -0.0011   0.2030
[0 1 0 1 0]  0.0031    0.0528
[0 1 1 0 0]  -0.0005   0.0435
[1 0 0 1 0]  0.0024    0.0314
...
```

That's much better. Now, if we run our trained ansatz five times, with a high probability, the optimal solution will be found at least once. We could try it by simply composing our circuit, binding the parameters, and measuring for a set of runs:

```
from qiskit import QuantumCircuit
from qiskit import Aer, execute
from qiskit.visualization import import plot_histogram

qc = QuantumCircuit(num_assets,num_assets)

# VQE Two Local ansatz
qc.compose(ansatz, inplace=True)

# Measures
for i in range(0, num_assets):
    qc.measure(i, i)

pqc = qc.bind_parameters(best_parameters)

# Number of shots to the circuit
nshots = 10

# execute the quantum circuit
backend = Aer.get_backend('qasm_simulator') # the device to run on
result = execute(pqc, backend, shots=nshots).result()
```

We could then collect the results and check the outcome.

```
counts  = result.get_counts(pqc)
plot_histogram(counts)
```

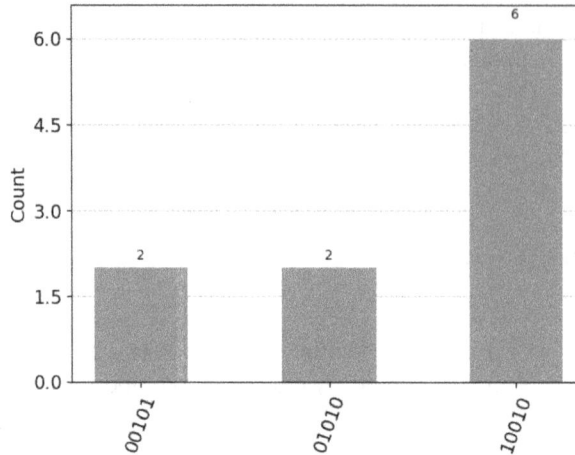

Figure 5.8 – The probability output by quantum states

Conclusion

When scaling to larger portfolios, computing the optimal result might be too expensive compared to quantum approaches. Still, as we have seen, even when quantum-computing those large combinatorial problems, they come at the cost of needing a complete certainty of the outcome.

It is important to understand that these techniques require, as happens in traditional machine learning approaches, a good understanding of how the best architecture for our ansatz plays in our favor. And in many cases, this will come from the experience of fitting against different types of portfolios and stock combinations. Not all assets show similar behaviors. This will require exploring the vast extension of potential ansatzes, repetitions of schemes in those ansatzes, and optimization techniques that require fewer iterations to find the best parameters.

Even though gate-based quantum devices may offer a generalist approach to quantum computation, it is undeniable that, nowadays, quantum annealers provide devices capable of handling larger portfolios without the hustle of looking for and training variational approaches.

The next chapter will introduce the credit risk analysis domain. An introduction will be provided on the theory and how to solve it classically and with quantum approaches.

6
Credit Risk Analytics

Problems such as credit scoring, fraud detection, churn prediction, credit limit definition, and financial behavior forecasting (among others) are constant challenges for banks and financial institutions, which permanently research for more accurate results and ways to decrease business-related risk when providing services. Most of these problems can be tackled by using machine learning to classify users who are likely to, for example, not pay their bills on time or commit fraud. In this chapter, the quantum machine learning side of these scenarios will be explored, using a permanent benchmark with classical counterparts for most of the cases.

In the current economic situation, where the stability of the markets is unpredictable and the way people work is always changing (thanks to the rise of the "gig economy"), it is harder to increase a credit product portfolio and cover a larger number of customer cohorts without increasing the risk for businesses. Exploring QML and ML methods side by side could leverage the current decision-making architectures of different banks, neobanks, fintechs, and other financial institutions that consider in their structures the possibility of lending money to companies or individuals.

As we mentioned previously, the ML alternative is very well suited for cases where we have evidence (data) but cannot fully grasp the underlying model or logic manually. One of the most well-known machine learning techniques to address these kinds of projects relates to supervised learning. Credit scoring systems are a common part of decision-making methods that are executed in finance. They use boosted decision trees (LGBM and XGBoost), random forests, support vector machines, clustering methods, and some regression models to get results that can be used to make decisions and automate scoring procedures. Similarly, QML algorithms can be tested and compared under the same scenario and eventually provide a business advantage. Typical classification algorithms in the quantum spectrum are **Quantum Neural Networks (QNNs)**, **Quantum Support Vector Classifiers (QSVCs)**, and **Variational Quantum Classifiers (VQCs)**. The code and rationale expressed in this chapter can help data science departments or any machine learning-related professionals in the finance sector who are usually trying to improve their models, finding ways to determine the right approach to extract more benefit from the available computational power.

Data exploration and preparation to execute both ML and QML models

As mentioned before, in this chapter, we will walk you through the implementation of hybrid quantum-classical algorithms and how they behave in a real-world scenario in finance, but before you start playing with them in a professional setup, you should think – or at least review – some the following concepts.

Data enrichment refers to the process of enriching or supplementing an existing dataset with extra information. Data enrichment in the context of credit scoring systems is the use of additional data sources to supplement extra variables and features that could come from a credit bureau or a non-traditional source (e.g., mobile data mining) in order to increase the accuracy of credit risk assessments.

By incorporating additional data sources like public records (digital footprints), social media behavior, financial history, open finance, and other alternative data sources, data enrichment can help bridge the gaps in information for a thorough analysis of customers. For instance, a lender might utilize a third-party service to verify a borrower's job, income, and assets by obtaining data from financial institutions, tax authorities, and credit card institutions.

Creditors can make more informed choices regarding creditworthiness and lower the risk of default or delinquency by incorporating new data from credit bureau reports. Moreover, data enrichment may assist lenders in identifying new client categories and creating more customized solutions based on borrower profiles.

To summarize, the typical data sources of a credit scoring system can be aggregated into three main groups:

- **Internal data**: Most financial institutions will provide credit to current customers that use checking or current accounts. Analyzing this behavior should be the base for any further decision.

- **Financial behavior data**: Retrieve all the financial data required to assess the financial behavior of an organization or individual, considering their payment history, risk scores, current debts, demographics, and current financial products in use.

- **Out-of-the-box data**: This includes data that comes from different sources compared with the sources of traditional bureaus (for example, Equifax). It is well known that some financial institutions use psychological factors, smartphone metadata, and users' digital footprints to add a significant number of variables and features in decisioning models.

Features analysis

Feature analysis is the process of determining the most influential factors or features on the performance of a machine learning model. In the context of credit scoring systems, feature analysis is the process of discovering the most predictive characteristics that can be utilized to make correct credit decisions and discriminate correctly between potential good or bad payers.

Credit scoring models that employ machine learning often incorporate a number of characteristics or descriptive variables, including payment history, credit usage, credit tenure, and types of credit used. Nevertheless, not all of these characteristics may be equally significant in predicting credit risk, and some characteristics may have a greater influence than others.

Feature analysis aids in identifying the most influential variables that impact credit risk and prioritizing them in a model. Several approaches, including correlation analysis, decision trees, and gradient boosting algorithms, can be used to determine the characteristics that have the highest predictive potential.

By concentrating on the most essential variables, machine learning models for credit scoring can increase precision and lower the chance of default or delinquency. Feature analysis can also assist lenders in establishing more tailored risk management strategies by enhancing their understanding of the determinants of credit risk.

It is essential to remember that feature analysis techniques are an ongoing process, and the most relevant factors may change as economic conditions, customer behavior, and other variables alter. Thus, machine learning models for credit scoring must be continually updated and adjusted to account for the ever-changing nature of credit risk.

The most well-known strategies and methods applied to execute the feature analysis are as follows:

- **Feature selection**: This is a non-trivial process that can have a tremendous impact on the final results, depending on the case. There is a myth about machine learning projects that more data and variables are always good, which is true, but not all of the information will be useful for the ML model. In some scenarios, it is actually better to reduce those features to allow a better prediction (Ji et al.). To execute these processes, there are a few techniques that consider the use of genetic algorithms, or simply analyze the importance, correlation, and variance of the features to decide which ones add more value to the predictive process. Typically, this stage is included in the data science procedure called **Exploratory Data Analysis** (**EDA**), which involves the investigation of datasets to extract the best data from them as input for subsequent operations.

- **Feature engineering**: Once the data and the features are available, the original variables might not be enough to develop good results under your specific target or key demographics. If so, you may be required to build new features that can come as a result of a calculation from the original variables (e.g., if we have the customer's transactions, additional features can be generated that consider the average value of the transactions and the same with the median, maximum amount, and minimum amount). These new columns inn the datasets can have a high impact on the machine learning model's **Key Performance Indicators** (**KPIs**) later on.

Data preprocessing

The process of modifying and preparing data for use in machine learning models is known as data preprocessing. In the context of credit scoring systems, data preparation entails cleaning, converting, and preparing credit data so that it may be efficiently utilized to train machine learning models.

Credit data can sometimes be incomplete and disorganized, with missing numbers, inconsistent formats, and other difficulties that might hinder the effectiveness of machine learning models. Techniques for data preparation can assist in addressing these challenges and preparing data for modeling.

By utilizing data pre-treatment approaches, machine learning models for credit scoring can be trained more efficiently and yield more accurate results. Here are two of the most relevant approaches:

1. **Oversampling**: It is common that financial datasets are imbalanced with regard to the target variable that a model is predicting. Having distributions of 95% non-defaulters and 5% defaulters could represent a significant difficulty for ML architectures. There are different techniques to mitigate this problem that will allow you to increase one of the classes or simply provide more statistical copies of your initial dataset. A typical strategy is to use the **Synthetic Minority Oversampling Technique (SMOTE)** or synthetic oversampling in general, with the application of several sub-strategies. By using these kinds of techniques, a financial dataset can be balanced to represent an equal portion of good and bad payers; therefore, the ML training process can be impacted positively in terms of the data points and patterns to be analyzed.

2. **Encoding**: Usually, data comes in different forms and data types. To be able to process them within an ML or QML algorithm, we need to ensure that all features are numerical, and frequently, a portion of the variables are originally categorical. To be able to continue the process, there are a few methods to encode categorical data as numerical data, such as one-hot encoding, label encoding, binary encoding, and feature hashing. Moreover, QML models pose the challenge of translating classical data samples into quantum states, which is a whole field by itself. We will explore some common embedding and feature maps within the regime of the techniques we will explore, but keep in mind that many different techniques exist on how encoding can be tackled, from basic feature mapping to **Quantum Generative Adversarial Networks (qGANs)**, such as embeddings, as we saw in *Chapter 4* with the stock price distribution case.

In the upcoming subsections, as mentioned earlier, the primary focus will be on model implementations, and it should be assumed that the dataset has been prepared in accordance with all the previous concepts.

Real business data

One of the barriers in QML, when applied to industry cases, is the lack of open source examples that use representative data to recreate a true business scenario. Most of the tutorials and open code repositories use demo datasets to show the architecture of the models, usually with interesting results that are difficult to replicate later. In the case of the exercise in this chapter, we will use a synthetic copy of real small and medium businesses' financial behavior so that the results and the data treatment can truly mimic an authentic bank or fintech scenario at the time, classifying customers by their financial risk.

Synthetic data

Synthetic data is meant to revolutionize artificial intelligence, according to experts such as Gartner (`https://www.gartner.com/en/newsroom/press-releases/2022-06-22-is-synthetic-data-the-future-of-ai`). Trained on real-world data samples, data generators are able to create samples of realistic synthetic data points that are statistical replicas of the original ones. The model first discovers the patterns, correlations, and statistical characteristics of the sample data so that it can then fake samples similar to those. It is basically the same technology behind all the buzz there has been around deepfake technology but, in this case, used for corporate tabular data. One of the benefits of using synthetic data is the ability to curate the original dataset fixing bias, data sample balance, and missing data, as the generator is able to overcome these issues by learning the relationship between the features, composing a realistic data sample (Figueira et al.). It is particularly relevant when customer data is involved in the process, as this can pose privacy-related issues that may be a burden to an already complex analytic project. Luckily for us, given that synthetic data refers to no specific individual, if properly synthesized, it would be free of any regulatory restriction.

Synthetic data looks and has the same meaning as the actual data sample used to train the algorithm. Since the synthetic dataset includes the same insights and correlations as the original, it is a great stand-in for the original. Taking this into account, the extracted information can be used safely as training data to build machine learning models and test data, such as when testing a credit scoring or fraud detection system (Assefa et al.).

The main benefits of this method for generating new data are as follows:

- It avoids **General Data Protection Regulation** (**GDPR**) and other legal constraints when data is shared between institutions or is simply used to train ML models under different environments, without the risk of PII data leakage.

- It detects more efficiently outliers in cases such as fraud. Fraudulent actions are a small fraction of the total activities tracked by a bank. Due to the data size, it is difficult for a machine learning model to learn from this sort of dataset in order to identify new instances of fraud, and inaccurate findings may be a consequence. Undersampling and oversampling are two methods to deal with imbalanced datasets. Undersampling is the process of deleting (in this example) non-fraud observations to get a balanced dataset. In contrast, oversampling generates fresh examples of fraudulent behavior that mimic genuine fraud. The ML model may then be trained on the balanced dataset to provide more precise outcomes. In order to get a balanced dataset, synthetic data creation methods might be employed to generate fictitious cases of fraud.

- It improves existing machine learning models, since most of the algorithms related to supervised learning and deep learning are usually data-hungry. Even if a financial institution has sufficient data to train an ML model, data quantity has a significant impact on the accuracy of ML models. Synthetic data can be used to expand the size of a dataset dramatically.

Case study

The exercise that will be applied in this chapter is built on synthetic public data from **small and medium businesses** (**SMBs**) that has been released on the Kaggle data science platform by the company NayaOne (`https://www.kaggle.com/datasets/nayaone/sme-uk-businesses-financial-statistics`). The dataframe's structure is composed of 10 distinct CSV files, each of which contains information about a different aspect of a firm, as follows:

- Account Receivable: Entails the money owed by clients for billed goods or services

- Businesses: A list of companies and their details

- COVID: The financial data of firms during pandemic waves

- Credit Account History: Refers to the history of a credit account

- Credit Card History: Entails a record of the business's credit card activity and associated debt

- Credit Rating: A quantitative evaluation of a borrower's creditworthiness in general or relative to a financial obligation

- Director: An individual from the United Kingdom who holds a director role in the businesses presented in the dataset

- Factoring: Data related to the process when a firm sells its accounts receivable to a third party at a discount in a factoring transaction, which is a kind of debtor financing

- Loan: Details on paid and outstanding loans taken out by an organization

When all the CSV files are put together, they give a total of 269 variables. The target variable that determines whether a company is a "good" or "bad" payer is based on how the company actually behaved when it had debts, classifying them into four distinct groups, namely the following:

- **A potential defaulter in terms of loans**: In the context of loans, a debt is considered overdue if there was at least one delay in the payment of the loan installments

- **A potential defaulter in terms of credit cards**: A credit card account is deemed overdue if there was at least one payment delay

- **A defaulter**: The corporation is deemed to have defaulted on the loan when the loan status variable is recorded as "default"

- **Late payers**: A delinquent mark was assigned to all firms with more than four late payments in the previous five years

All these previous rules defined good behavior in SMBs for 71.46% of the cases and bad behavior for the remaining 29.54%. Of course, as is customary, all the variables used to calculate the target class variables were dismissed from the dataset to avoid highly correlated features.

Provider of the data

NayaOne is a disruptive start-up from the UK that was founded in 2019. Its revolutionary goal is to provide a single point of access to hundreds or even thousands of synthetic data points, enabling machine learning models for the finance industry to be built without having to wait months for the proprietary data to be ready. Using NayaOne's platform, every insurtech, fintech, or bank can prototype ML models or architectures in weeks rather than months or years.

On top of the benefits of faster prototyping to match an ideal time to market, the cost of experimentation can be reduced by at least 80%.

Features

The areas of the features used for the model are the following, based on an EDA and feature selection analysis:

- **Company details**: For example, `primary_sector`
- **Financial services currently in use**: For example, `factoring_provider`
- **Unit economics**: For example, `revenue`
- **Payments and transactions**: For example, `cant_invoices`
- **Credit reports and evaluations**: For example, `payment_index`
- **Human resources**: For example, `new_recruitments`

Finally, 164 features were chosen as being very important to train the model after all the techniques were applied.

Implementation of classical and quantum machine learning algorithms for a credit scoring scenario

Applying machine learning and quantum machine learning for credit scoring challenges requires the development of a prediction model that can properly determine an individual's or company's creditworthiness. Typically, this procedure, as shown in the steps described previously, includes data collection, data enrichment, data preparation, feature engineering, feature selection, model selection, model training, model evaluation, and subsequently, deployment. In this section, we will cover most of the previous concepts and procedures, assuming that the data is already encoded to numerical variables and the feature has been selected.

Data preparation

First, the data needs to be loaded. This data will come in one of the more well-known formats in the industry, which is CSV. The information that will load into the notebook, as previously detailed, is in a classical format, so we can handle the first steps of our architecture with pandas and scikit-learn without issues.

Step one of the preprocessing is loading the CSV, defining the X and y values of the experiment, and later, splitting the train and test sets:

```
import pandas as pd

# Data loading from a CSV file
fulldata = pd.read_csv('../../data/nayaone_synthetic_data.csv')

# Transforming data to float
data = fulldata.astype(float)
data.head(10)
```

At the moment, to load your data, it's important to split the dataset into two groups – the dataset that will be used to train a model and the dataset that will be used to evaluate the model fitness. By having a dataset that has never been used to train a model, we aim to set realistic measures for when our models will face real incoming data coming when operating in the real world. This dataset already contains identifiers to split those two sets from the merged CSV file:

```
data_train = data.groupby([data.index, 'train']).filter(lambda x:
x['train'] == 1.).reset_index()
data_test = data.groupby([data.index, 'train']).filter(lambda x:
x['train'] == 0.).reset_index()
```

After this, it is simple to split those two sets into feature and target attributes. Columns not containing relevant information or that could fake our ability to predict over a further test set, given that the label information is encoded, need to be removed from the attributes that our model will be able to retrieve in reality:

```
# Separate X and y considering dropping not useful columns
X_train = data_train.drop(['target', 'Unnamed: 0', 'train']
,axis="columns")
y_train = data_train['target']
X_test = data_test.drop(['target', 'Unnamed: 0', 'train']
,axis="columns")
y_test = data_test['target']
```

It's important to always review the distribution of the target variable because if it is highly imbalanced, it could drive the model towards a simplified decision that all samples must be treated like the majority of them. In such cases, other oversampling techniques may be necessary to increase the performance of the model and balance it with the different sample groups within the dataset. In the example shown here, the dataset is balanced enough (70–30 between our two main classes of individuals) in preparation for the next sections, those related to the model's architecture:

```
# Review the balance of the target variable in train
y_train.value_counts(normalize=True)*100


0.0     69.953052
1.0     30.046948



# Review the balance of the target variable in test
y_test.value_counts(normalize=True)*100


0.0     71.636364
1.0     28.363636
```

Preprocessing

The preprocessing stage is one of the most important steps in any machine learning project and model's architecture. In hybrid quantum-classical algorithms, the input also needs to be transformed from classical features to quantum states, which are usually called quantum encodings or quantum embeddings. During this section, these ideas will be explained in detail, but first, we will focus on the classical preprocessing methods that will be extended during the quantum coding part.

After the train and test datasets have been obtained, the preprocessing step, especially the dimensionality reduction, will take place. As previously mentioned, not all attributes hold the same amount of information, and it is crucial to concentrate the majority of it to avoid burdening the model with unnecessary work in determining the relevance of features. Tree-based models, for example, do take into consideration the information gain each attribute provides (Tangirala 2020), and neural networks, for example, will render into zero value weights to those attributes that do not contribute to improving the decision. However, certain techniques, such as the ones we will explore, lack this capacity, and it is important we make a realistic exercise, easing the work required by the subsequent model training steps.

There are a few techniques that can be used in this regard, and in the context of QML, they diminish the number of variables to be encoded into quantum devices, with fewer qubits to run classification tasks. Recall that this is relevant also because of the capacity of some quantum devices, which range from 10 or 100 qubits, while datasets can expand to thousands of features for each data point.

The two most utilized techniques are as follows:

- **Principal component analysis (PCA) (Bro & Smilde 2014)**: By analyzing the covariance matrix and expressing it in terms of linear combinations between various features, thereby generating orthogonal axes or principal components, PCA provides an ordering where the bottom principal components can be removed, as they encode a minimal amount of information. With this technique, the number of components or features that we want to extract from the process is a parameter that we can define, with the only constraint being that the features should not surpass the original number of variables.

- **Linear discriminant analysis (LDA) (Izenman 2013)**: LDA is a supervised algorithm that reduces the feature space by considering class labels. LDA focuses on target separability and tries to define the characteristics that better map this separable space. If LDA is used, there is a limitation on the number of features that could come from the reduction, since LDA can only provide $N - 1$, where N is the number of classes available.

The diagram in *Figure 6.2* highlights the main difference between the two techniques. In this case, LDA will be used because it has a proven record of surpassing PCA, with a reduced number of qubits and a binary classification (Mancilla and Pere 2022). The main constraint is that, previously, the database would have been split with the objective to extract more than one component per set and to have at least two components for the 2-qubit approach that followed.

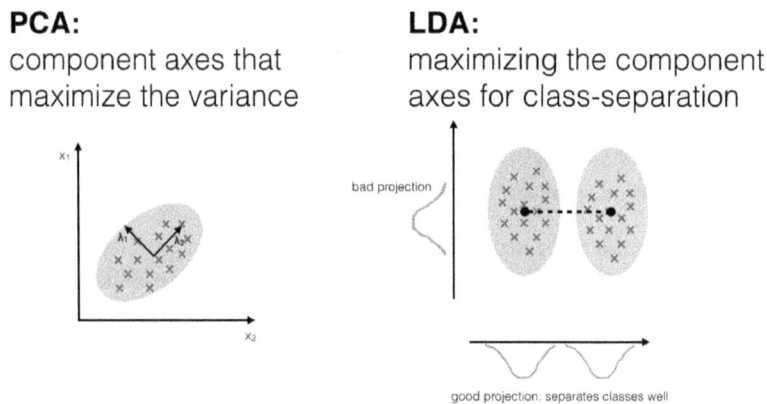

Figure 6.2 – A comparison between PCA and LDA

Image source: https://sebastianraschka.com/Articles/2014_python_lda.html

For the sake of simplicity, X_train and X_test will be split in half, allocating 50% of the features to the features_a set and the rest to features_b. Since we have 167 features, 83 will be allocated in one half and 84 in the other. It is highly recommended that this process is replaced by clusters, variable types groups, data sources, or a correlation definition:

```
# Hard split by half on the dataframe for the LDA dimensionality
reduction

# Train split
features_a = X_train.iloc[:,:83]
features_b = X_train.iloc[:,83:]

# Test split
features_a_test = X_test.iloc[:,:83]
features_b_test = X_test.iloc[:,83:]


from sklearn.discriminant_analysis import LinearDiscriminantAnalysis
as LDA

# LDA fit with the separated groups
lda1 = LDA(n_components=1, solver='svd').fit(features_a, y_train)
lda2 = LDA(n_components=1, solver='svd').fit(features_b, y_train)

# LDA train transformation
features_lda_1 = lda1.transform(features_a)
features_lda_2 = lda2.transform(features_b)


# LDA test transformation (using train fit)
features_lda_1_test = lda1.transform(features_a_test)
features_lda_2_test = lda2.transform(features_b_test)

# Arrays to dataframe for join in a single dataframe
features_lda_1 = pd.DataFrame(features_lda_1)
features_lda_2 = pd.DataFrame(features_lda_2)
features_lda_1_test = pd.DataFrame(features_lda_1_test)
features_lda_2_test = pd.DataFrame(features_lda_2_test)

# Join of dataframes
x_train_lda = pd.concat([features_lda_1, features_lda_2], axis=1)
x_test_lda = pd.concat([features_lda_1_test, features_lda_2_test],
axis=1)
```

Another factor that is common is scale disparity. It is important that we make our models agnostic to scale and able to focus on the information encoded into our features. It is also convenient when dealing with neural networks, as normalization always helps with their convergence.

In this case, we will replicate the information in different dataframes, adjusted to the target techniques we will use in the following sections:

```
from sklearn.preprocessing import StandardScaler, MinMaxScaler,
normalize

## QSVC
minmax_scaler = MinMaxScaler().fit(x_train_lda)
X_train_qsvc = minmax_scaler.transform(x_train_lda)
X_test_qsvc = minmax_scaler.transform(x_test_lda)

## SVC
strd_scaler = StandardScaler().fit(x_train_lda)
X_train_svc = strd_scaler.transform(x_train_lda)
X_test_svc = strd_scaler.transform(x_test_lda)

## VQC
strd_scaler = StandardScaler().fit(x_train_lda)
X_train_vqc = strd_scaler.transform(x_train_lda)
X_test_vqc = strd_scaler.transform(x_test_lda)
y_train_vqc = pd.DataFrame(y_train)
y_test_vqc = pd.DataFrame(y_test)

## Quantum Neural Network
minmax_scaler = MinMaxScaler().fit(x_train_lda)
X_train_nn = minmax_scaler.transform(x_train_lda)
X_test_nn = minmax_scaler.transform(x_test_lda)
y_train_nn = y_train.to_numpy()
y_test_nn = y_test.to_numpy()
```

It is important to highlight that this transformation should only affect the scale of the data, as their distribution and the relationship between different attributes associated with each sample of our dataset should remain intact. It mostly affects the way in which each algorithm is trained and tries to make this task easier by scaling the information (Singh and Singh 2020).

Quantum Support Vector Machines

The **Support Vector Classifier** (**SVC**) and **Quantum Support Vector Classifier** (**QSVC**) are the first models that will be used to look at our synthetic dataset, and we will see how a quantum algorithm versus a classical algorithm can work to find potential defaulters. One of the most widely used techniques is known as **Support Vector Machines** (**SVM**) (*Hearst et al., 1998*), which make use of hyperplanes in order to find separable spaces within our data regime. These hyperplanes are responsible for separating our N-dimensional information into different spaces, trying to maximize the margin between samples from the regions split by the hyperplane itself. By softening this margin constraint and allowing some samples to be misclassified, we allow the model to generalize from the dataset itself. This softened version is what we will call an SVC.

Thanks to the abstraction level that Python libraries such as scikit-learn provide, its usage is as simple as calling a fit function to pass the dataset and target data:

```
from sklearn.svm import SVC

# Instantiate the SVC
svc = SVC()

# Training
svc.fit(X_train_svc,y_train)

# Testing
svc_score = svc.score(X_test_svc, y_test)
print(f"SVC classification test score: {svc_score}")

SVC classification test score: 0.7927272727272727
```

As previously mentioned, it is important to pay attention to relevant metrics that will help us better understand the actual fitness of the model besides that single metric:

```
from sklearn import metrics

# Classification report of SVC
expected_y_svc  = y_test
predicted_y_svc = svc.predict(X_test_svc)

# Print classification report and confusion matrix
print("Classification report: \n", metrics.classification_
report(expected_y_svc, predicted_y_svc))

Classification report:
              precision    recall  f1-score    support
```

0.0	0.85	0.85	0.85	194
1.0	0.65	0.65	0.65	81
accuracy			0.79	275
macro avg	0.75	0.75	0.75	275
weighted avg	0.79	0.79	0.79	275

This is when the relevance of unbalanced datasets shows its ugly face, as we can see that our accuracy is mostly driven by our ability to detect non-defaulting customers.

Given the nature of SVMs and their requirement to handle space separability, one of the initial proposals in the realm of QML essentially leverages the inherent high-dimensional encoding offered by quantum states. **Quantum Support Vector Machines (QSVMs)** (Rebentrost et al. 214) encode classical data into quantum states so that after a measurement is obtained, encoded samples show better separability – in this case, performed by classical means.

One of the main benefits of the QSVM approach is how data points are represented in a quantum feature space, due to the use of quantum kernels (visualized in *Figure 6.3*). Usually, businesses can face non-linear separable data, and the use of classical kernel methods is not enough to properly divide two classes in the case of binary classification models. With the usage of quantum kernels, data points can be distributed in a Hilbert space so that they can be divided more efficiently with the algorithm (SVC). In *Figure 6.3*, you can see a visual example of a workflow that presents both approaches (classical and quantum) and how data could be represented in the different feature spaces to gain linear separability (`https://quantum-journal.org/papers/q-2021-08-30-531/`).

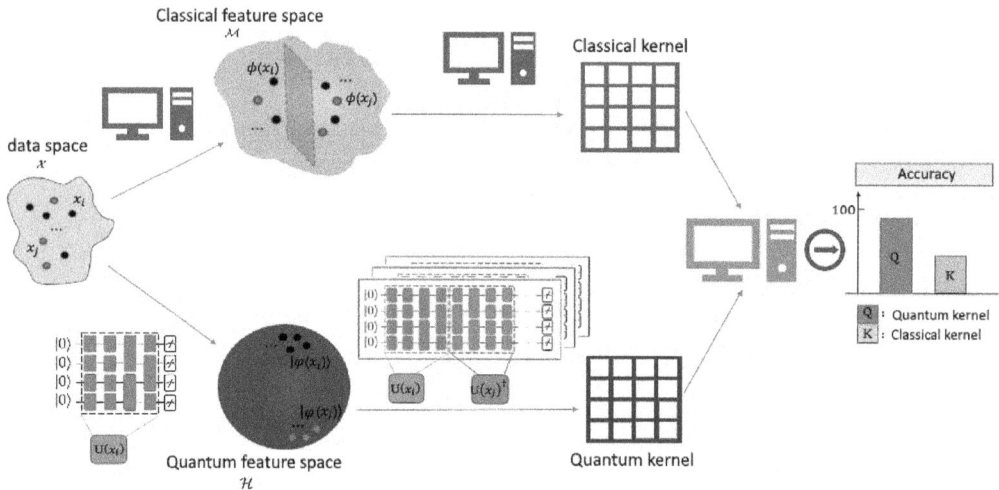

Figure 6.3 – A comparison of how classical and quantum kernels embed data points

Therefore, one of the first steps we will face when attempting a QSVM classifier is encoding classical data into a feature map that performs the actual quantum encoding for us. There are several options we can choose from, and the gain we will obtain will come from arbitrary decisions on the number of repetitions each feature map is performed with. This is a common issue we can face in data science projects, where some decisions will be based on experience of given datasets or scenarios.

Simply put, a quantum feature map encodes conventional data into a quantum state space by employing a quantum circuit. The number of times a circuit is repeated during encoding is called "depth," and it is a parameter that can be changed. QML on classical data requires the encoding of data into quantum states to be applied later to the quantum algorithm.

Qiskit provides a set of candidate feature maps we can use for our task of running a classification model. Most of them are based on Pauli operators, rotating according to our data features. That is one of the reasons why data needs to be preprocessed so that its numerical representation can be introduced as rotation angles in our feature map. Using combined Z rotations along the Z axis of each qubit is a common case that can be invoked, as seen here:

```
from qiskit.providers.aer import AerSimulator
from qiskit.utils import QuantumInstance
from qiskit.circuit.library import ZZFeatureMap

# Defining backend and feature map to be used
backend = QuantumInstance(
    AerSimulator(method='statevector'),
    seed_simulator=algorithm_globals.random_seed,
    seed_transpiler=algorithm_globals.random_seed,
)

# ZZ feature map
feature_map = ZZFeatureMap(feature_dimension=num_qubits, reps=3)

# Feature map circuit print
feature_map.decompose().draw(output = "mpl")
```

reps makes reference to the number of instances a feature map is repeated and is one of those hyperparameters that we might need to play with in order to find its best option. *Figure 6.4* shows the representation of our selected feature map composed of a set of rations (*P* gates in pink) and entangling CNOT gates.

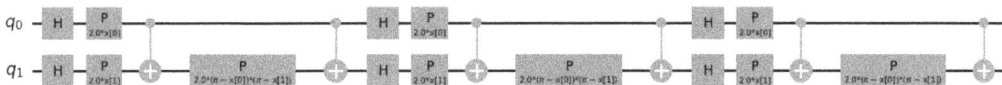

Figure 6.4 – The ZZFeature map with three repetition schemes

The *X* variables within the boxes in *Figure 6.4* represent the features of our dataset, which are used as a rotation weight that will drive the initial state of the circuit (|00> for the 2-qubit case) toward the one used as input in our SVC classifier.

Qiskit also provides higher-level abstractions for these QML tasks, so it is not required to produce the whole code for known techniques, as is the case with QSVM:

```
from qiskit_machine_learning.kernels import QuantumKernel
from qiskit_machine_learning.algorithms import QSVC


# Defining quantum kernel and qsvc
kernel = QuantumKernel(feature_map=feature_map, quantum_
instance=backend)
qsvc = QSVC(quantum_kernel=kernel, C=C)


# Training
qsvc.fit(X_train_qsvc,y_train)


# Testing
qsvc_score = qsvc.score(X_test_qsvc, y_test)
print(f"QSVC classification test score: {qsvc_score}")


QSVC classification test score: 0.7927272727272727
```

Even though it may seem like the same result has been obtained, we could check the classification report as we did before:

```
# Classification report of QSVC
expected_y_qsvc  = y_test
predicted_y_qsvc = qsvc.predict(X_test_qsvc)


# Print classification report and confusion matrix
print("Classification report: \n", metrics.classification_
report(expected_y_qsvc, predicted_y_qsvc))


Classification report:
              precision    recall  f1-score   support

        0.0       0.88      0.82      0.85       194
        1.0       0.63      0.73      0.67        81


   accuracy                           0.79       275
  macro avg       0.75      0.77      0.76       275
weighted avg       0.80      0.79      0.80       275
```

We can see some of the decisions have moved between the different classes, losing precision and gaining recall in some cases, but we could, by simple encoding, improve our detection of defaulters by two percentual points.

It might seem like a small gain, but considering the figure we saw at the beginning of this chapter, a 2% increase in detection is a huge improvement in terms of revenue. It's definitely a technique worth trying out, given how simple its adaptation from the classical regime is.

QNNs

Following the same structure as the previous comparison, we will now process our dataset of good customers and defaulters through quantum and classical neural networks. Neural networks of all kinds and shapes populate almost every machine learning initiative that a corporation may try (*Bishop 1994*). These models are versatile for a plethora of tasks, and their general framework allows for all kinds of architecture suitable for specific tasks – convolutional neural networks for artificial vision (*Khan et al., 2018*), recurrent neural networks for natural language understanding (*Yao et al., 2013*), or generative adversarial networks for synthetic data generation (*Park et al., 2018*).

Risk assessment is not absent from similar exercises (*Khashman 2010*), so given these are popular choices, we must try at least. Popular Python frameworks such as TensorFlow and its higher order abstraction, thanks to Keras, simplify much of the code needed to train a bioinspired trendy model. The code below follows an architecture where input data is passed through a series of layers in decreasing number of neurons (60, 40, 20 and 1), down to the point where the outcome of the last neuron determines the class input sample may belong to. That is why a Sigmoid function is defined for that last step.

Densely connected layers are our choice for this example and a **Rectified Linear Unit** (**ReLU**) is the neuron of choice (*Agarap 2018*), but as previously discussed, these decisions are not driven by any specific process, other than experience and trials in similar scenarios where this architecture proved successful:

```
# Keras
from keras.models import Sequential
from keras.layers import Dense

# Fit the model with specific layers and activations
model = Sequential()
model.add(Dense(60,input_dim=X_train_
nn.shape[1],activation='relu',kernel_initializer='normal'))
model.add(Dense(40,activation='relu'))
model.add(Dense(20,activation='relu'))
model.add(Dense(1,activation='sigmoid'))

# Model compiled
```

```
model.compile(loss='binary_crossentropy', optimizer='adam',
metrics=['accuracy'])
history = model.fit(X_train_nn, y_train, batch_size=batch,
                epochs=50, validation_data = (X_test_nn, y_
test),verbose=1)
```

Training will yield a high accuracy score (above 90%), but the test dataset is the one that provides realistic expectations of the model's ability to predict:

```
# Testing
nn_score = model.evaluate(X_test_nn, y_test)
print("NN test accuracy score: %.2f%%" % (nn_score[1]*100))


NN test accuracy score: 80.36%


# Classification report of NN
expected_y_nn  = y_test
predicted_y_nn = (model.predict(X_test_nn) > 0.5).astype("int32")


# Print classification report and confusion matrix
print("Classification report: \n", metrics.classification_
report(expected_y_nn, predicted_y_nn))


Classification report:
              precision    recall  f1-score   support

         0.0       0.86      0.87      0.86       194
         1.0       0.67      0.65      0.66        81

    accuracy                           0.80       275
   macro avg       0.76      0.76      0.76       275
weighted avg       0.80      0.80      0.80       275
```

Even though accuracy might seem to have increased, we have sacrificed the ability to identify non-defaulters and defaulters, which, even though they give a more balanced dataset, are not as efficient as we would like for our business needs.

Given that we already have an encoding sorted out, based on our previous exercise using ZZFeatureMap, it would be good to have a scheme where the whole model gets embedded into the quantum device so that once the data is represented in this feature map, the ability of quantum devices to disentangle complex relationships can be exploited fully. This can be done by QNNs (*Ezhov and Ventura, 2000, and Farhi and Neven, 2018*), a data embedding that is followed by a **Parameterized Quantum Circuit (PQC)** or ansatz, whose measurement sets the class that each sample belongs to:

```
from qiskit import QuantumCircuit
from qiskit.circuit.library import ZZFeatureMap, RealAmplitudes

# Declare the feature map
feature_map = ZZFeatureMap(num_inputs)

# Declare the ansatz
ansatz = RealAmplitudes(num_inputs, reps=2)

# Construct the quantum circuit
qc = QuantumCircuit(num_inputs)
qc.append(feature_map, range(num_inputs))
qc.append(ansatz, range(num_inputs))
qc.decompose().draw('mpl')
```

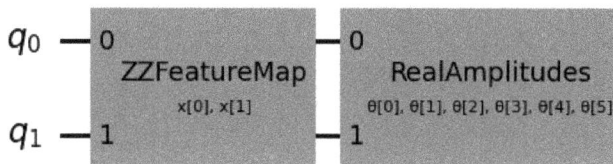

Figure 6.5 – A QNN obtained by the preceding code

As can be seen in the obtained circuit, the feature map only has two inputs belonging to the features in our dataset, but the PQC has five parameters that we need to determine in order to proceed. The way to perform such a task is by variationally adapting the output of the QNN model so that it minimizes a cost function, the mismatch between our labeled data, and the measured classical bit in our case.

Qiskit Machine Learning provides a whole machinery that will do the heavy lifting for us so that once the QNN structure is declared by these two steps (the feature embedding and the PQC), we just need to invoke a set of routines that will obtain the final model for us:

```
from qiskit.providers.aer import Aer
from qiskit_machine_learning.algorithms.classifiers import
NeuralNetworkClassifier
from qiskit_machine_learning.neural_networks import CircuitQNN
from qiskit.algorithms.optimizers import L_BFGS_B

# Maps bitstrings to 0 or 1
def parity(x):
    return "{:b}".format(x).count("1") % 2

# Defining quantum instance
quantum_instance = QuantumInstance(Aer.get_backend("aer_simulator"),
shots=shots)

# Declare the QNN circuit
circuit_qnn = CircuitQNN(
    circuit=qc,
    input_params=feature_map.parameters,
    weight_params=ansatz.parameters,
    interpret=parity,
    output_shape=2,
    quantum_instance=quantum_instance,
)


# Declare the classifier
circuit_classifier = NeuralNetworkClassifier(
        neural_network=circuit_qnn, optimizer= L_
BFGS_B(maxiter=maxiter), loss='absolute_error'
)
circuit_classifier.fit(X_train_nn,y_train_nn)

y_pred = circuit_classifier.predict(X_test_nn)

# print classification report and confusion matrix for the classifier
print("Classification report: \n", metrics.classification_report(y_
test_nn, y_pred))

Classification report:
                precision    recall   f1-score    support

        0.0         0.90       0.67      0.77        194
```

1.0	0.51	0.83	0.63	81
accuracy			0.72	275
macro avg	0.71	0.75	0.70	275
weighted avg	0.79	0.72	0.73	275

VQC

Finally, we will analyze the benefits of using a VQC, which only exists on the quantum side of machine learning; therefore, a comparison can't be made under the same principles. The VQC (*Havlíček et al. 2019*) is nothing more than a generalization of previously seen cases of QSVC and QNN. It allows for a broader description of the aforementioned concepts on data embedding and circuit parameterization but with a less restrictive setup, allowing any architecture to be deployed. The only restriction concerns the variational nature of obtaining the parameters for our ansatz and the outcome restricted to the task of classification.

Even though previously Qiskit-based approaches have been used, for this more generic setup, PennyLane is our framework of choice. This is mostly because of its functionality of differential programming that enables similar mechanisms for numerical gradient calculations, such as the ones popularized by TensorFlow and PyTorch, but also because of its access to gradient-based trainers such as Adam (*Kingma and Ba, 2014*).

Our circuit setup will follow a similar description as the previous example, with some differences in embedding and ansatz choices:

```
# PennyLane
import pennylane as qml
from pennylane import numpy as np
from pennylane.templates.embeddings import AngleEmbedding
from pennylane.optimize import AdamOptimizer

# Device
dev = qml.device('default.qubit', wires = num_qubits)

# Our generic candidate circuit
def circuit(parameters, X_train_vqc):
    for i in range(num_qubits):
        qml.Hadamard(wires = i)

    # Angle embedding for classical embedding
    AngleEmbedding(features = X_train_vqc, wires = range(num_qubits),
rotation = 'Y')

    # This will be our PQC of choice
```

```
    qml.StronglyEntanglingLayers(weights = parameters, wires =
range(num_qubits))

    # And measuring on 0 qubit we will get if it corresponds to one or
other label
    return qml.expval(qml.PauliZ(0))
```

`Angle` embedding encodes the dataset features into the angles of Y rotations and `StronglyEntanglingLayers` follows a scheme of single rotations and multiple CNOT entangling gate operations, which perform a circular link between all qubits (Schuld et al. 2020).

Once again, the circuit will be linked to a device that PennyLane calls a QNode:

```
# QNode: Device + Circuit
vqc = qml.QNode(circuit, dev, diff_method="backprop")
```

PennyLane allows fine-grained control over the different functions that will be used within the training of the model so that we can, for example, decide on the level of hybridization between classical and quantum means without much effort. In this example below, a classical bias neuron is added to the VQC scheme:

```
# VQC functions
def variational_classifier(weights, bias, x):
    return vqc(weights, x) + bias
```

The bias effect allows for a broader range of approximations when added, so it should work in our favor:

```
def square_loss(labels, predictions):
    loss = 0
    for l, p in zip(labels, predictions):
        loss = loss + (l - p) ** 2

    loss = loss / len(labels)
    return loss

def cost(weights, bias, X, Y):
    predictions = [variational_classifier(weights, bias, x) for x in
X]
    return square_loss(Y, predictions)
```

Once our score loss function is defined, we need to define an accuracy metric that will also be used as the criteria for parameter selection within the main loop:

```
def accuracy(labels, predictions):

    loss = 0
```

```
    for l, p in zip(labels, predictions):
        if abs(l - p) < 1e-5:
            loss = loss + 1
    loss = loss / len(labels)

    return loss

# Optimizer declaration and batch parameter
opt = AdamOptimizer(stepsize=0.1, beta1=0.9, beta2=0.99, eps=1e-08)
batch_size = batch

weights = weights_init
bias = bias_init

wbest = 0
bbest = 0
abest = 0

for it in range(50):

    # Weights update by each optimizer step

    batch_index = np.random.randint(0, len(X_train_nn), (batch_size,))
    X_batch = X_train_nn[batch_index]
    Y_batch = y_train_nn[batch_index]
    weights, bias, _, _ = opt.step(cost, weights, bias, X_batch, Y_
batch)

    # Accuracy computation
    predictions = [np.sign(variational_classifier(weights, bias, x))
for x in X_batch]

    acc = accuracy(Y_batch, predictions)

    if acc > abest:
        wbest = weights
        bbest = bias
        abest = acc
        print('New best')

    print(
        "Iter: {:5d} | Cost: {:0.7f} | Accuracy: {:0.7f} ".format(
            it + 1, cost(weights, bias, X_batch, Y_batch), acc
        )
```

```
    )

# X_test and y_test transformation to be analyzed
Yte = np.array(y_test_vqc.values[:,0] * 2 - np.ones(len(y_test_vqc.
values[:,0])), requires_grad = False)
Xte = np.array(normalize(X_test_vqc), requires_grad=False)


# Testing
predictions = [np.sign(variational_classifier(wbest, bbest, x)) for x
in Xte]
accuracy_vqc = accuracy(Yte, predictions)


print(f'VQC test accuracy score: {np.round(accuracy_vqc, 2) * 100}%')


VQC test accuracy score: 79.0%

# Classification report of VQC
expected_y_vqc  = Yte
predicted_y_vqc = predictions


# Print classification report and confusion matrix
print("Classification report: \n", metrics.classification_
report(expected_y_vqc, predicted_y_vqc))


Classification report:
              precision    recall  f1-score   support

        -1.0       0.89      0.79      0.84       194
         1.0       0.61      0.77      0.68        81

    accuracy                           0.79       275
   macro avg       0.75      0.78      0.76       275
weighted avg       0.81      0.79      0.79       275
```

Our final score shows an increased ability to detect defaulters, but even though the number of low-risk individuals has decreased, it still reaches the levels of the initial SVM and QSVM approaches.

Classification key performance indicators

In each one of the algorithms tested so far, you can see that there is a classification report that gives us the possibility to understand how good a model is in terms of predicting each class correctly. Deciding the **Key Performance Indicator** (**KPI**) to evaluate the model's performance is not a trivial decision. Most people assume that accuracy is the most important measure to see whether a model is working properly or not, with regard to the objective of predicting a specific class. Imagine that your credit scoring dataset is imbalanced, with a proportion of 5% defaulters and 95% good customers that pay on time. If the model predicts that all the test set is good and there are no defaulters, you will have 95% accuracy, which is bad.

As we mentioned before, it is common to face imbalanced datasets in the financial sector, so we usually need to look at a classification report to see which metric is the best to measure. The classification report shows the precision, recall, F1 score, and support per class. Digging deeper, it's important to see first that there are four ways to evaluate whether the predictions are good enough or not. These are as follows:

- **True Negative (TN):** The case was originally negative and the model predicted negative
- **True Positive (TP):** The case was originally positive and the model predicted positive
- **False Negative (FN):** The case was originally positive but the model predicted negative
- **False Positive (FP):** The case was originally negative but the model predicted positive

These four measures are the result of the model, and usually, you can see them reflected in a data visualization format called a confusion matrix, as shown in *Figure 6.6*.

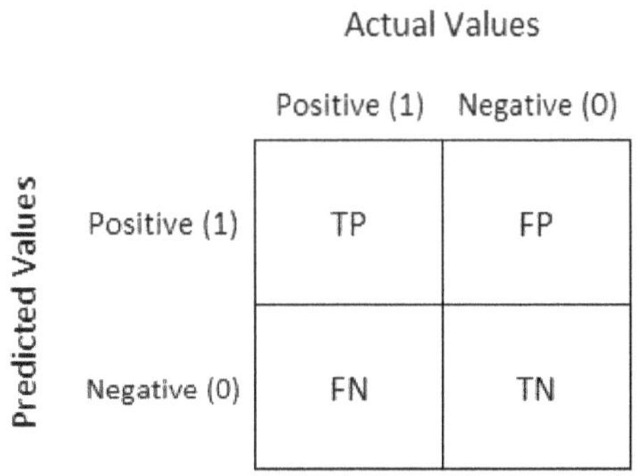

Figure 6.6 – The confusion matrix

Using these metrics, we can calculate the classification report outcome, which are as follows:

- **Precision (TP/(TP + FP))**: This is the capacity of a classifier to avoid incorrectly labeling instances as positive when they are truly negative. It considers the set of rightfully predicted instances (**TP**) with respect to the number of samples defined as a positive class (**TP + FP**).

- **Recall (TP/(TP+FN))**: This is a classifier's capacity to locate all positive examples. Considering all samples in the positive class of the dataset or population, rates the correctly identified positives (**TP**) with respect to the positive population (**TP + FN**).

- **F1-score (2*(Recall * Precision) / (Recall + Precision))**: This is a weighted harmonic mean of accuracy and recall, where the highest possible score is 1.0 and the lowest possible score is 0.0. F1 scores are lower than accuracy measurements, since their computation includes precision and recall. As a general rule, the weighted average of F1 should be utilized to compare classifier models rather than global accuracy.

- **Support**: This is the number of real instances of a class in a given dataset.

All of these numbers are given automatically by libraries such as Scikit-Learn, but it is very important to understand them before deciding if the model is working well or not.

Balanced accuracy, or ROC-AUC score

In this exercise, we will add another metric to the classification report that is related to the same baseline of the confusion matrix numbers, as can be seen in *Figure 6.7*. To measure the performance of an imbalanced dataset in a test set, we cannot rely on accuracy, as it may provide inaccurate estimators, prioritizing the class that is predominant and drastically failing to detect the less present one.

The **receiver operating characteristic** (**ROC**) curve is a plot or graph representing the performance of the classification at all thresholds (the cut-off probability to declare an instance as part of a specific class). Basically, this curve is based on two parameters, based on the metrics mentioned previously, which are the **True Positive Rate** (**TPR**), equivalent to recall, and the **False Positive Rate** (**FPR**):

True Positive Rate	False Positive Rate
$TPR = \dfrac{TP}{TP + FN}$	$FPR = \dfrac{FP}{FP + TN}$

Plotting the TPR against the FPR values in opposing axes, we obtain a plot, also known as a curve (hence the name).

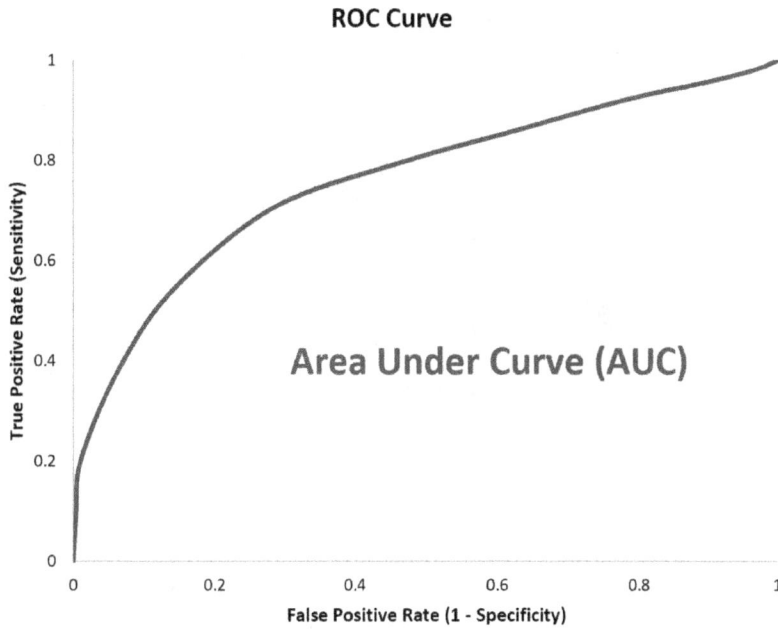

Figure 6.7 – An ROC curve representation

AUC is an acronym for **Area Under Curve**, referring to the ROC curve. Thus, AUC measures the full two-dimensional area underneath the complete ROC curve (consider integral calculus) and has a score from 0 to 1. There is no consensus about the specific AUC score number to define a model as good enough or not, but here are some considerations (assuming that higher is better):

- **AUC score of 0.50**: Not useful
- **AUC score 0.51–0.70**: Not enough discrimination to be a performant model
- **AUC score 0.71–0.80**: Acceptable as good enough discriminant
- **AUC score 0.81–0.90**: Excellent discriminant
- **AUC score >0.90**: An outstanding discriminant or an indicator of model overfitting

In the case of binary classification models, the AUC score is equal to the balanced accuracy score. It represents the arithmetic mean between correctly classified samples in each category.

Conclusion

As mentioned earlier, even if accuracy is a common measure from the classification report that most people will look at, the way to treat this kind of imbalanced data scenario is to compare the models using a balanced accuracy score, or AUC score, which in this case are the same, since it is a binary classification challenge.

Model	Accuracy	Balanced Accuracy	F1-score
QSVC	79	77	67
SVC	79	75	65
QNN	72	75	63
NN	80	78	69
VQC	75	65	49

Created with Datawrapper

Figure 6.8 – A comparison of classification results between classical and hybrid quantum-classical methods

At first glance, the results do not appear to be conclusive about the benefits of using hybrid quantum-classical for classification problems that the finance sector may face. However, the purpose of the exercise in this chapter is to get people to think about their own business challenges and do more research, since we can see that quantum machine learning could be at least equal or slightly better than classical ML methods (e.g., QSVC versus SVC). When any incremental benefit is achieved in terms of the model's capacity to detect each class properly, even if it seems a small increase, its impact on a business can actually mean high figures of saving or earnings significant in a competitive market.

On top of the architecture developed for this classification example, there are several more adjustments that can be explored to increase the performance of the hybrid algorithms. Some of them are as follows:

- Test different preprocessing methods such as normalization or dimensionality reductions
- Explore better procedures to apply the division in the dataset for the LDA step
- Analyze different methods to execute feature selection in terms of the quantum enhancement of the architecture
- Evaluate more feature maps to encode the data in quantum states
- Customize feature maps manually to measure the best approach for the individual problems faced

- Increase the qubits used to detect whether there is an advantage or disadvantage when a higher number of quantum bits are used

- Train a quantum kernel to be optimized

- Change iterations and shots for the sake of finding the best parameters, with regard to the model classification result

- Execute the algorithms in different types of simulators and quantum hardware to evaluate the impact of the backends in the final result

After deciding to dive into these types of implementations, it's critical to remember that the preprocessing and encoding steps of the quantum algorithms application process can be the key to retrieving successful results. We will see in *Chapter 7* how and which cloud provider we can use to run this type of project. We will learn how to use different hardware and how to access them through the cloud.

Further reading

- *Agarap, A. F. (2018). Deep learning using rectified linear units (relu). arXiv preprint arXiv:1803.08375.*

- *Assefa, S. A., Dervovic, D., Mahfouz, M., Tillman, R. E., Reddy, P., & Veloso, M. (2020, October). Generating synthetic data in finance: opportunities, challenges and pitfalls. In Proceedings of the First ACM International Conference on AI in Finance (pp. 1–8).*

- *Bishop, C. M. (1994). Neural networks and their applications. Review of scientific instruments, 65(6), 1803–1832.*

- *Bro, R., & Smilde, A. K. (2014). Principal component analysis. Analytical methods, 6(9), 2812-2831.*

- *Crook, J. N., Edelman, D. B., & Thomas, L. C. (2007). Recent developments in consumer credit risk assessment. European Journal of Operational Research, 183(3), 1447–1465.*

- *Crouhy, M., Galai, D., & Mark, R. (2000). A comparative analysis of current credit risk models. Journal of Banking & Finance, 24(1-2), 59–117.*

- *Ezhov, A. A., & Ventura, D. (2000). Quantum neural networks. In Future directions for intelligent systems and information sciences (pp. 213–235). Physica, Heidelberg.*

- *Farhi, E., & Neven, H. (2018). Classification with quantum neural networks on near term processors. arXiv preprint arXiv:1802.06002.*

- *Figueira, A., & Vaz, B. (2022). Survey on synthetic data generation, evaluation methods and GANs. Mathematics, 10(15), 2733.*

- *Havlíček, V., Córcoles, A. D., Temme, K., Harrow, A. W., Kandala, A., Chow, J. M., & Gambetta, J. M. (2019). Supervised learning with quantum-enhanced feature spaces. Nature, 567(7747), 209–212.*

- *Hearst, M. A., Dumais, S. T., Osuna, E., Platt, J., & Scholkopf, B. (1998). Support vector machines. IEEE Intelligent Systems and their applications, 13(4), 18–28.*

- *Izenman, A. J. (2013). Linear discriminant analysis. In Modern multivariate statistical techniques (pp. 237–280). Springer, New York, NY.*

- *Ji, G., & Zhu, Z. (2020). Knowledge distillation in wide neural networks: Risk bound, data efficiency and imperfect teacher. Advances in Neural Information Processing Systems, 33, 20823–20833.*

- *Khan, S., Rahmani, H., Shah, S. A. A., & Bennamoun, M. (2018). A guide to convolutional neural networks for computer vision. Synthesis lectures on computer vision, 8(1), 1–207.*

- *Khashman, A. (2010). Neural networks for credit risk evaluation: Investigation of different neural models and learning schemes. Expert Systems with Applications, 37(9), 6233–6239.*

- *Kingma, D. P., & Ba, J. (2014). Adam: A method for stochastic optimization. arXiv preprint arXiv:1412.6980.*

- *Mancilla, J., & Pere, C. (2022). A Preprocessing Perspective for Quantum Machine Learning Classification Advantage in Finance Using NISQ Algorithms. Entropy, 24(11), 1656.*

- *Moritz, P., Nishihara, R., Wang, S., Tumanov, A., Liaw, R., Liang, E., ... & Stoica, I. (2018). Ray: A distributed framework for emerging {AI} applications. In 13th USENIX Symposium on Operating Systems Design and Implementation (OSDI 18) (pp. 561–577).*

- *Park, N., Mohammadi, M., Gorde, K., Jajodia, S., Park, H., & Kim, Y. (2018). Data synthesis based on generative adversarial networks. arXiv preprint arXiv:1806.03384.*

- *Rebentrost, P., Mohseni, M., & Lloyd, S. (2014). Quantum support vector machine for big data classification. Physical review letters, 113(13), 130503.*

- *Schuld, M., Bocharov, A., Svore, K. M., & Wiebe, N. (2020). Circuit-centric quantum classifiers. Physical Review A, 101(3), 032308.*

- *Sergeev, A., & Del Balso, M. (2018). Horovod: fast and easy distributed deep learning in TensorFlow. arXiv preprint arXiv:1802.05799.*

- *Singh, D., & Singh, B. (2020). Investigating the impact of data normalization on classification performance. Applied Soft Computing, 97, 105524.*

- *Tangirala, S. (2020). Evaluating the impact of GINI index and information gain on classification using decision tree classifier algorithm. International Journal of Advanced Computer Science and Applications, 11(2), 612–619.*

- *Yao, K., Zweig, G., Hwang, M. Y., Shi, Y., & Yu, D. (2013, August). Recurrent neural networks for language understanding. In Interspeech (pp. 2524–2528).*

7

Implementation in Quantum Clouds

This chapter will dig deeper into the options for executing our algorithms in quantum devices or at least solutions that will go beyond the capabilities of our classical devices. For the sake of simplicity, most of the algorithms you have seen so far used some kind of local simulation to mimic how the outcome would look when running on a real quantum computer.

When developing our approaches, we have the means to locally simulate the behavior of an ideal quantum computer while taking from the mathematical description each operation requires. But at the end of the day, the goal is to be able to send our work to a quantum device that will leverage the potential of actual quantum computing.

Given that owning a quantum computer is something very few privileged people will be able to do, we will highlight how cloud access has been an important way of leveraging those still experimental resources.

We will also illustrate several examples demonstrating how to utilize cloud resources and cloud-hosted quantum devices to execute the previously mentioned examples from *Chapters 4, 5,* and *6*. By doing so, you will not only become familiar with the distinct workflow it may entail but also understand the advantages of employing these resources when working on the scale that most companies demand for their proof-of-concept or innovation projects.

Lastly, considering that the cloud operates on a pay-per-use model, we will examine the financial implications of utilizing cloud services for our project. We will also explore intriguing approaches to initiate quantum projects and implementations on cloud-hosted services, even with a limited budget.

Chapters 8 and *9* will dig deeper into different types of devices and simulators we might be using, as well as how to deal with the noise most devices will introduce into our abstracted circuits. Finally, *Chapter 10* will get us into the strategies we can utilize to start using quantum computing as an added value asset in our organization and grow with a sensible adoption strategy that will not harm our corporation's finances, nor the pace at which the institution may be adopting these disruptive but promising new paradigms as part of their business processes.

This chapter will cover the following topics:

- Challenges of accessing the cloud quantum computing platform and implementing an algorithm
- Major quantum technology providers
- Cost estimation when using a cloud provider

Challenges of quantum implementations on cloud platforms

As we mentioned previously, most of the examples shown previously leverage the fact that quantum computing can be mimicked by our classical resources (using simulators). As an example, in *Chapter 5*, we used the following routine:

```
backend = Aer.get_backend('qasm_simulator')
result = execute(quantum_circuit, backend, shots=10).result()
counts  = result.get_counts(quantum_circuit)
```

We utilized a `qasm_simulator`, an implementation that can execute the operations defined in our quantum circuit and provide the expected outcome as dictated by the mathematical principles governing quantum computing.

We would like to take this very same circuit to a quantum computer, but it is not as easy as purchasing one on Amazon. We can purchase commercially available devices, but the price might be too high for most organizations.

D-Wave

In 2011, D-Wave Systems announced the world's first commercially available quantum computer – a 128-qubit quantum annealing device. They have been able to scale their Chimera topology up to 2,000 qubits, and the new architectures have surpassed this barrier, with up to 8,000 qubits promised for late 2023/early 2024. Considering that the cost of their initial device reached a seven-zero figure (https://www.engadget.com/2011-05-18-d-wave-one-claims-mantle-of-first-commercial-quantum-computer.html) and its chassis reminds us of old mainframe infrastructures, as can be seen in *Figure 7.1*, which requires a data center to put it in, it was clear it was not going to be mass-produced:

Figure 7.1 – A technician working on a D-Wave Systems machine

IBM Quantum

Something similar happened to IBM when they started creating their initial chips. In 2018, they released their first commercial product, IBM Q System One, as shown in *Figure 7.2*, which is a 20-qubit commercially available quantum computer:

Figure 7.2 – IBM's Q System One device

But before this achievement, they were already aware of the needs of many research institutions and universities already working in the field of quantum computers. They wanted to use an actual device, but they would need to build their own to run their experiments.

That is why, in early 2016, IBM decided to connect one of their experimental devices to a cloud service so that independent organizations could submit their experiments to their first available quantum computer. This milestone gave birth to the rich cloud quantum computing ecosystem we know today.

In early 2017, a team at Rigetti Computing was able to program a set of instructions into IBM's device using the pyQuil Python wrapper of the Quil Quantum Instruction Set Architecture (*Smith et al., 2016*).

Like in many emergent industries, several standards can still be found. IBM decided to leverage its own. We have made reference to it in previous chapters. Still, **Open Quantum Assembly Language (OpenQASM)**, which is already on its third version, was initially referenced in a publication (*Cross et al., 2017*) and the code of IBM's Quantum Information Software Toolkit (*Qiskit - Anis, Md Sajid, et al., 2021*), becoming one of the most mature frameworks for implementing quantum programs and communicating with a wide variety of cloud-available devices.

Qiskit can abstract our quantum code from the final device it will run on, but given this quite diverse landscape of devices, we might need to remember that certain frameworks will fit our needs better, depending on the final hardware meant to be used.

One of the most evident examples is when D-Wave Systems' devices were the ones to be used. These are quantum annealing devices. Therefore, gate operations do not apply to them yet (`https://techcrunch.com/2021/10/05/d-wave-plans-to-build-a-gate-model-quantum-computer`).

Their devices are freely accessible via their service offering, known as Leap (*Figure 7.3*; `https://cloud.dwavesys.com/leap/login`):

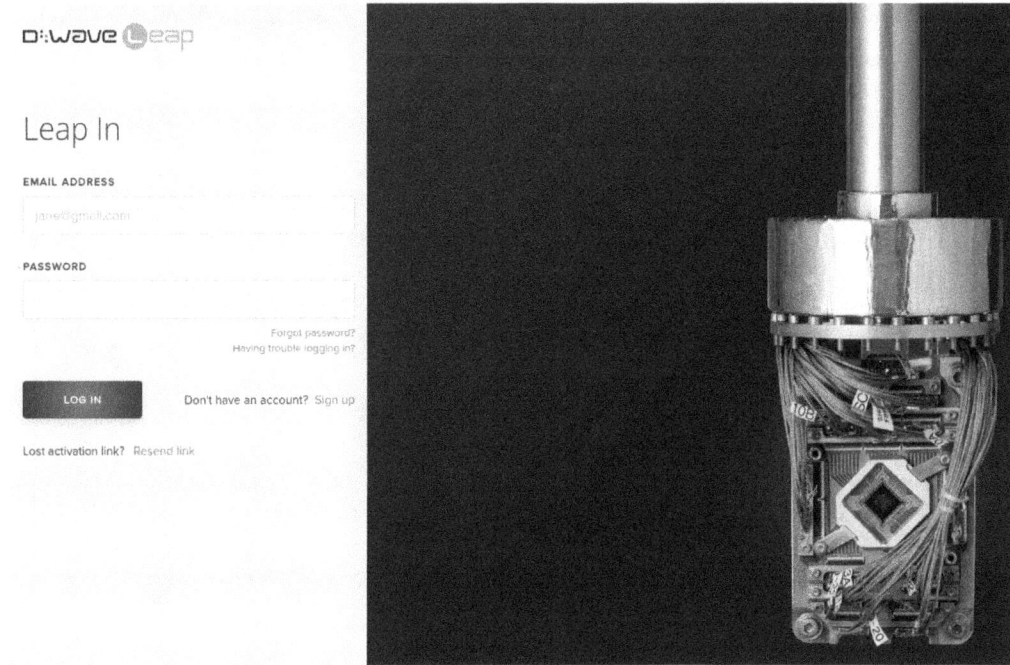

Figure 7.3 – D-Wave Systems' cloud-accessible service, Leap

You can simply sign up, and you will be granted monthly time to run your experiments. In fact, within the different plans, you can access the Developer Plan (*Figure 7.4*), which only requires a GitHub account to be synchronized with D-Wave's Leap service – it provides recurrent usage of their devices for up to 20 minutes a month. Considering that the running time of their solver only requires milliseconds, it allows for quite a few experiments to be run before you run out of time:

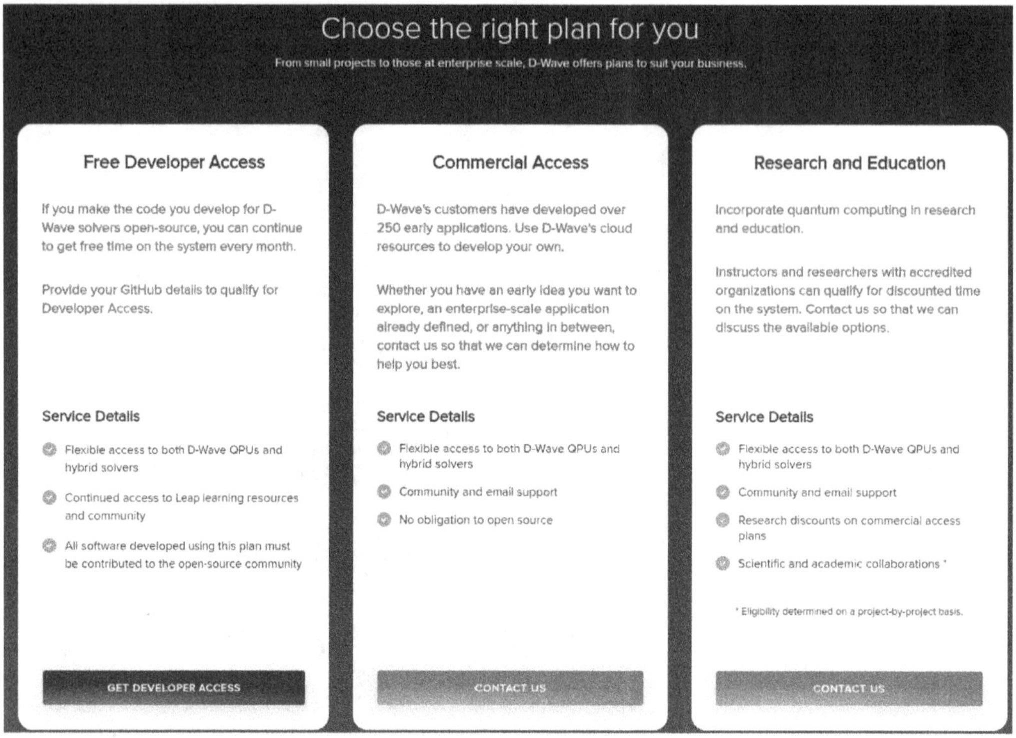

Figure 7.4 – D-Wave's cloud service usage plans

Two main options are available when interacting with Leap. The simplest one is directly using their cloud-based development environment. By providing the URL to an existing GitHub repository where the code will be taken from and committed to guarantee it is not lost, an ephemeral browser-accessible IDE will be created where your account credentials will be made available. This enables a ready-to-work environment for any registered user:

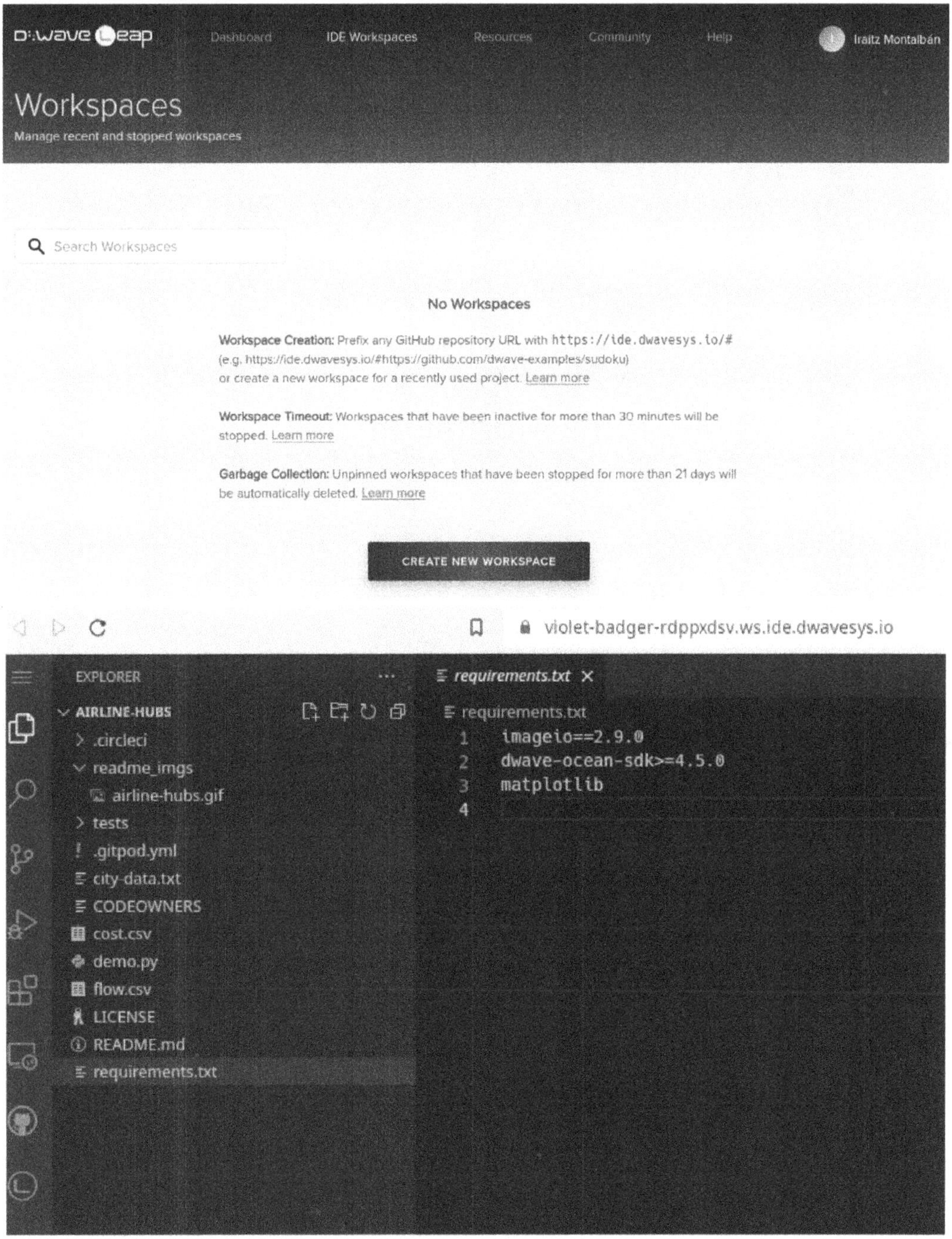

Figure 7.5 – A Leap workspace with an airline example loaded in an example IDE

This will also ensure that D-Wave's Ocean Software Development Kit is installed and ready to use.

Of course, you could install the SDK on a local Python setup and log into the account by using a Leap-provided token that should be accessible via the Leap interface, as shown in *Figure 7.6*:

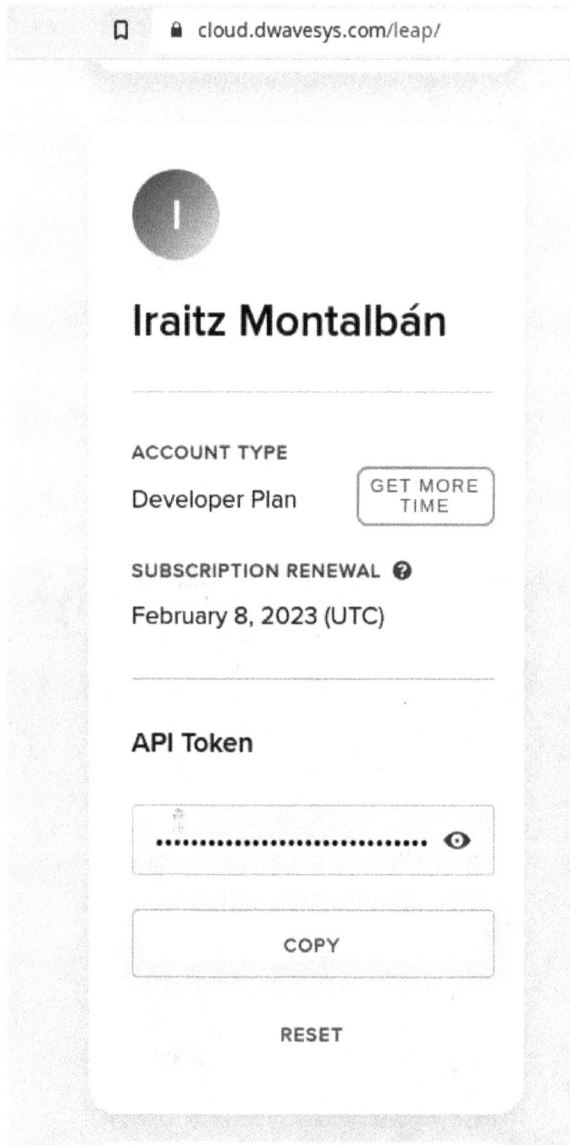

Figure 7.6 – Leap dashboard, where you can find the token for remote authentication

Ocean SDK's documentation already provides instructions on how this can be done locally so that interaction with the cloud service is done programmatically (`https://docs.ocean.dwavesys.com/en/latest/overview/install.html`).

This is how we remotely solved our portfolio optimization in *Chapter 5* using a non-owned D-Wave device, free of charge.

Like D-Wave, IBM offers free access to some of their devices via their cloud-accessible service (`https://quantum-computing.ibm.com/`). You can register using a wide variety of credentials so that if you're using a LinkedIn or GitHub account, you have a simplistic way to access their solutions (free or pay-as-you-go).

Once registered, a set of services will be shown so that you can choose the appropriate one according to your level of expertise. *Figure 7.7* shows all the different services available:

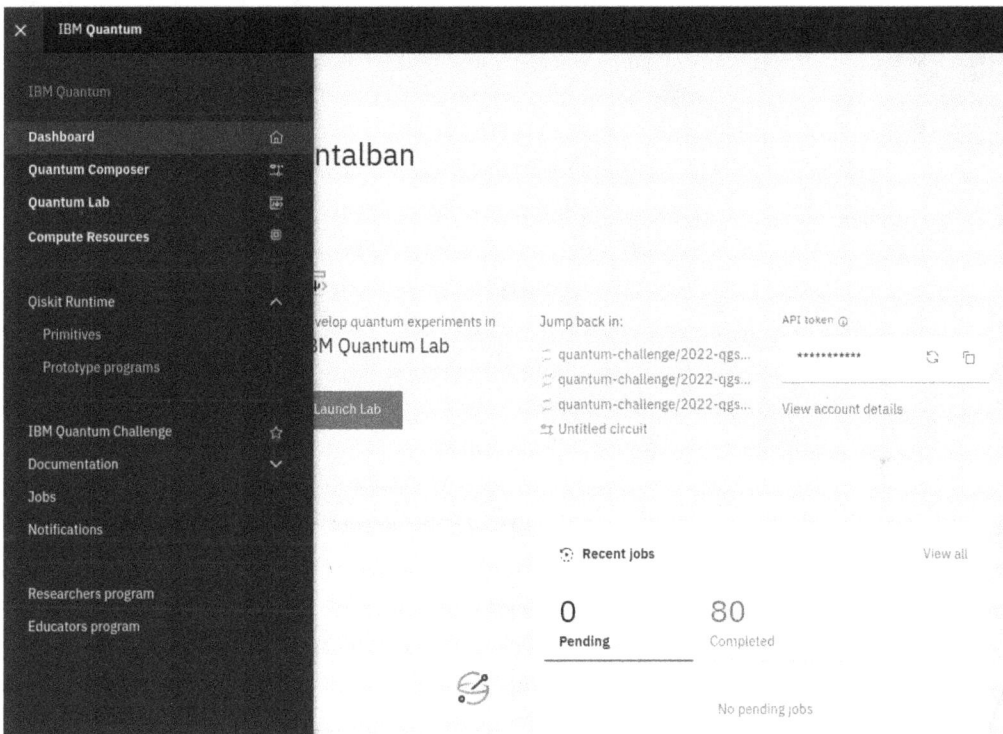

Figure 7.7 – IBM Quantum dashboard showing the different available services

One of the first things we will realize is that there is also a token option, so remote job submission is also available – in this case, using IBM's Qiskit framework. This is often the token that's referred to when the instructions are set to a local setup (`https://github.com/Qiskit/qiskit-ibmq-provider#configure-your-ibm-quantum-credentials`).

IBM also provides a tool for creating quantum circuits: Quantum Composer. It's probably the easiest way to start *coding* our first examples. *Figure 7.8* shows how, by dragging and dropping gate figures into Quantum Composer's central console, different plots or even Qiskit and OpenQASM codes are shown. It simplifies the transition from the graphical designer to code-based implementations, which will be useful when you're aiming for more complex examples or projects like the ones we covered in *Chapters 4* to *6*:

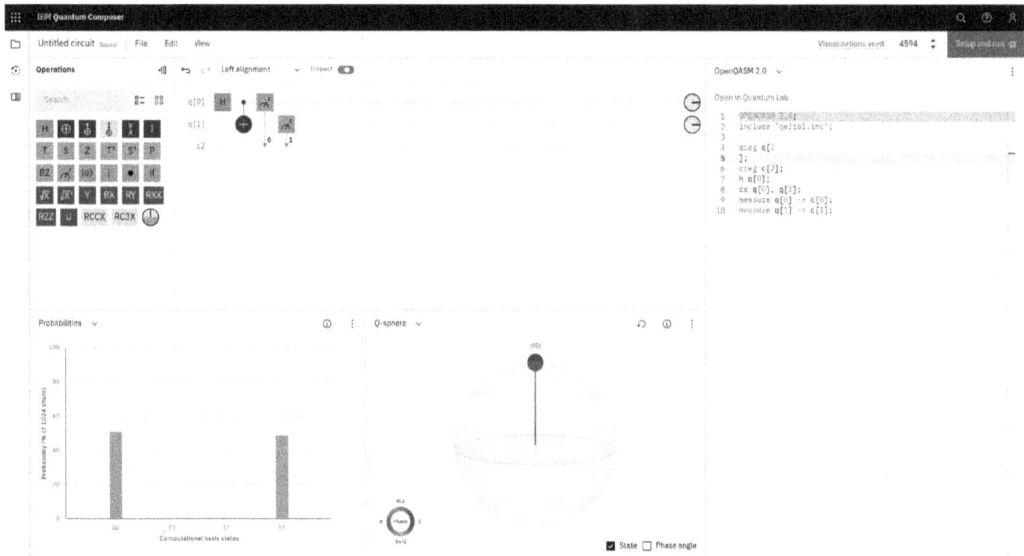

Figure 7.8 – IBM's Quantum Composer graphical interface for starting quantum algorithm programming

On the top left-hand side of the preceding figure, we can see that it also allows us to submit our circuit to a device. We can select the device according to the number of qubits we might require and the waiting queue (many people will be sending circuits to the same shared device), so we can choose the least busy one (*Figure 7.9*):

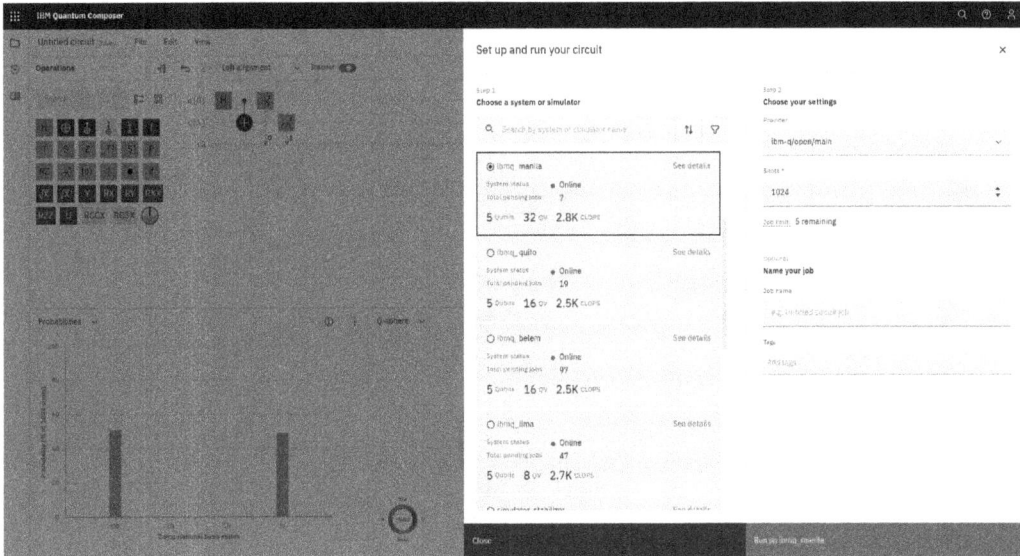

Figure 7.9 – Circuit submission from Quantum Composer to one of the available devices

Once the job is sent to the device, the queue will progress, and our results will be made available. Within the same console, the set of jobs we have sent can be listed, and more information can be requested if we click on the job itself (*Figure 7.10*):

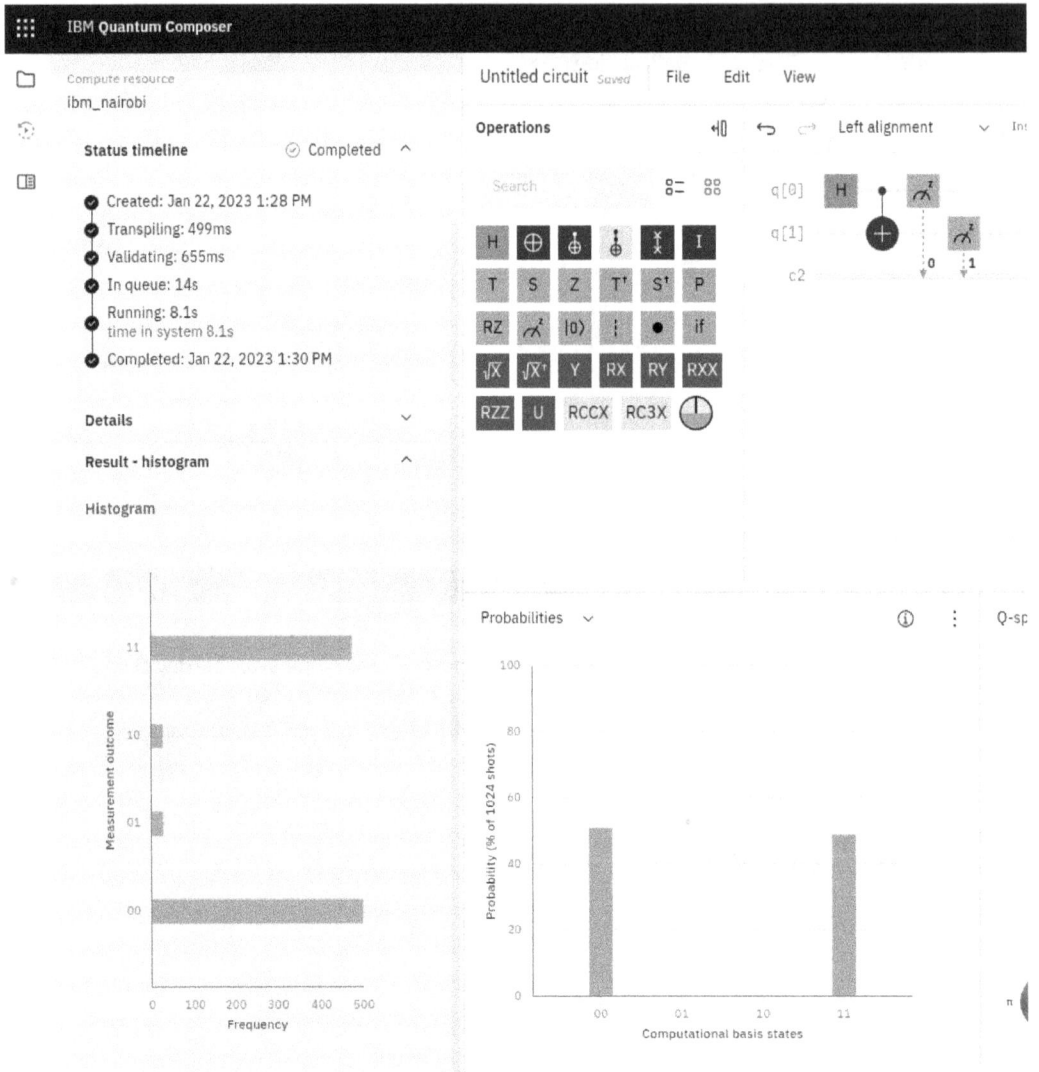

Figure 7.10 – Actual results obtained from the ibm_nairobi device

IBM keeps a list of all the jobs we have submitted; therefore, old results can be recovered from the cloud service. A really useful feature is when someone has to send a set of examples so that they can be later analyzed. Most of our examples will take time to run, not only because they might be variationally trained and therefore need to call the device many times, but because the queue for the device may increase and take quite some time until our circuit runs on the device (the priority in the queue is determined by the number of requests you make in a certain time).

Two interesting things we would like to highlight at this point are that if we look at the plots in *Figure 7.10*, the one from the devices shows values on states that were not present when we simulated the results (the right-hand side plot in *Figure 7.10*). This is because of the effect of noise and the different types of errors that are introduced when running on real devices. We will cover this in more detail in *Chapters 8* and *9*. Still, it is interesting that we highlight that real devices will not behave like the ideal simulators we have been using in some of the examples and will introduce results that are not supposed to be there.

Another interesting fact is that, if we get to the details of the job we just submitted, the circuit we sent and the one that runs are not the same, as can be seen in *Figure 7.11*. Computationally speaking, they are, because the composition of Z rotations and square root X provides the same effect as the Hadamard gate, but this is changed because the H operation is unavailable on the device. Not all operations performed in the theoretical setup are available on the devices. There are even more qubits than the ones we want to use. Therefore, there is always a step we cannot omit when moving to the real device; this is called *transpilation*.

Transpilation is the process of adapting our theoretical algorithm to the specific gates and topology of a chip that may not perfectly map what we require. This process tries to find the best way to map the quantum circuit using some heuristics and different optimization levels. By doing this programmatically, we can balance the time it takes to fit the algorithm and the depth or the number of operations it will be translated into. Simply put, the transpile job will reduce complex gates into basic ones to map the hardware architecture.

The more operations we introduce, the more noise the circuit will be subjected to, and more inaccurate results may appear in our final reading. That is why this step is so important for researchers; they invest so much time in finding better ways to improve it. In *Chapter 9*, we will look at some of the latest advances in this process, which is known as *error mitigation*:

Circuit

[Diagram]   [Qasm]   [Qiskit]

Original circuit   **Transpiled circuit**

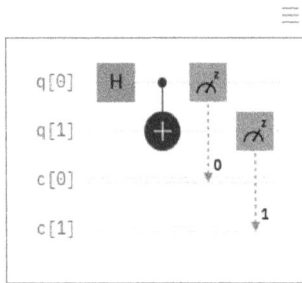

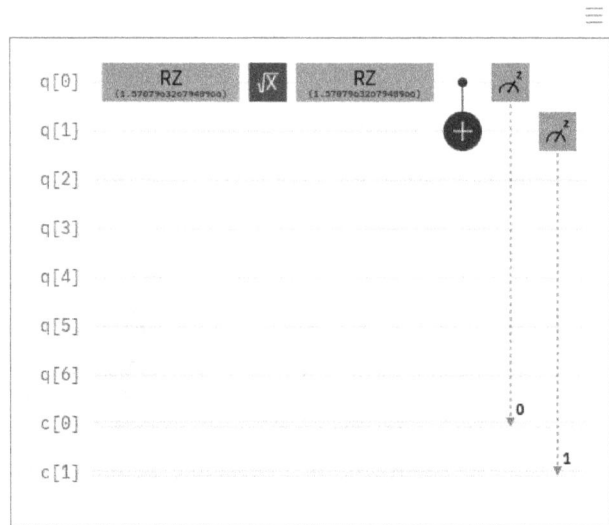

Figure 7.11 – Submitted circuit and the actual circuit that runs on ibm_nairobi

Within the options available in IBM's cloud offering, there's the option to deploy a workspace so that we can work from there without worrying about local installations and account settings. The Quantum Lab option (*Figure 7.12*) allows us to deploy a hosted JupyterLab environment that's already configured with the latest Qiskit version and our account loaded so that submitting jobs becomes easy:

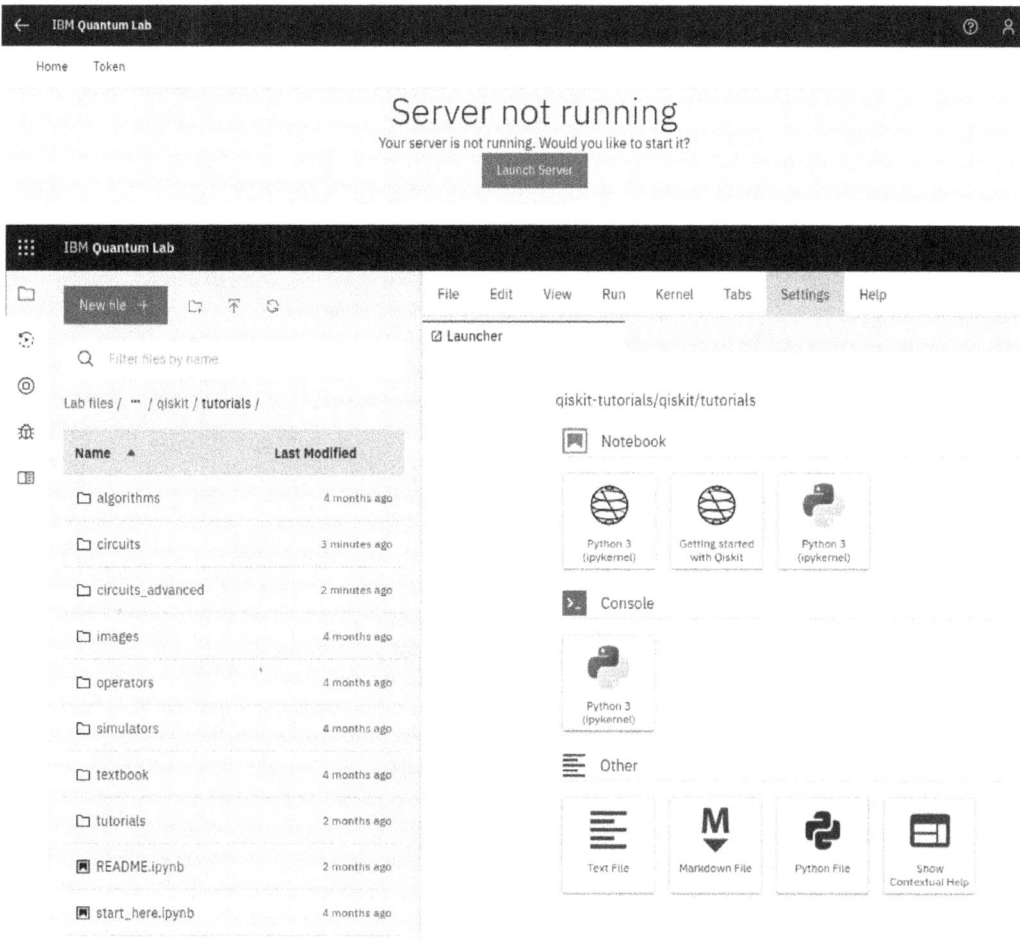

Figure 7.12 – IBM Quantum Lab workspace creation and available tutorials

Any of the examples we have previously coded can be easily transferred to this workspace, given that Jupyter notebooks can be transferred just by clicking on the upload option (up-facing arrow in *Figure 7.12*). Suppose we click on the first **Notebook** option available that says **Python 3** under Qiskit's logo. In that case, a new Jupyter notebook instance will be shown where some common libraries and the way we can load our account credentials will appear:

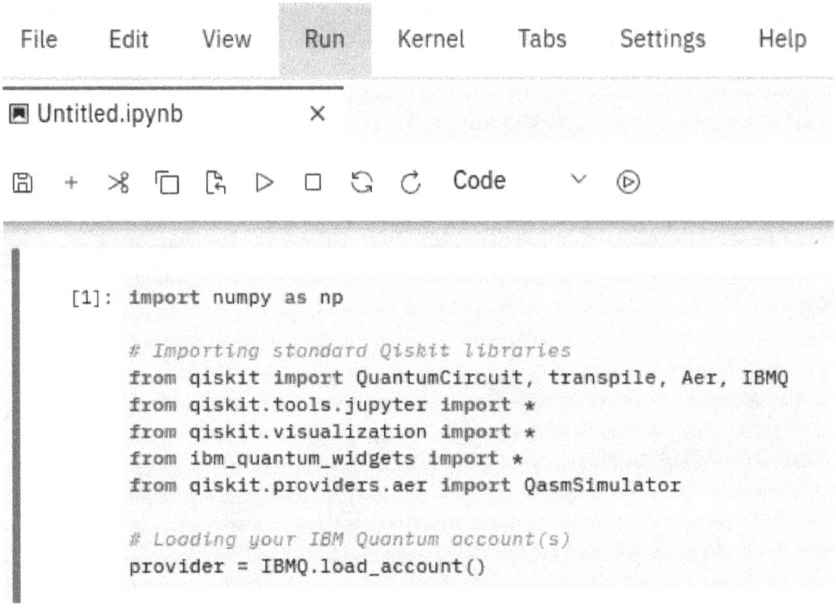

File	Edit	View	Run	Kernel	Tabs	Settings	Help

▣ Untitled.ipynb   ✕

▣ + ✂ ⬜ ⬚ ▷ □ ⟳ ⟲   Code   ⌄ ⊙

```
[1]: import numpy as np

     # Importing standard Qiskit libraries
     from qiskit import QuantumCircuit, transpile, Aer, IBMQ
     from qiskit.tools.jupyter import *
     from qiskit.visualization import *
     from ibm_quantum_widgets import *
     from qiskit.providers.aer import QasmSimulator

     # Loading your IBM Quantum account(s)
     provider = IBMQ.load_account()
```

Figure 7.13 – Default cell made available when Qiskit-supporting notebooks are created

Figure 7.13 shows the code to load the default provider to access all the available backends. They can then be requested:

```
provider.backends()
```

```
[<IBMQSimulator('ibmq_qasm_simulator') from IBMQ(hub='ibm-q', group='open', project='main')>,
 <IBMQBackend('ibmq_lima') from IBMQ(hub='ibm-q', group='open', project='main')>,
 <IBMQBackend('ibmq_belem') from IBMQ(hub='ibm-q', group='open', project='main')>,
 <IBMQBackend('ibmq_quito') from IBMQ(hub='ibm-q', group='open', project='main')>,
 <IBMQSimulator('simulator_statevector') from IBMQ(hub='ibm-q', group='open', project='main')>,
 <IBMQSimulator('simulator_mps') from IBMQ(hub='ibm-q', group='open', project='main')>,
 <IBMQSimulator('simulator_extended_stabilizer') from IBMQ(hub='ibm-q', group='open', project='main')>,
 <IBMQSimulator('simulator_stabilizer') from IBMQ(hub='ibm-q', group='open', project='main')>,
 <IBMQBackend('ibmq_manila') from IBMQ(hub='ibm-q', group='open', project='main')>,
 <IBMQBackend('ibm_nairobi') from IBMQ(hub='ibm-q', group='open', project='main')>,
 <IBMQBackend('ibm_oslo') from IBMQ(hub='ibm-q', group='open', project='main')>]
```

Figure 7.14 – Freely available device and simulator options within IBM's Quantum Lab

Figure 7.14 shows the output of the backend function and lists devices and simulators. These are classical resources mimicking an available quantum computer, so we can choose the backend that best fits our requirements.

Having covered two of the most popular cloud-based resources for quantum computing, you may think that going provider by provider and testing different device types may become a nightmare of tokens, configurations, and frameworks to be used.

That is the reason why key players have also started enabling cloud-based quantum computing but from a slightly different perspective. AWS and Azure, being the cloud providers for the majority of corporations around the globe, aim to make it easier to access technology in general. That is the way they primarily joined the quantum community – as hubs providing access not only to their actual offering but also to third-party providers so that you can access a plethora of options via their services.

This is why, in the next two sections, we will concentrate on AWS and Azure while showcasing the different options and ways to access those computational means so that any quantum developer can make the most out of the existing broad offerings.

Amazon Braket

Amazon Web Services (**AWS**) decided to create both a service and a framework for quantum computation under the same name.

The Amazon Braket service, like in previous examples, makes quantum computing devices that go beyond the actual offering of AWS available to any user. As far as we know, AWS is not working on any hardware device of its own. So, how can they offer a quantum computing platform? Well, they partnered with some key niche players providing said hardware that decided to give access through a third party instead of adding that extra workload of maintaining a customer-accessed platform to their business model.

Anybody with an AWS account can access the Braket service within their account, though not all regions currently offer this option, as shown here:

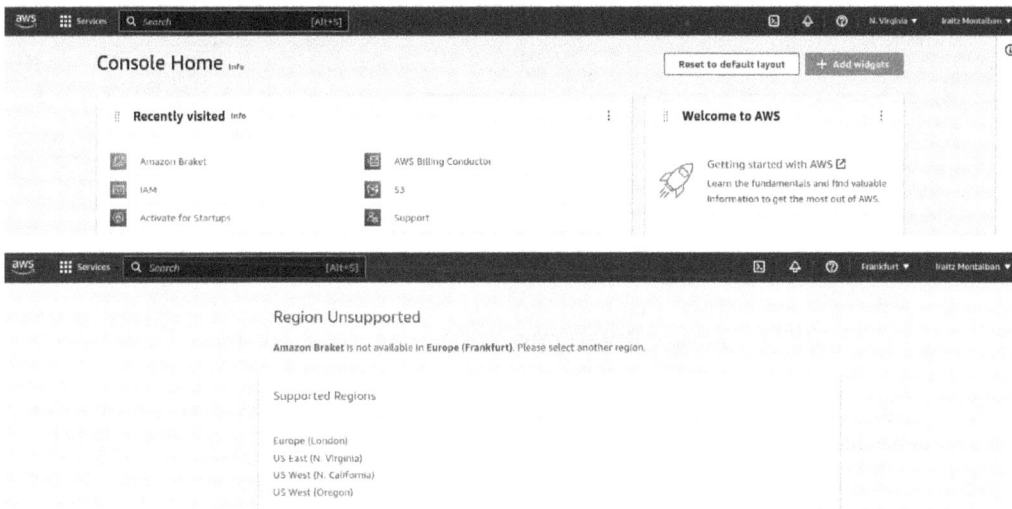

Figure 7.15 – Amazon Braket shown within the AWS service console, highlighting region options

The console resembles the ones we saw previously as it also provides an overview of available devices, notebooks that can be run on a workspace created for remote development, and a list of jobs that were previously running within the service:

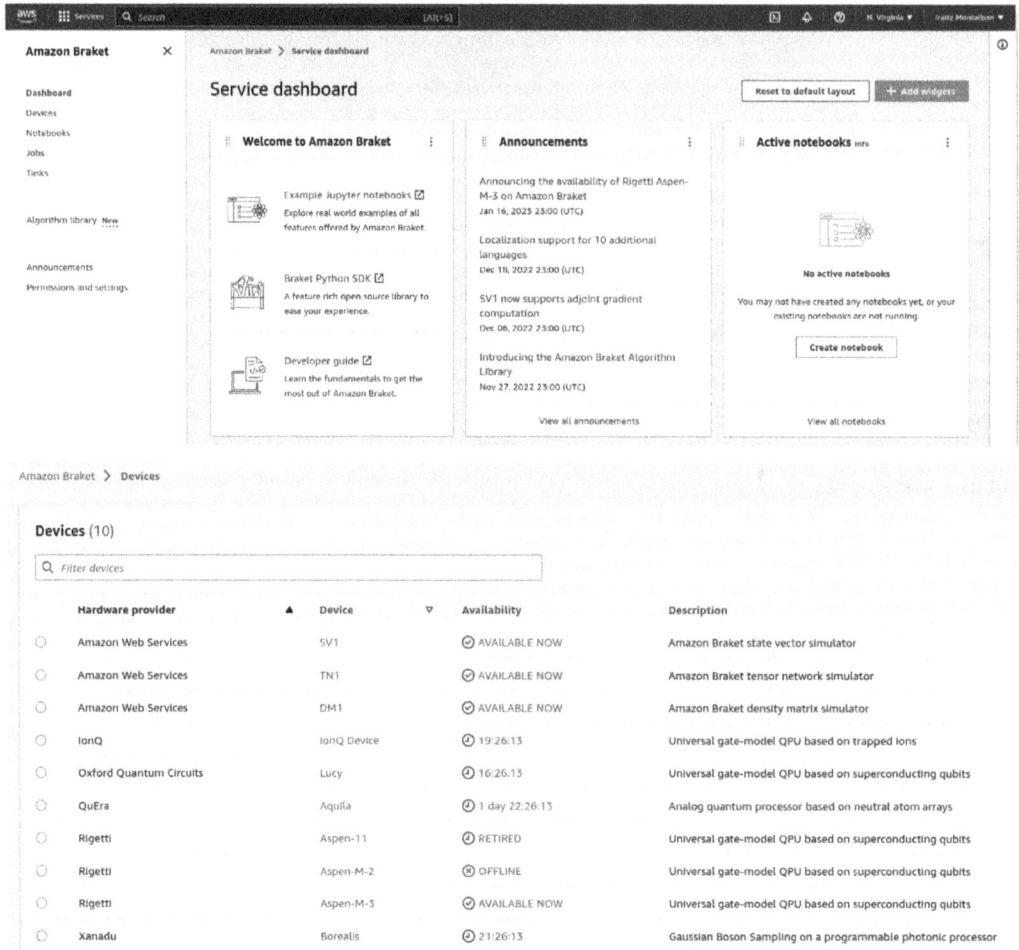

Figure 7.16 – Amazon Braket's main console and available devices

One of the key benefits of using AWS Braket instead of independent direct access services provided by any quantum hardware company is that it acts as a hub. So, by using the same connectivity interface, a customer can directly access a plethora of services of many different types.

It also provides a set of libraries containing implementations of some canonical algorithms that we reviewed in *Chapter 2*. As shown in *Figure 7.17*, they are provided via Amazon Braket's Python SDK, an open source framework provided by AWS:

```
3    # Licensed under the Apache License, Version 2.0 (the "License"). You
4    # may not use this file except in compliance with the License. A copy of
5    # the License is located at
6    #
7    #     http://aws.amazon.com/apache2.0/
8    #
9    # or in the "license" file accompanying this file. This file is
10   # distributed on an "AS IS" BASIS, WITHOUT WARRANTIES OR CONDITIONS OF
11   # ANY KIND, either express or implied. See the License for the specific
12   # language governing permissions and limitations under the License.
13   from typing import Dict
14
15   import numpy as np
16   from braket.circuits import Circuit
17   from braket.devices import Device
18   from braket.tasks import QuantumTask
19
20
21   def bernstein_vazirani_circuit(hidden_string: str) -> Circuit:
22       """Bernstein-Vazirani circuit on a hidden string. Creates a circuit that finds the hidden
23       string in a single iteration, using number of qubits equal to the string length.
24
25       Example:
26           >>> circ = bernstein_vazirani_circuit("011")
27           >>> print(circ)
28           T  : |0|1| 2 |3|4|Result Types|
29           q0 : -H---C---H---Probability--
30                     |       |
31           q1 : -H---|---C-H-Probability--
32                     |   |   |
33           q2 : -H-I-|-H-|---Probability--
34                     |   |
35           q3 : -H-Z-X---X--------------
36           T  : |0|1| 2 |3|4|Result Types|
37
38       Args:
39           hidden_string (str): Hidden bitstring.
40
41       Returns:
42           Circuit: Bernstein-Vazirani circuit
43       """
44       num_qubits = len(hidden_string)
45
46       bv_circuit = Circuit()
47       bv_circuit.h(num_qubits)
48       bv_circuit.z(num_qubits)
49       bv_circuit.h(range(num_qubits))
```

Figure 7.17 – Amazon Braket's algorithm library and Berstein Vazirani implementation example

This framework is more general, given the technologies Amazon Braket is meant to support beyond the superconducting chip IBM is focusing on. It makes sense that IBM's framework is mostly thought to help increase device usage. Still, Amazon is forced to cover a much wider spectrum within its offering. Here, we can find neutral atoms, photonic devices, and trapped-ion services that require different ways to interact and impose the computation to be done.

To understand why this is important, many restrictions associated with the process of transpiling the logical circuit initially coded into a specific device setup depend on particular aspects of the device. One of the most basic ones is qubit connectivity, which forces different translations. This connectivity differs from provider to provider (and also backends), as shown here:

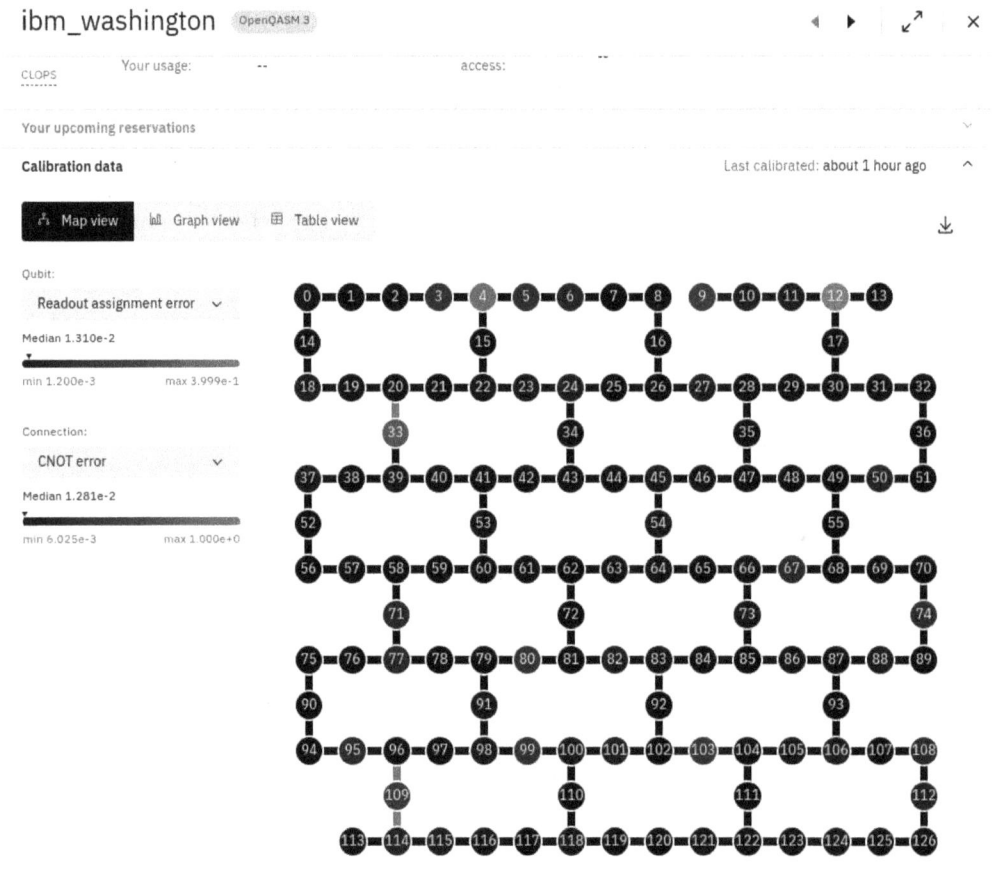

Rigetti — Aspen-M-3
Universal gate-model QPU based on superconducting qubits

Rigetti quantum processors are universal, gate-model machines based on tunable superconducting qubits.

Rigetti's latest Aspen-M processor is based on scalable multi-chip technology, and features enhanced readout capabilities that contribute to better overall circuit fidelities independent of depth and width. Aspen M systems show fast processing times, fast gate times for multiple entangling gate families, rapid sampling via active register reset, and parametric control.

The Aspen chip topology is octagonal with 3-fold (2-fold for edges) connectivity and features both CPHASE and XY entangling gates that allow developers to optimize programs for performance and minimize circuit depth. Rigetti's optimizing quil-c compiler transforms abstract quantum algorithms into this set of native gates and produces optimal circuit implementations to be carried out on a Rigetti QPU. These gates offer fast (40ns and 220ns) 1Q and 2Q gate times and program execution rates within qubit coherence times measuring 28 and 22 us for T1 and T2 respectively.

More about this device

Hardware provider	Region	Location
Rigetti	us-west-1	California, USA
Availability	Next available	Cost
• Everyday, 04:00:00 - 06:00:00 UTC	09:22:27	$0.30 / task + $0.00035 / shot
• Everyday, 15:00:00 - 16:00:00 UTC	Status	Qubits
	ONLINE	79

Device ARN
arn:aws:braket:us-west-1::device/qpu/rigetti/Aspen-M-3

Pulse control
Supported

Topology

Figure 7.18 – Superconducting chip topology for IBM Washington (below) and Rigetti Aspen-M-3 (above)

There are also some differences, such as the native quantum gates that the provider will accept. For example, Hadamard gates, which are used for state superposition, can hardly be achieved if you don't combine other actions that can be realized in hardware, as shown in *Figure 7.11*. But it has more profound implications when the underlying technology changes. For example, ion-trapped devices can connect "many-to-many" qubits arbitrarily (*Figure 7.19* – connections representation) and are better suited for problems that show all-to-all connectivity schemes. This is, for example, the case for portfolio optimization, which requires you to evaluate the covariance between all potential assets (*Chapter 5*):

IonQ

Universal gate-model QPU based on trapped ions

Ion's trapped ion QPUs are built on a chain of trapped 171Yb+ ions, spatially confined via a microfabricated surface electrode trap within laser. This allows for high-quality single and two-qubit transitions and all-to-all connectivity. Initialization is performed via optical pumpir

IonQ compiles and optimizes your high-level quantum logic gates into the smallest possible set of laser pulses to realize your program or

For single-qubit gates, IonQ uses the GPI gate, the GPI2 gate and the GZ gate. The GPI and GPI2 gates are simply Rabi oscillations made k beam, creating a "virtual" operation.

For entangling, two-qubit gates, IonQ uses the Mølmer-Sørenson gate. This entangling gate and the single-qubit gates above constitute a motion to create entanglement.

More about this device ↗

Hardware provider	Region
IonQ	us-east-1
Availability	Next available
Weekdays, 13:00:00 - 02:00:00 UTC	⏱ 18:18:30
Device ARN	Status
📋 arn:aws:braket:::device/qpu/ionq/ionQdevice	⊘ ONLINE
Pulse control	
⊗ Not supported	

Topology

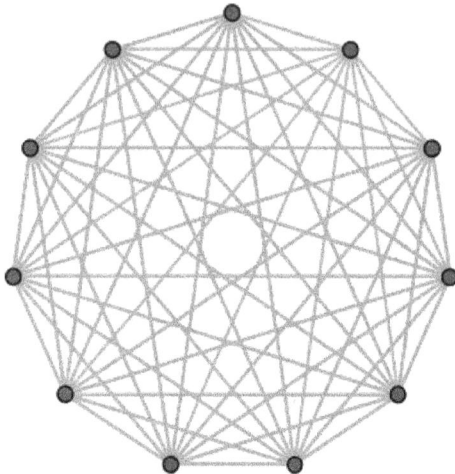

Figure 7.19 – IonQ trapped-ion device topology

Or in the case of neutral atom devices, similar to what happens in D-Wave systems, analog coding has to be submitted instead of gate-based algorithms, which requires some specific knowledge on how this needs to be done (`https://docs.aws.amazon.com/braket/latest/developerguide/braket-quera-submitting-analog-program-aquila.html`). This is also one of the reasons why Amazon Braket was developed as it allows us to extend those specific requirements as new services are enabled within the platform.

Given the usage and maturity of Qiskit within the quantum computing community, Amazon also released a plugin so that any Qiskit-encoded routine can be sent to Amazon Braket-enabled devices. This helps us interface with some of those devices that offer gate-based computation without the need to learn about a third framework.

You can use the following code to install the Amazon provider-enabling plugin:

```
pip install qiskit-braket-provider
```

Qiskit circuits can be sent to Amazon devices. Similar to what we did in the case of the IBM-enabled provider in *Figure 7.14*, we can instantiate Amazon Braket as a provider:

```
from qiskit_braket_provider import AWSBraketProvider
provider = AWSBraketProvider()
```

We can also ask for available devices to be used as backends:

```
ionq_device = provider.get_backend("IonQ Device")
rigetti_device = provider.get_backend("Aspen-M-3")
oqc_device = provider.get_backend("Lucy")
```

It is important to pause here. As we mentioned previously, our circuit may need to be translated into the specifics of the final device. So, depending on each case, certain adaptations may need to be performed.

Also, consider that each device has a different cost scheme, but they will all require a billing structure so that the cost of running any example will be charged at the end of the billing period.

It is particularly relevant that we pay attention to the pricing of each device because, when using variational algorithms, the number of interactions required to fit the parameters could increase dramatically, which will directly affect the cost of each job.

To figure out how much a specific algorithm could cost on a given device, we must be aware of the resources and operations required to run our candidate quantum circuit.

PennyLane, given its role when dealing with variational algorithms, has a really useful resource called a tracker that can keep track of the jobs being sent to the device. We could leverage this resource to perform our estimations in combination with AWS's SDK and the PennyLane plugin:

```
pip install amazon-braket-sdk amazon-braket-pennylane-plugin
```

We would proceed as usual and create a circuit, but in this case, using the `bracket.local.qubit` device as our target device:

```
import pennylane as qml
from pennylane import numpy as np

wires = 2  # Number of qubits
dev = qml.device("braket.local.qubit", wires=wires)

def circuit(params):
    qml.Hadamard(wires=0)
    qml.RY(params[0], wires=0)
    qml.CNOT(wires=[0, 1])
    return qml.expval(qml.PauliZ(1))

qnode_local = qml.QNode(circuit, dev)
```

Now, we can call the circuit to perform the operation surrounding it with the `qml.Tracker` object, as shown here:

```
params = np.array([0.1], requires_grad=True)
```

We can use `qml.Tracker(dev)` as the tracker:

```
    print("Expectation value of circuit:", qnode_local(params))

>>> Expectation value of circuit: -0.09983341664682821
```

Apart from producing the expected result via the tracker, we can request the tasks that were sent to the device:

```
print(tracker.history)
{'executions': [1], 'shots': [None], 'braket_task_id': ['0f6c047e-
fb58-48d5-bc85-1ff4a1538115'], 'batches': [1], 'batch_len': [1]}
```

For example, if we perform a gradient calculation, which, for a parameter-shift routine, will require executions of the circuit, we will see that this is encapsulated within different batch calls:

```
with qml.Tracker(dev) as tracker:
    print("Gradient of circuit:", qml.grad(qnode_local)(params))

print(tracker.history)
>>> Gradient of circuit: [-0.99500417]
>>> {'executions': [1, 1, 1], 'shots': [None, None, None], 'braket_
```

```
task_id': ['2d68103f-3817-422c-9100-6b59b236a614', 'e44a156f-c78f-
4a57-8426-0fa0c6133d76', 'abba84cb-3ff5-4b44-b8b9-cdae7ba16ed8'],
'batches': [1, 1], 'batch_len': [1, 2]}
```

Remote devices offer more information to the tracker object, and therefore for executions. The computation time is obtained in milliseconds. The bill can then be expressed in milliseconds and can be obtained from the `history` field. Of course, you must do the final calculations according to the target device and its pricing scheme.

Task tracking becomes the key. When translating a task into a device-specific execution, the cost schemes will be obtained accordingly. When pushed to the device, we can realize the implications of different algorithms and training schemes and their associated costs.

Figuring out our cloud costs is one of the most challenging tasks for quantum computers and classical resources. That is why Microsoft considered this a core part of their service and tried to provide simpler ways so that their users could access this billing information at any time.

Azure

Microsoft has a wide corporate market size and is well aware of how quantum computing technology may disrupt some operational workloads of business users. Given their cloud offering, they decided to compete with AWS in a similar setup via their Quantum Workspace offering.

In this case, Microsoft decided to also create a framework according to their needs, Q#, that follows a similar approach to previous C# and J# proprietary languages within the more general .NET framework (`https://learn.microsoft.com/en-us/azure/quantum/overview-what-is-qsharp-and-qdk`).

To enable this service, you must create a quantum workspace from an available subscription, which is the billing unit Microsoft uses to bill purchased services. Quantum Workspace is the service that provides access to the quantum devices that you can use, the coding environment, which is once again a notebook-based approach (using the omnipresent Jupyter Notebook engine), and additional information on quotas, resources, and everything that might be needed to perform your quantum circuit executions:

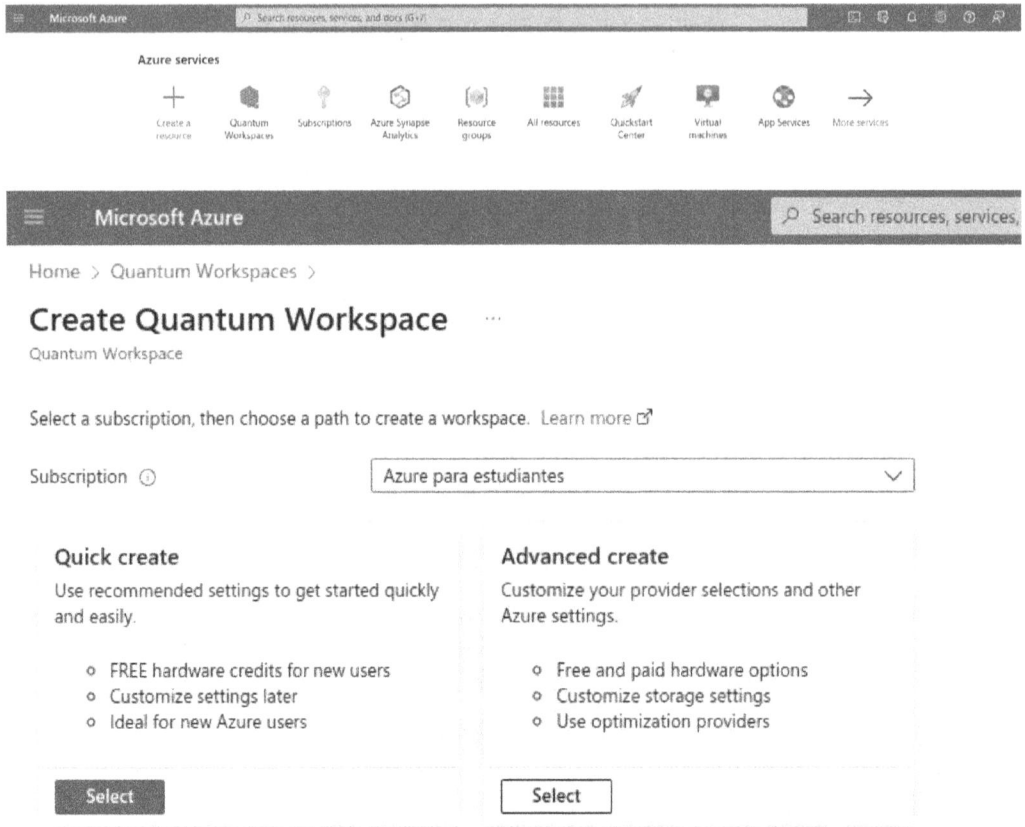

Figure 7.20 – The Azure portal and Quantum Workspace creation page

By default, a Microsoft Azure account provides free credits, different for each device, as part of the agreement with those hardware providers. This helps users test the different providers before deciding which type of plan they need. The plans are pay-per-use, but there are monthly service options. Similar to previous options and quantum devices, a notebook service is offered so that you can experiment, and a job list is provided so that you can retrieve any past jobs (core services are present on the main screen of the service, as shown in *Figure 7.21*):

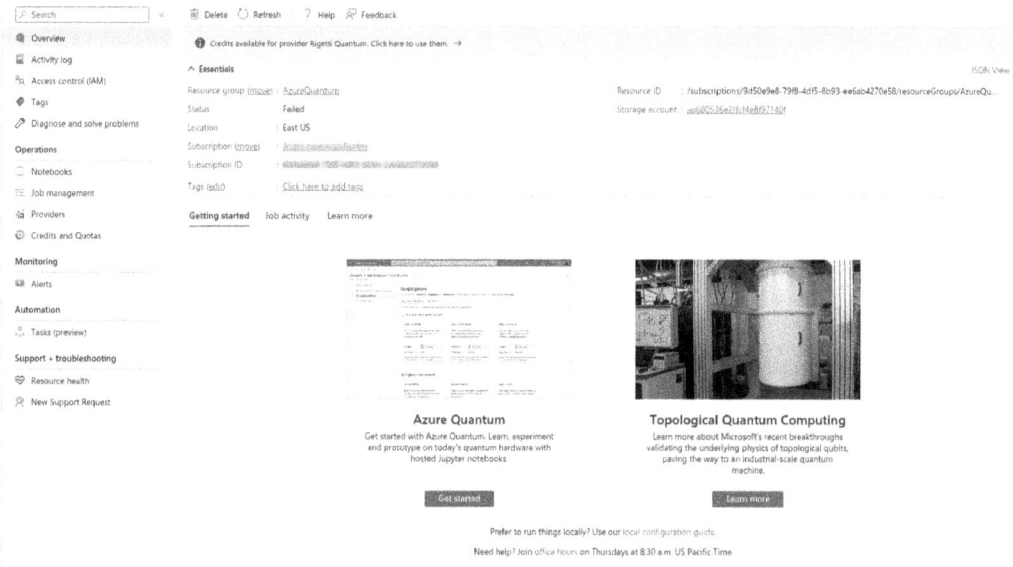

Figure 7.21 – Azure's Quantum Workspace main page with management options on the left-hand side menu

The available options show fewer service providers than Amazon's offering:

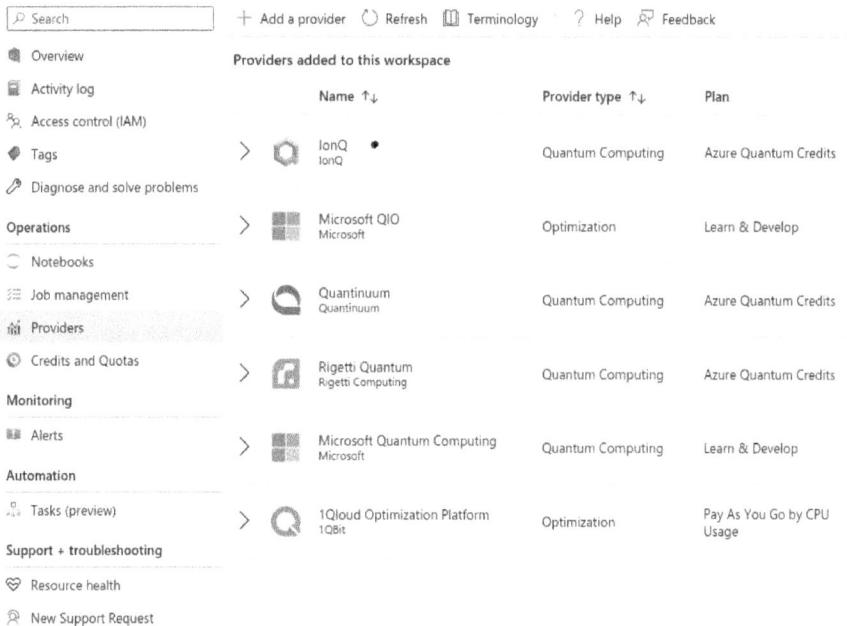

Figure 7.22 – Available Azure Quantum Workspace service providers

Apart from actual hardware devices, Azure also offers services for optimization routines. The user avoids the procedure needed to encode and solve a given problem. This is a trend we have seen before in the case of D-Wave's Hybrid solver or IBM's Qiskit Runtime. The level of abstraction for the user is increased, so they only have to worry about the problem to be solved. Quite an interesting trend indeed.

Being aware of the maturity of frameworks such as Qiskit instead of forcing users to learn about yet another quantum computing framework, Microsoft released a Qiskit plugin so that any Qiskit circuit could be sent to enabled devices:

```
pip install azure-quantum[qiskit]
```

Once it has been installed, we need to register our Quantum Workspace as the provider from which we want to obtain the backend. This can be done using the following code. These lines need to be added to the beginning of any experiment:

```
from azure.quantum.qiskit import AzureQuantumProvider
provider = AzureQuantumProvider (
resource_id = "/subscriptions/<suscription_id>/resourceGroups/
AzureQuantum/providers/Microsoft.Quantum/Workspaces/<workspace>",
    location = "eastus"
)
```

The backend information is obtained from the main window of Quantum Workspace (browser) and is meant to identify the region and subscription it has been deployed to:

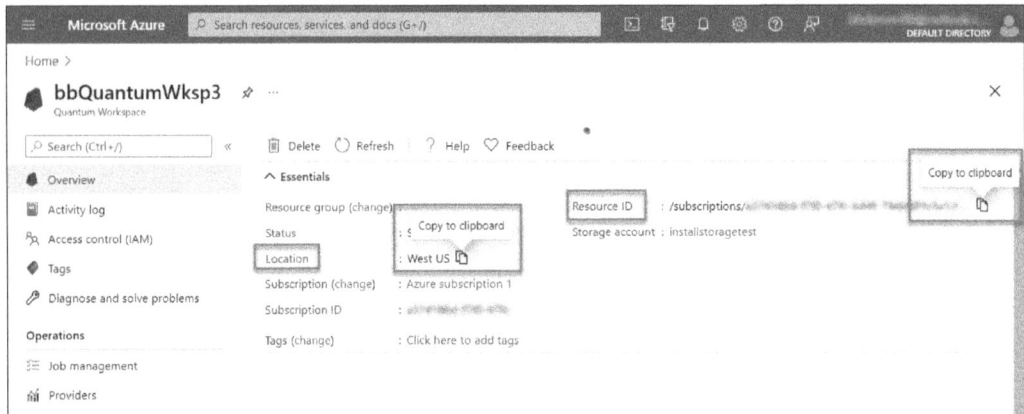

Figure 7.23 – Azure Quantum Workspace main window with access information highlighted

Thanks to this, all devices that were seen in *Figure 7.22* can be invoked so that our candidate circuit can be submitted to run on those:

```
ionq_simulator_backend = provider.get_backend("ionq.simulator")
ionq_qpu_backend
  = provider.get_backend("ionq.qpu")
```

Before running any circuit, it might be relevant to check the cost that running the circuit involves. To make it accessible via code, we can use Azure Resource Estimator, which only requires the circuit and backend it will be running on to assess the potential costs of our execution:

```
cost = backend.estimate_cost(circuit, shots=1024)
```

Microsoft offers a solid view of how they envision their services to be used (*Figure 7.24*), including resource estimation, which will become key information for longer-term and cost-efficient usage of quantum resources:

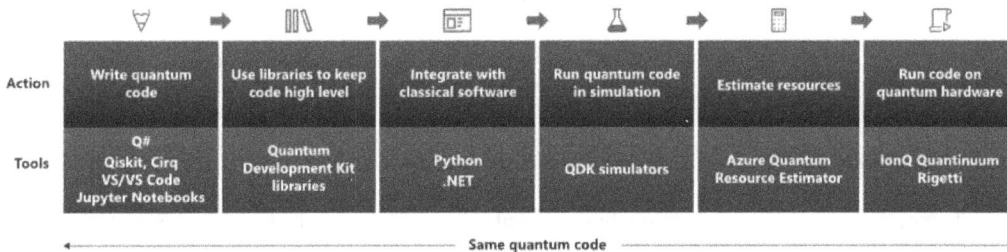

Figure 7.24 – Quantum development pipeline envisioned by Microsoft

This resource estimator, as we saw in the case of Amazon, prevents the user from expending substantial amounts of money before any execution is done. More examples of how to use Azure resources beyond the algorithm implementation can be found in their notebook gallery (*Figure 7.25*):

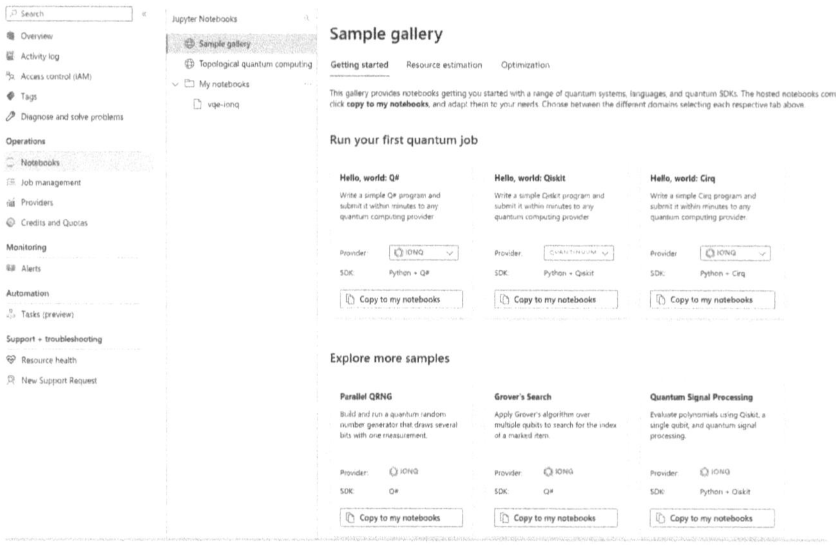

Figure 7.25 – Example of available notebooks within each Quantum Workspace

Cost estimation

We briefly mentioned resource estimation, but we would like to highlight the importance of this ability when aiming for a sustainable adoption strategy.

Quantum computing is at an early stage, requiring continuous and complex maintenance tasks to provide the best possible service. This is something that classical computing resources have mastered for a long time. Due to the limited ecosystem of hardware providers and the status of the technology, specifically, when aiming for real hardware, we will see costs ramp up significantly, even for the simplest providers. That is why resource estimation is such a crucial step in any QC pipeline, particularly if the model's training requires iterations:

IonQ

Universal gate-model QPU based on trapped ions

IonQ's trapped ion QPUs are built on a chain of trapped 171Yb+ ions, spatially confined via a microfabricated surface electrode trap within a vacuum chamber. Gates are performed via a two-photon Raman transition using a pair of counter-propagating beams from a mode-locked pulsed laser. This allows for high-quality single and two-qubit transitions and all-to-all connectivity. Initialization is performed via optical pumping, and readout is performed with a combination of a resonant laser, a high numeric aperture lens, and photomultiplier tubes.

IonQ compiles and optimizes your high-level quantum logic gates into the smallest possible set of laser pulses to realize your program on trapped ions, mapping your gates onto ideal pairs for execution using up-to-the-minute continuous calibrations.

For single-qubit gates, IonQ uses the GPI gate, the GPI2 gate and the GZ gate. The GPI and GPI2 gates are simply Rabi oscillations made by driving the qubits on resonance using laser beams in a Raman configuration. The GZ gate is performed by advancing/retarding the phase of this laser beam, creating a "virtual" operation.

For entangling, two-qubit gates, IonQ uses the Mølmer-Sørenson gate. This entangling gate and the single-qubit gates above constitute a universal gate set. By irradiating any two ions in the chain with a predesigned set of pulses, it is possible to couple ions' internal states with the chain's normal modes of motion to create entanglement.

More about this device [↗]

Hardware provider	Region	Location
IonQ	us-east-1	Maryland, USA
Availability	Next available	Cost
Weekdays, 13:00:00 - 02:00:00 UTC	⌛ 04:30:42	$0.30 / task + $0.01 / shot
Device ARN	Status	Qubits
▣ arn:aws:braket:::device/qpu/ionq/ionQdevice	⊘ ONLINE	11

Quantinuum
Quantinuum

Access to Quantinuum trapped-ion systems

Select Plan / Pricing *

Plan	◉ **Azure Quantum Credits**	◉ **Premium**	◉ **Standard**
	The Azure Quantum Credits program provides sponsored access to Quantinuum hardware through Azure. You will not be charged for usage created under the credits program, up to the limit of your credit grant.	Monthly subscription plan with 17K Quantinuum H-System Quantum Credits (HQCs) / month, available through queue Request Access ↗	Monthly subscription plan with 10K Quantinuum H-System quantum credits (HQCs) / month, available through queue Request Access ↗
Features	System Model H1 Syntax Checker Quantinuum System Model H1 Emulator Quantinuum System Model H1, Powered by Honeywell	Quantinuum System Model H1 Syntax Checker Quantinuum System Model H1 Emulator Quantinuum System Model H1	Quantinuum System Model H1 Syntax Checker Quantinuum System Model H1 Emulator Quantinuum System Model H1
Limits	Up to $500 of Quantinuum compute, unless you have received an additional project-based grant. While availability lasts, credits must be used within 6 months. Learn more about quota for credits.	17K H-System Quantum Credits (HQCs) / month	10K H-System Quantum Credits (HQCs) / month
Pricing	€0 per month Plus: HQC: €0 per hqc EHQC: €0 per hqc	$ 175,000 USD / Month	$ 125,000 USD / Month

Figure 7.26 – Cost for Quantinuum on Azure (below) and IonQ in AWS (above)

As an example, we could take the European Call Pricing from *Chapter 4* and extract its underlying quantum circuit, which we already know is composed of a block encoding, the log-normal distribution of the asset, and the block performing the function computing the pay-off function:

```
european_call_pricing = EuropeanCallPricing(
    num_state_qubits=nqubits,
    strike_price=strike,
    rescaling_factor=0.05,
    bounds=(low, high),
    uncertainty_model=dist_circ,
)

problem = european_call_pricing.to_estimation_problem()
problem.state_preparation.draw('mpl')
```

The problem we might face is that, depending on the device we choose, we might not be able to understand what the P(X) and F blocks represent in terms of operations, as shown in Figure 7.27. We will need to translate it into a combination of basic gates that the device can comprehend, as high-level abstraction blocks typically cannot be directly executed on a real device. Consequently, we will also estimate the potential cost associated with this translation process, as it is a common occurrence.

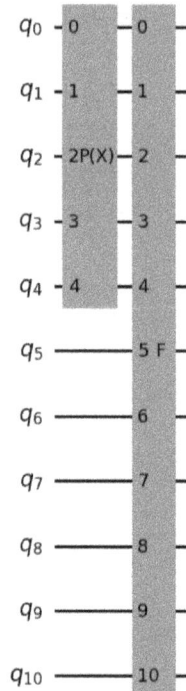

Figure 7.27 – European Call Pricing problem circuit showing high-level abstraction blocks for the circuit

For the Quantinuum device, we could use a combination of rotations, identity, CNOT, and Hadamard gates and request the translation of the circuit based on those operations:

```
from qiskit import transpile

result = transpile(problem.state_preparation, basis_gates=['id', 'ry',
'rx', 'rz', 'cx', 'h'], optimization_level=1, seed_transpiler=1)
```

Then, we can select the device so that it can perform the estimation on the resulting circuit:

```
backend = provider.get_backend("quantinuum.qpu.h1-1")
costs = backend.estimate_cost(result, shots=1)

print(f" Estimated cost for a single shot is of {costs.estimated_
total}{costs.currency_code}")

Estimated cost for a single shot is of 5.449HQC
```

In this case, a single circuit pass would consume 5.5 Quantinuum credits, which, for a standard subscription, would sum up close to $70. If we consider that the amplitude estimation routine could require several iterations over the same circuit, we may need a couple of hundred dollars just for an asset pay-off evaluation. Of course, then comes the ability to compress this circuit so that fewer operations would still render the same state preparation. However, this is mostly the core activity of research institutions and is less likely to be something our analysts will invest time in.

This is why we must perform some calculations and thoroughly evaluate the expected return on investment before we naively submit our training routine to a cloud provider that will be happy to serve requests at those prices.

Summary

The transition from on-premises to cloud-hosted has been a complicated journey for many organizations, including the switch to be made from owning the computing resources to pay-per-use modalities common today. Quantum computing made its initial foray directly into the cloud. Different platforms give access to services and providers with efficient costs. Many institutions have facilities to onboard into this quantum journey.

Quantum hardware is problem-focused and increases the complexity and decisions to be made as you must decide what option, out of the plethora of devices, is the most convenient for your problems. Estimators help companies evaluate the cost of using this new type of machine, providing them with an efficient way to estimate the budget required per study.

No technology has faced such a wide, almost *free-of-charge* offering to learn and adapt than quantum computing. Hardware providers enable their latest devices in those cloud services and help boost the field for researchers and business users. The role of the different communities around the libraries used to manipulate such hardware is highly important. It brings an important volume of notebooks and tutorials to self-learn quantum computing.

There are already providers offering 2- and 3-qubit desktop systems at competitive prices (`https://www.discovermagazine.com/technology/a-desktop-quantum-computer-for-just-usd5-000`), but this will mostly remain as an educational resource, given that the cloud is where most organizations seem to be locating their infrastructure. It simplifies any integration effort to be made by your when self-hosting this type of resource.

To summarize, there are several challenges associated with implementing quantum computing on cloud platforms, including the following:

- **Accessibility**: Quantum computing resources are currently only available through specialized cloud providers, which can be difficult for some users to access. General cloud providers are already easing this with their early adoption of QC hubs.

- **Scalability**: Quantum computing systems require specialized hardware and infrastructure, which can be difficult to scale up as demand for quantum computing resources increases.

- **Interoperability**: Different quantum computing platforms have different programming languages and interfaces, making it difficult for developers to work with multiple systems.

- **Security**: Quantum computing systems are vulnerable to certain types of attacks, such as quantum hacking, which can expose sensitive information.

- **Noise and errors**: Quantum computers are more susceptible to noise and errors than classical computers, making it difficult to obtain accurate results from quantum algorithms.

- **Cost**: Quantum computing resources are still relatively expensive, making it difficult for some organizations to afford the necessary hardware and infrastructure.

In any case, this high-paced technology has just started being useful, and the applications that bring competitive advantage will uncover the paths those resources will end up adopting.

Further reading

Many providers are already shaping their offerings so that new as-a-service paradigms will emerge in the following years.

Oxford Quantum Circuits has already embraced the concept of **Quantum Computing as a Service (QCaaS)** (`https://www.techradar.com/news/quantum-computing-as-a-service-is-going-mainstream`), whereas other companies like QCentroid are targeting a wider audience by offering off-the-shelf solutions tailored to industry-specific applications through their **Quantum-as-a-Service (QaaS)** platform (`https://marketplace.qcentroid.xyz/`).

When thinking about cloud-accessible resources, one of the most interesting cases is the one posed by the variational quantum algorithm, where a constant interchange between classical and quantum resources must be sorted out. Given the queue times we have seen, we must be aware that any remote training of the ansatz will face important delays per iteration if we attempt to train on an actual device remotely.

Given the existing benefits that companies derive from classical machine learning models, Quantum Computing is likely to be integrated as an auxiliary tool for addressing difficult-to-solve problems. Doing so in competent architectures is what will require senior roles to step up over the hype in the field and make sensible decisions regarding the adoption and long-term strategy. Companies are already doing their part to ease the decision process for these early adopters.

To solve that issue, IBM decided to create Qiskit Runtime. Runtimes are routines with some well-known algorithms where additional information is sent to the remote execution engine, which takes charge of both the classical and the quantum parts. It provides closer interaction between two sides of the algorithm, thus rendering much more efficient running times. An example workflow can be seen in *Figure 7.28*:

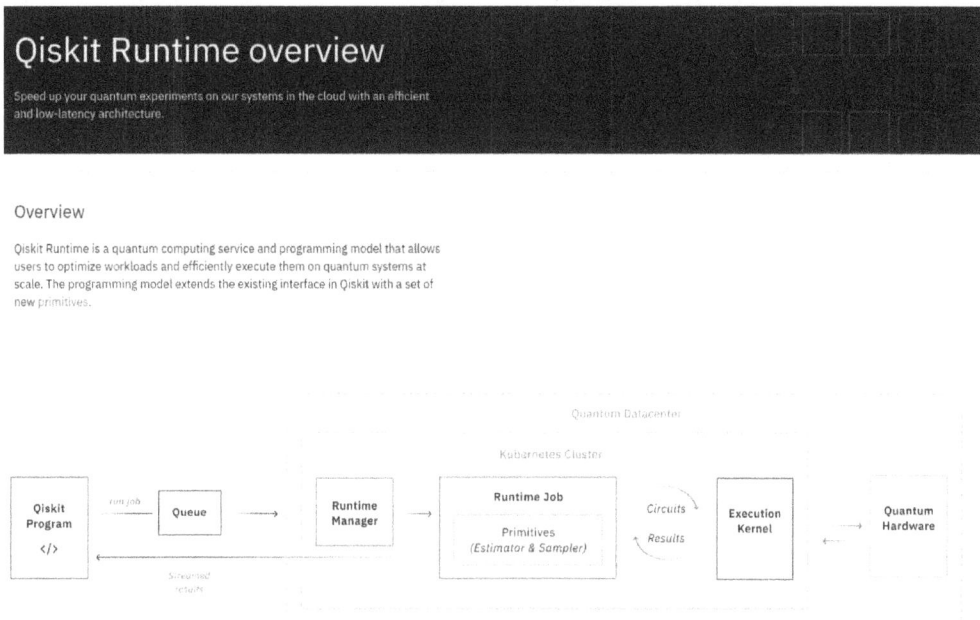

Figure 7.28 – Qiskit Runtime as envisioned by IBM for efficient workload balancing

This offering comes with a cost scheme that you need to consider, even though a lite option is available with up to 3 hours of free access:

Standard	IBM Quantum Systems access	1,60144 € EUR/Qiskit Runtime Seconds

Figure 7.29 – IBM Qiskit Runtime pricing as of January 2023

D-Wave also realized that by combining classical and quantum operations on their end, they could extend their portfolio and reduce the time needed to solve certain problems that required intermediate classical steps. This is what is hidden behind their Hybrid solver – classical routines interacting with a quantum annealer so that the combination of both creates a broader range of problems to be solved.

By definition, their solver efficiently solves binary quadratic models but adds classical routines. Discrete and constrained models can also be solved by allocating quantum and classical resources to each process step (https://docs.dwavesys.com/docs/latest/doc_leap_hybrid.html).

In all probability, the progression of these remote solvers will eventually manifest as a streamlined service, wherein problems are submitted and the service provider's engine determines the optimal combination of resources. If not for the advancements that quantum devices can offer in specific problem domains, it would be challenging to discern their involvement in the process. Nevertheless, this approach will simplify usability and abstraction for business users who are primarily focused on finding solutions and may not be as concerned with the technical intricacies employed to achieve them.

References

Cross, A. W., Bishop, L. S., Smolin, J. A., & Gambetta, J. M. (2017). Open quantum assembly language. arXiv preprint arXiv:1707.03429.

Anis MS, Abraham H, AduOffei RA, Agliardi G, Aharoni M, Akhalwaya IY, Aleksandrowicz G, Alexander T, Amy M, Anagolum S. (2021). Qiskit: An open-source framework for quantum computing. Qiskit/qiskit.

Smith, R. S., Curtis, M. J., & Zeng, W. J. (2016). A practical quantum instruction set architecture. arXiv preprint arXiv:1608.03355.

Part 3:
Upcoming Quantum Scenario

This section highlights the crucial role of classical means and high-performance hardware in achieving a short-term quantum advantage, offering insight into key approaches that shape the quantum-classical landscape. It further explores the potential evolution of noisy intermediate-scale hardware based on different provider strategies, emphasizing its long-term implications. Lastly, it addresses the challenges of implementing quantum computing in fintech firms and banks, providing guidance to ensure successful, low-risk project execution.

This part has the following chapters:

- *Chapter 8, HPCs and Simulators Relevance*
- *Chapter 9, NISQ Quantum Hardware Evolution*
- *Chapter 10, Quantum Roadmap for Banks and Fintechs*

We will cover the following main topics:

- Local simulation of quantum hardware with noise

- Distributed approaches to running local emulators

Local simulation of noise models

First, we must distinguish between the three naming conventions we will use during this chapter and the following ones. Previously, we talked about how quantum algorithms can be run on a classical device before being sent to a real quantum device, but there are some different ways in which this classical execution can be done. Problems such as the ones we have posed have been around for a while, and classical computing has evolved in many different ways to bring solutions to the technology at hand during this time. As we will see, this may also bring some challenges related to the specifics of the different classical setups we will cover. Mimicking quantum mechanical evolution is a non-trivial task; that was how quantum computing was proposed as a potential solution.

Simulators are the classical means of processing information in the way an ideal quantum computer would do so. Recall that quantum information theory is not a new task brought about by the availability of quantum hardware. Lots of work was done even before the first quantum device was created (*Bennet and Shor, 1998*). By defining the quantum information and determining the set of operations to be employed, the sequence that applies these operations to our quantum states is what we refer to as algorithms or circuits in the quantum domain. Simulators make the mathematical apparatus used in quantum computing computationally available. We have not discussed those terms much since *Chapter 1*, but remember that a quantum state is, in simple terms, a vector that encodes the wave function of a given system. As an example, we can represent the basic 0 state as a column vector, as shown in the following equation:

$$|0\rangle = \begin{pmatrix} 1 \\ 0 \end{pmatrix}$$

Hence, computationally, we could represent it as follows:

```
import numpy as np

ket0 = np.array([[1.0], [0.0]])
```

On the other hand, operations, such as the CNOT or Hadamard gates, which are used to create superposed states, are nothing other than the matrices that perform the evolution from one state into its product state. A Hadamard gate, for example, is represented by the following matrix:

$$H = \frac{1}{\sqrt{2}} \begin{pmatrix} 1 & 1 \\ 1 & -1 \end{pmatrix}$$

The following code can express its coded version:

```
hadamard = np.dot(1/np.sqrt(2), np.array([[1.0, 1.0], [1.0, -1.0]]))
```

Since each operator (quantum gate) can be represented as a matrix, it is simple to perform those operations with classical resources, so long as we have sufficient resources. Memory, in particular, becomes relevant as the system's size grows. The representation for a quantum computer is two to the power of N matrices, and vectors will need to be handled to perform such computations. We can benefit from the work we've done on vectorization and sparse matrix handling, but at this point, our classical devices will reach their limits with these techniques.

For example, applying a Hadamard gate to our basic 0 state qubit would yield a state in a superposition of the 0 and 1 states. This action can be simulated by creating the dot product of the previously defined objects:

```
>>> np.dot(hadamard, ket0)
array([[0.70710678], [0.70710678]])
```

This is the superposed quantum state:

$$|\psi\rangle = \tfrac{1}{\sqrt{2}}\Big(|0\rangle + |1\rangle\Big)$$

With that, we have performed our first simulation. Starting from the initial state, most devices are initialized with a Hadamard gate operator (H), producing the output state. We could extend it so that all basic gates and states can be represented and thus work at higher levels of abstraction. This is mostly what quantum simulators do when we use them to run an algorithm. Frameworks such as Qiskit or Pennylane offer this set of operations as abstractions to this matrix product of operations so that it is easy for us to use those by simply using those definitions.

How many classical resources are needed to simulate a quantum system? Well, this is where things become interesting – you can expect many qubits to be simulated on a normal laptop and many bit operations to be performed. But the truth is that 16-qubit algorithms may already consume more than the available memory on a common laptop. As an example, 16 qubits would encode the available options for 16 assets of the portfolio optimization task we reviewed in *Chapter 5*. This is a small problem that can be easily solved using classical computers but that would, on its quantum version, consume up to the 16 GB available on a regular laptop using any of those previously mentioned frameworks. So, how can classical computers handle that, and how can quantum simulators get out of hand at the same size?

The amount of information you are processing when simulating quantum mechanical systems is much more than the simple sum of assets and derived information you could have encoded into those quantum objects. Quantum mechanical dynamics occur in more complex spaces, which require many more resources to reproduce whole system dynamics faithfully. But that also means fewer quantum resources are necessary to encode larger pieces of classical information (*Bowen, 2001*). Hopefully, thanks to this very same fact, we can compute things differently, and that is when the advantage arises. Making use of quantum domain characteristics such as superposition or entanglement, we can do things a little bit differently, such as evaluating all potential combinations via single-step operations (*Brassard et al. 2002*) or making solutions cancel out between them, amplifying the best candidates, as we did in the examples in *Chapters 4*, *5*, and *6*.

With that, we have covered the basics of how different quantum computing is from classical computing. Therefore, you must know that classical systems have limitations when it comes to mimicking those dynamics. That is why so much effort has been put into creating computers that work at a quantum mechanical level so that there is no loss due to the classical "emulation" of those effects.

While mimicking real quantum devices, we can take things one step further and allow our classical simulations not only to work as an ideal quantum computer but also as a specific device. When simulating specific devices, we would like to mimic all their restrictions regarding connectivity or error statistics. In the current state of the NISQ era (*Preskill, 2021*), it is important that we faithfully characterize the specifics of our target device.

Emulator is the word used when simulators mimic quantum dynamics within a given set of restrictions associated with specific quantum hardware. In the case of IBM's superconducting chips, for example, we can retrieve their model from Qiskit and use existing local simulators limited to the functioning of the real device. This means that not all possible two-qubit gate operations can be performed between any two qubits, plus operations will fail sometimes, with what we call errors, thus producing noise (inaccuracies):

```
from qiskit.providers.fake_provider import FakeVigo
from qiskit.visualization import import plot_error_map

emulator = FakeVigo()
plot_error_map(emulator)
```

Figure 8.1 is a representation of the error map for the fake Vigo.

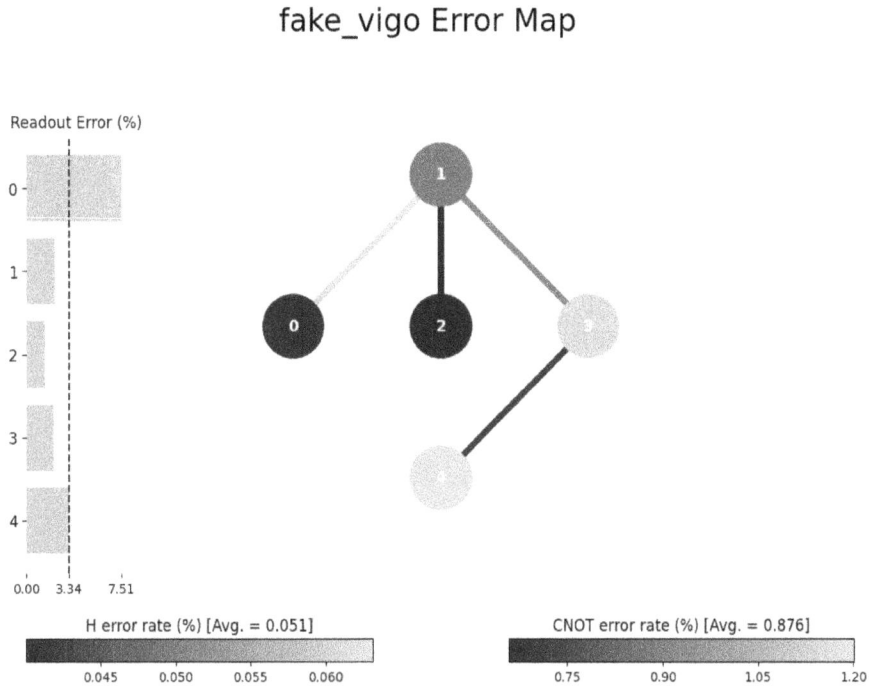

Figure 8.1 – IBM Vigo chip description highlighting qubit connectivity
and error upon H, CNOT, or measurement operations

By running our circuits against this fake instance instead of a simulator, we will face the same issues as we would when using the real device and obtain results closer to the ones obtained with it without waiting in the actual device queue. That is why, when a quantum circuit needs to be sent to an actual device (or an emulator mimicking the real hardware), a transpilation step is needed. We need a step that translates our theoretical and device-agnostic algorithm into the available gates and provides connectivity to the hardware.

If we take the example of the two-qubit bell state we presented in *Chapter 1*, as shown in *Figure 8.2*, we could add a transpilation step to that `fake_vigo` device and see what is drawn:

```
from qiskit import QuantumCircuit

qc = QuantumCircuit(2)
qc.h(0)
qc.cx(0, 1)
qc.draw('mpl')
```

The last line of code outputs the circuit shown in *Figure 8.2*. It represents one of the Bell states.

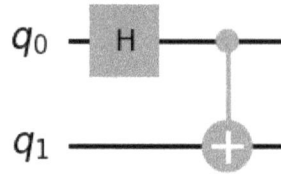

Figure 8.2 – Bell state circuit

The circuit needs to be broken into gates implemented on the quantum computer. To do that, the circuit needs to be transpiled:

```
from qiskit import transpile

qc = transpile(qc, emulator)
qc.draw('mpl')
```

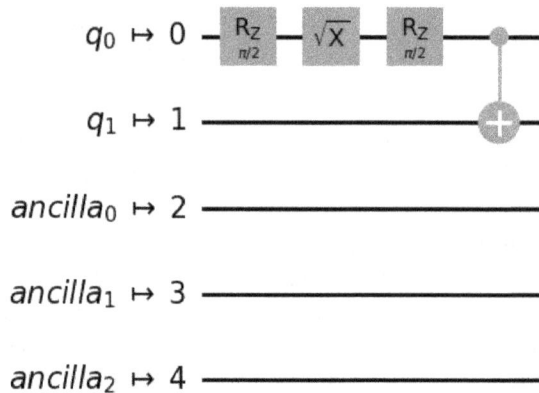

Figure 8.3 – Circuit transpiled based on the Bell state with the emulator configuration

These discrepancies come from the fact that the Hadamard gate is not a native operation in the device, even though its error is shown in *Figure 8.1*. We need to transform the circuit into native gate operations so that their combination produces the same effect as an H gate would. We also need to specify what will happen to the rest of the qubits that are part of the hardware specification but not of the circuit.

This fact, of course, extends to all devices, not only IBM's, as each manufacturer and the underlying technology are different. Moreover, each chip will show different error statistics at different moments in time, and this is because they are being worked on and improved upon. Therefore, device models may need to be updated every once in a while, so the last snapshot of the device is used.

Lastly, we have quantum *devices*, the actual services we showed in *Chapter 7*, which can ultimately be used to run our algorithms.

Like in any sensible project development, it is relevant to understand the difference between the three options and know when it makes sense to leverage each one.

Simulators help us conceptualize algorithms and particular implementations so that we can envision the expected outcome for a given use case. The classical resources will limit us, but, as we will see, there are plenty of options for squeezing these resources as much as possible before moving forward.

The ultimate goal of a quantum algorithm is for it to be run on quantum hardware. As much as we could work on classical resources, we would find limitations as we moved forward at the scale of our problems. Quantum devices are scarce, and we may need to adapt a theoretical algorithm to the specific hardware. But given that these are scarce and are doing that work locally, emulating a device is a suitable option before moving forward.

Device emulation makes us aware of the changes our theoretical algorithm will face, and the results will be much closer to the actual expected outcome when it's run on the device. For variational approaches and QML, which not only require many iterations to fit parameters also but where the parameter fitting may substantially change due to device behavior, these are really valuable resources. Having a faithful representation or model of the device is also key. Even though some providers will charge for the emulator, most can be accessed freely or mimicked using some of the software we have explored so far. Some of the devices shown in *Chapter 7* are classically emulated quantum device representations. Providers such as Quantinuum offer access to their devices and emulators, often offering less waiting time so that researchers can balance their workload between the emulator and the actual device.

Most libraries and frameworks offer resources to create noise models to be added to standard simulators (`https://qiskit.org/documentation/tutorials/simulators/3_building_noise_models.html`). But what if our algorithm requires more classical resources than the ones we can provide on our laptops? Next, we will explore some interesting options we may need to consider from the range of available classical resources to get the most out of those devices.

Distributed computing approaches to quantum simulation

One way we could get the most classical resources is by leveraging distributed frameworks for quantum computing.

Nowadays, they are omnipresent in all large organizations. Some distributed computing frameworks, such as Apache Spark and Ray, have been extensively used for large dataset wrangling or deep learning model training (*Meng et al. 2016, Moritz et al. 2018*). Not far from it, quantum computing simulators can leverage the distributed ecosystem by splitting the mathematical operations that need to be performed. Splitting a system that should operate as a whole as a set of independent operations requires us to understand how splittable our problem at hand is.

This is why most of the frameworks that deal with distributed quantum computing simulation come from research teams, even in large organizations such as Intel (*Guerreschi et al. 2020*) and Baidu (*Zhao et al. 2021*).

As quantum hardware matures, device-independent frameworks will likely proliferate, but there is still a lack of consensus that renders into isolated or hardware-specific frameworks for distributed computation. This is the reason why Microsoft researchers have created **Quantum Intermediate Representation** (**QIR**) and the QIR Alliance (`https://www.qir-alliance.org/`) is to help deliver an industry standard that can help boost that interoperability between hardware providers and quantum computing scientists.

The creation of an industry-wide standard will also help boost work done on cloud-based quantum computation for quantum deep learning (*Kwak et al., 2022*) and emerging quantum versions for federated learning (*Li et al, 2021*), which is already present as a solution for fighting against organized crime and collaborative financial crime detection (*Suzumura et al., 2021*).

While these standards and distributed frameworks evolve at the maturity of their classical counterparts, there is still room for computational efficiency in simulating complex systems, which is what we will dig into in the next section.

Tensor networks for simulation

Tensor networks are new to many people approaching quantum computation but were created a while back. Even though initial steps were made in the early 90s to help deal with large systems in the field of condensed matter physics, this rapidly extended to other fields, such as high-energy and many-body physics. This exploded during the early 2000s as a whole family of methods and algorithms suited to particular use cases of studying entanglement at many different levels (*Biamonte and Bergholm, 2017; Órus, 2019*).

Entanglement is one of the key properties that makes quantum computing highly intriguing, powerful, and challenging to comprehend and develop intuition about. Tensors, as mathematical objects, provide a consistent framework for handling relationships between sets of objects related to an N-dimensional vector space. Due to the dimensionality that some problems in certain areas of physics pose, the tensor network framework allows researchers to decompose these complex structures into tensor products, which can be contracted and expanded so that they can be handled more efficiently.

Knowing the relevance of tensor networks in the field of quantum computing, some providers have already taken a step forward and developed their frameworks so that researchers can leverage them. This is the case of the Pennylane creators, Xanadu, and their Jet framework (*Vincent et al. 2022*).

Here, we will simulate a two-qubit circuit producing a Bell state using the Jet framework as an exercise. The resemblance between the circuit and the tensorial representation, as can be seen in the following figure, should help you envision the similarity between both approaches. The efficiency of computing will become apparent when the scale of the circuit is increased:

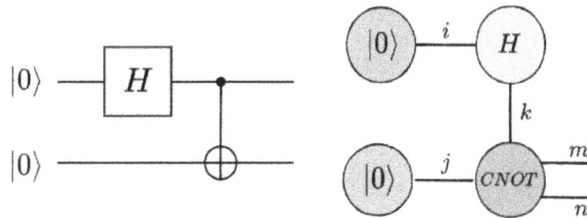

Figure 8.4 – A quantum circuit producing a two-qubit entangled bell state (left); tensor network representation highlighting the indexes to be used in the following code example (right)

As we did previously, we will need to create the two 0 states that will kickstart our circuit state (initialization). In this case, we will need to indicate the index and dimensionality of our states:

```
import jet

dim = [2]
ket0 = [1, 0]

# Initializing our qubits
qbit0 = jet.Tensor(["i"], dim, ket0)
qbit1 = jet.Tensor(["j"], dim, ket0)
```

Similarly, the Hadamard gate is represented by the matrix operator, and the indexes indicate where it is placed for our initial states:

```
Hadamard = jet.Tensor(["i", "k"], [2, 2], [1/np.sqrt(2), 1/np.sqrt(2),
1/np.sqrt(2), -1/np.sqrt(2)])
```

It does not matter if the k index has not appeared before, as it will be the link to further actions. The last action will be the **Control NOT (CNOT)** operation, which acts on the second qubit only if the first one (also called the control qubit) is in state |1>. It is characterized by the following matrix:

$$CNOT = \begin{bmatrix} 1 & 0 & 0 & 0 \\ 0 & 1 & 0 & 0 \\ 0 & 0 & 0 & 1 \\ 0 & 0 & 1 & 0 \end{bmatrix}$$

So, we can compose it by selecting which elements of the matrix are the ones that should be replaced with a value of 1, given that the matrix is initialized with 0 values:

```
CNOT = jet.Tensor(["k", "j", "m", "n"], [2, 2, 2, 2])
CNOT.set_value((0, 0, 0, 0), 1) # |00> -> |00>
CNOT.set_value((0, 1, 0, 1), 1) # |01> -> |01>
CNOT.set_value((1, 0, 1, 1), 1) # |10> -> |11>
CNOT.set_value((1, 1, 1, 0), 1) # |11> -> |10>
```

With these four elements, we can compose our tensor network, linking each element by the indexes that are common to the rest. We could, for example, simply impose the Hadamard action on the first qubit (similar to what we did in the first exercise) and ask for its contraction:

```
tnet = jet.TensorNetwork()
tnet.add_tensor(qbit0)
tnet.add_tensor(Hadamard)
tnet.contract()
```

This will yield an equal superposition of |0> and |1> states:

```
Size = 2
Indices = {k}
Data = { (0.707107,0)   (0.707107,0) }
```

We can see how the obtained tensor is the one referenced by the k index. Just by concatenating further actions and asking for the final contraction, we can effectively simulate the full chain of actions until the circuit produces the final state:

```
tnet = jet.TensorNetwork()

tnet.add_tensor(qbit0)
tnet.add_tensor(qbit1)
```

```
tnet.add_tensor(Hadamard)
tnet.add_tensor(CNOT)
tnet.contract()

Size = 4
Indices = {m  n}
Data = {(0.707107,0)   (0,0)   (0,0)   (0.707107,0)}
```

In the two-qubit case, we can see how the first ($|00>$) and last ($|11>$) are states with probability amplitudes above zero and of equal value. They should coincide with the Bell state encoded by the circuit in *Figure 8.3*, which can be represented in Dirac notation, as shown here:

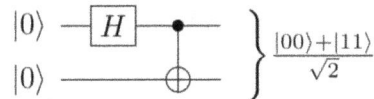

Figure 8.5 – Quantum circuit producing an entangled bell state (source: Wikipedia)

Due to its fundamental functioning, many providers already offer the fundamentals of it as a simulator so that users can work at higher abstraction levels. We can find it as an option with some cloud vendors, as in the case of AWS cloud devices, as shown in the following figure:

Amazon Web Services — TN1

Amazon Braket tensor network simulator

TN1 is a fully managed, high-performance, tensor network simulator. For certain types of circuits, TN1 can simulate up to 50 qubits, with a circuit depth of 100 gates or less. It is particularly powerful for sparse circuits or circuits with local gates. Circuits with all-to-all gates are better suited for the universal state vector simulator, SV1. TN1 operates in two phases. First, the "rehearsal phase" attempts to identify an efficient computational path for your circuit, so that TN1 can estimate the runtime of the next stage, which is called the "contraction phase." If the estimated contraction time exceeds the TN1 runtime limit, TN1 does not attempt contraction. TN1 is always available, it executes circuits on demand, and it can run multiple circuits in parallel.

More about this device ↗

Hardware provider	Region	Location
Amazon Web Services	eu-west-2, us-east-1, us-west-2	—
Availability	Next available	Cost
Everyday, 00:00:00 - 23:59:59 UTC	⊘ AVAILABLE NOW	$0.275 / minute
Device ARN	Status	Qubits
⬚ arn:aws:braket:::device/quantum-simulator/amazon/tn1	⊘ ONLINE	50

Figure 8.6 – AWS TN1 tensor network simulator description page

It costs up to 0.275 dollars per minute but can perform on up to 50 qubits and 100 gate circuit instances. Both SV1 and DM1 devices, which can classically simulate circuits as well, are limited to up to 34 qubits and 17 qubit circuits, respectively (also being cheaper options).

Given that it all seems to boil down to tensor multiplications (vectors for states and matrices for operators in general), there is an evident step to squeeze our classical resources up to their limit, which is done by exploiting all available classical resources when performing those computations. Tensor networks are great for simplifying the required computation, but still, the hardware needs to be provided. This is when classical resources for vector and matrix computation join the quantum computing party.

GPUs

As mentioned previously, GPUs also play a key role in short-term quantum computing. Initially, GPUs were designed for matrix operations, which are required when rendering images on a computer. Mid-90s manufacturers such as Nvidia (`https://en.wikipedia.org/wiki/NV1`) released their first working cards and have been actively innovating since then. The gaming industry made sure GPU manufacturers had continuous improvements to be delivered both software and hardware-wise, making those devices more and more performant for their main tasks.

Looking at adjacent fields, GPU manufacturers realized that it was becoming more and more difficult to train models on a CPU for machine learning specialists, particularly in computer vision. And with the explosion of large-scale models and the deep learning era, it was obvious that there was a niche market to exploit for their product. Their ability to boost deep learning tasks comes from the fact that performing matrix operations efficiently is their main purpose. In general, computers process images as tensors, performing convolutions on them to identify cats or dogs (for example), detect objects in the image, or segment the objects on it.

Given that matrix operations are at the core of the mathematical concept of quantum computing, a few providers such as Nvidia focused on how they could help boost this field, which later released an SDK specialized for quantum computing that leverages the usage of its card architectures (`https://docs.nvidia.com/cuda/cuquantum/`). Not only that, but it also provided specialized frameworks for previously highlighted techniques and mathematical frameworks, making its GPU cards the cornerstone for current quantum computing research:

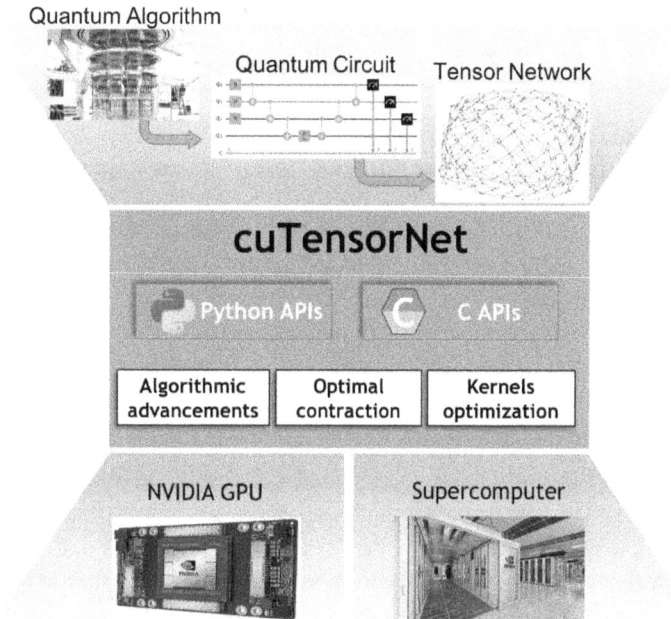

Figure 8.7 – Architecture for the GPU-based simulation framework described by NVIDIA

Thanks to its abstractions, most hardware providers and cloud computing vendors can seamlessly integrate state-of-the-art quantum simulation and emulation technology on its stack, making it available to the general public.

For those interested in diving a little bit deeper into the technology, frameworks such as Baidu's PaddlePaddle and Xanadu's Pennylane offer the option to run their simulations on top of Nvidia cards by allowing Python-intermediate libraries to interact with native CUDA libraries acting on the hardware. Even if it sounds complicated, it just takes a few lines of code to enable this boosting.

For example, when using Qiskit as the main framework, you can install the Aer simulator's version with GPU support:

```
pip install qiskit-aer-gpu
```

It will overwrite the standard `qiskit-aer` library, and all simulations will utilize GPU-backed processing for state vector simulations.

Xanadu and its QML framework, Pennylane, went in a different direction. It released a completely separate library called Lightning that, once installed with GPU support, allows users to invoke a GPU device so that all required calculations are sent to the GPU instead of the default CPU:

```
pip install pennylane-lightning[gpu]
dev = qml.device("lightning.gpu", wires=2)
```

Google went on a different journey, defining its specific hardware as optimized for low-dimensional matrices and the broader definition of tensors. These devices are called *tensor processing units* (https://cloud.google.com/tpu/docs/tpus) and are the natural evolution of this abstraction; they are particularly suited for AI and will most likely boost some of the workloads of its cloud-provided quantum computing service (https://quantumai.google/cirq/google/concepts). Thanks to the cloud's abstraction, it would most likely be hard to tell where our circuits were running if it was not for their price.

Summary

In this chapter, we saw that there are many ways to simulate a quantum computer before running it on an actual device. We saw that there are also some implications regarding the limited availability, errors, and specific characteristics of the real hardware to be considered and that classical computers are not yet done when it comes to quantum computing.

Establishing a strategy to validate our circuits, evaluate their potential, and decide where those algorithms will run requires understanding the set of options provided by almost all quantum companies.

Tensor networks provide a powerful mathematical framework to simulate complex systems efficiently. GPUs have also placed their bet. Even combining both has proven to be a valid approach for simulating large devices.

Distributed computation is anticipated to be the next hurdle to overcome, necessitating a certain level of technical expertise to harness its potential efficiently. Similar to the trajectory followed by tensor networks and GPUs, simplified approaches have emerged to exploit classical computing resources at various levels.

Vendors such as Nvidia already provide a distributed framework for data science called RAPIDS, which simplifies the end-to-end work, boosting the core activities related to data cleaning, transformation, and model training. It allows us to imagine a future where distributed GPU-enabled tensor network-rooted quantum computing simulators and emulators will be integrated within the actual ecosystem for end-to-end data-driven use case exploitation. Even when fault-tolerant quantum devices are available to the open public, this type of setting will provide a cost-efficient way to tackle some of the most complicated problems companies face nowadays.

Hybrid quantum computation will make use of all the research that has been developed so that meaningful advances in science and business will be accelerated in the near future.

Further reading

For those interested in diving deeper into some of the techniques mentioned in this chapter, here are some recommendations that should help you understand the basics.

One of the most interesting and challenging frameworks we have discussed is tensor networks. Many resources can be found in the literature. Still, two that we can recommend are the work by Biamonte and Bergholm from 2017, which provides a solid foundation to understand its potential better. For those more hands-on engineers, the Quimb (*Gray, 2018*) and Jet (*Vincent et al., 2022*) Python packages provide a fun way to learn and experiment.

Similarly, distributed computation has a path, and works by Zaharia et al. (2010) on Apache Spark and Moritz et al. (2018) on Ray are leading the path toward easy-to-implement distributed solutions.

Something particularly interesting is the contribution of the Baidu team to the existing PaddlePaddle framework (*Ma et al., 2020*). Not only have they provided an industrial-level framework for deep learning but they have also adapted part of it to include QML-related works, extending it to one of the most interesting hybrid QML platforms that's openly available: `https://github.com/PaddlePaddle/Quantum`.

It also specifies the possibility of performing said calculation on GPUs so that users get the most out of classical resources.

References

Bennett, C. H., & Shor, P. W. (1998). Quantum information theory. IEEE transactions on information theory, 44(6), 2,724-2,742.

Biamonte, J., & Bergholm, V. (2017). Tensor networks in a nutshell. arXiv preprint arXiv:1708.00006.

Brassard, G., Hoyer, P., Mosca, M., & Tapp, A. (2002). Quantum amplitude amplification and estimation. Contemporary Mathematics, 305, 53-74.

Bowen, G. (2001). Classical information capacity of superdense coding. Physical Review A, 63(2), 022302.

Guerreschi, G. G., Hogaboam, J., Baruffa, F., & Sawaya, N. P. (2020). Intel Quantum Simulator: A cloud-ready high-performance simulator of quantum circuits. Quantum Science and Technology, 5(3), 034007.

Gray, J. (2018). quimb: A Python package for quantum information and many-body calculations. Journal of Open Source Software, 3(29), 819.

Kwak, Y., Yun, W. J., Kim, J. P., Cho, H., Park, J., Choi, M., ... & Kim, J. (2022). Quantum distributed deep learning architectures: Models, discussions, and applications. ICT Express.

Li, W., Lu, S., & Deng, D. L. (2021). Quantum federated learning through blind quantum computing. Science China Physics, Mechanics & Astronomy, 64(10), 1-8.

Ma, Y., Yu, D., Wu, T., & Wang, H. (2019). PaddlePaddle: An open-source deep learning platform from industrial practice. Frontiers of Data and Computing, 1(1), 105-115.

Meng, X., Bradley, J., Yavuz, B., Sparks, E., Venkataraman, S., Liu, D., ... & Talwalkar, A. (2016). Mllib: Machine learning in apache spark. The Journal of Machine Learning Research, 17(1), 1,235-1,241.

Moritz, P., Nishihara, R., Wang, S., Tumanov, A., Liaw, R., Liang, E., ... & Stoica, I. (2018). Ray: A distributed framework for emerging {AI} applications. In the 13th USENIX Symposium on Operating Systems Design and Implementation (OSDI 18) (pp. 561-577).

Orús, R. (2019). Tensor networks for complex quantum systems. Nature Reviews Physics, 1(9), 538-550.

Preskill, J. (2021). Quantum computing 40 years later. arXiv preprint arXiv:2106.10522.

Suzumura, T., Zhou, Y., Kawahara, R., Baracaldo, N., & Ludwig, H. (2022). Federated Learning for Collaborative Financial Crimes Detection. In Federated Learning (pp. 455-466). Springer, Cham.

Vincent, T., O'Riordan, L. J., Andrenkov, M., Brown, J., Killoran, N., Qi, H., & Dhand, I. (2022). Jet: Fast quantum circuit simulations with parallel task-based tensor-network contraction. Quantum, 6, 709.

Zaharia, M., Chowdhury, M., Franklin, M. J., Shenker, S., & Stoica, I. (2010). Spark: Cluster computing with working sets. In the 2nd USENIX Workshop on Hot Topics in Cloud Computing (HotCloud 10).

Zhao, X., Zhao, B., Wang, Z., Song, Z., & Wang, X. (2021). Practical distributed quantum information processing with LOCCNet. npj Quantum Information, 7(1), 1-7.

9

NISQ Quantum Hardware Roadmap

When using our implemented circuits for the different options we have explored, one key factor is the relevance of noise to obtain meaningful results. Along these lines, we would like to take you through the work you might need to consider while adapting to each specific hardware vendor, the specifics of those devices, and the bets some of them have taken for their scaling roadmap so that you can choose your companionship for this journey wisely.

Previously, we have seen how simulators can be used with classical devices, with those simulators being free of any kind of noise, as we explained in *Chapter 8*. We could also include the limitations and noise models of different types of quantum devices so that emulation can occur. So, even though classical resources will be used to perform our computations, the system will introduce errors and specific characteristics related to the qubit coupling of real devices so that the outcome will resemble the effect of running on the actual hardware.

In any case, both simulators and emulators are limited by classical hardware and its ability to imitate the dynamics of a quantum circuit. And even though performant means are available today, as we saw in the previous chapter, this limitation will lead us to the actual hardware at some point. In particular, when focusing on realistic applications, we may need several qubits to encode the problems at hand.

Currently, companies such as IBM and D-Wave provide quantum hardware services that are in the order of 433 qubits, as in the case of IBM's superconducting chips, and 5,000 qubits, as in the case of D-Wave's annealing machines. It is complicated to get close to emulating something in that order. Recently, researchers of the AWS Quantum Computing Center learned they could perform a 44-qubit simulation (`https://aws.amazon.com/blogs/hpc/simulating-44-qubit-quantum-circuits-using-aws-parallelcluster/`) while leveraging their distributed computing cloud resources. You can see the problems we might face classically while simulating circuits at these scales.

Therefore, to leverage the potential of current quantum devices, we will need to deal with noise and potential errors while executing a quantum circuit.

Each vendor has proposed a roadmap for their device evolution, which allows for lower-level analog encoding, scaling by classically communicating quantum devices, or even going from specific functionality to broader - scope digitized devices, as in the case of D-Wave. But why? What is the basis for those decisions and how does it affect our roadmap for quantum computing adoption?

To better understand those decisions and help us design a strategy accordingly, this chapter will dig deeper into the following topics:

- The difference between physical and logical qubits
- Fault-tolerance versus the NISQ era
- Mitigation and scaling
- Annealing processes and other types of computations

This topic is a highly technical one, so the main idea is to enable you to understand and be aware of the challenges and limitations you could face when betting for specific devices and providers.

Logical versus physical qubits

Classical computing resources deal with faulty physical means or errors generated by all kinds of sources. Error-correcting codes have been extensively studied (https://en.wikipedia. org/wiki/Error_correction_code) concerning those needs. Richard Hamming (1950) was the first to propose error-correcting codes in early 1950. Classical error correction codes use the concept of redundancy or information replication to spot inconsistencies in the outcome of a given channel or computation result. This way, the error can be detected and even corrected to recover the mitigated outcome.

Taking this to the quantum regime faces two main challenges. The no-cloning theorem (*Lindblad 1999*) states that there is no way we can copy a quantum state if this state is unknown. Knowing this state would mean measuring it, and this event will force the state to collapse and lose all its quantum information. These two challenges require inventive solutions to deal with errors within the quantum regime, given that classical protocol will not be possible given these conditions.

If we look at, for example, IBM's 127-qubit superconducting device (ibm_washington), we will notice that information is provided, other than the coupling map between different qubits, as shown in *Figure 9.1*:

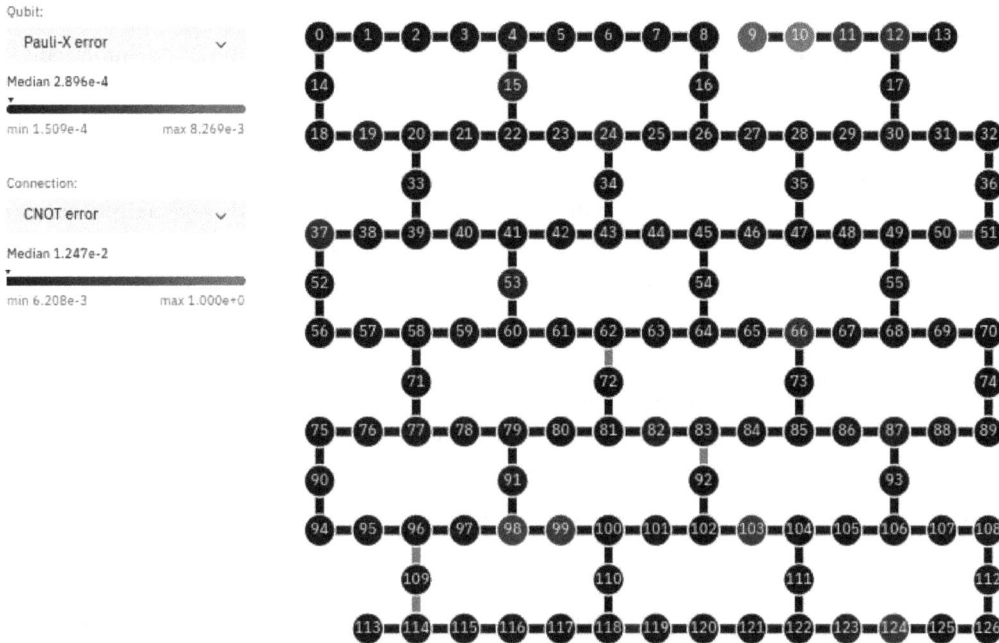

Figure 9.1 – Error map of IBM's Washington device equipped with 127 superconducting qubits (Eagle r1)

On the left-hand side of *Figure 9.1*, we can see the error rate of Pauli-X gates. It indicates how many times the effect of this operation does not affect the qubit it gets applied to. We can retrieve this information for each of the qubits in the device at a given time.

The other relevant piece of information in the preceding figure is the CNOT two-qubit operation, which is required for qubit-qubit interactions and generating entanglement. We can see that single qubit operations are at a reasonable median of a 10^{-4} error rate. Still, for the two-qubit entangling gates (CNOT), even though the median is low (10^{-2}), we can see it can raise to 100% probability in some couplings (look at qubits 96, 109, and 114), which means almost all entangling operations involving these three qubits will face failure by all means.

More importantly, we should consider how many of these instructions are involved in previously designed circuits. If we take the portfolio optimization use case we covered in *Chapter 5* as an example, each asset significantly increases the number of operations as we would need to cover its relationship with every other asset. More instructions will be needed to implement the circuit effectively. Circuit depth refers to the longest sequence of quantum gates (operations) that must be performed in sequence, from input to output. More formally, in a quantum circuit model, the depth of the circuit is the maximum number of time steps required to execute the circuit, assuming that gates acting on different qubits can be performed simultaneously. The deeper our circuits become, the more of these gates will be involved in the circuit. This fact creates a cumulative probability of noise being introduced into our system, due to which higher error rates will be faced. This is why the community focuses on creating shallower circuits to solve the same problems (*Bravyi et al. 2018*).

There are techniques to improve the effectiveness of our circuits that specifically deal with these sources of error. Ideally, we would like to abstract our circuits from the specific nature of the underlying hardware. From experience in the classical domain, error-detecting schemes and correcting codes have been proposed.

Let's consider the basic example of a bit-flip error or the Pauli-X error we mentioned previously. Consider the situation when a single qubit in the $|\psi\rangle$ state needs to be transmitted over a noisy channel, ϵ, which can also be pictured as the time taken for our circuit to run. The noise in this mean takes the effect of an X gate with probability p. Therefore, if we take that single qubit state over that mean, the final state we would obtain has a probability of $(1 - p)$ to be read as the expected outcome state, $|\psi\rangle$, and p for the flipped version, $(X|\psi\rangle)$.

Instead of using a single qubit to encode our state, we could replace the physical qubits (the actual hardware-based qubits) with a higher-level abstraction or logical version that utilizes three physical qubits instead.

The logical representation of our potential $|\psi\rangle$ state can be described with the following equations:

$$|0_L\rangle \equiv |000\rangle$$

$$|1_L\rangle \equiv |111\rangle$$

We can identify any bit flip by using an entangled state to describe our logical qubit. If we measured, for example, the $|010\rangle$ state at a given point in our channel, we would be able to detect the inconsistency of the state. It could only be one of those described previously, so something happened in the system. Given that we know the current status, we could recover the original state by using the redundant information in those extra physical qubits, known as the *syndrome qubits*:

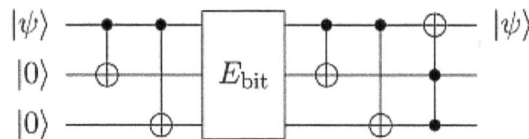

Figure 9.2 – Implementation of a 3-qubit physical code for bit flip detection and correction

This scheme performs that detection and correction over the initial $|\psi\rangle$ state as part of the qubit containing the information within the logical form. Error operations, which are represented by the $_{bit}$ block, can therefore be identified and even corrected if they can be mapped to operations, as we will see later. This was one of the first error-resilient codes proposed by Asher Peres (*Peres 1985, Peres 1996*).

These errors occur because qubits are not completely isolated from the environment. A quantum circuit, like the one shown previously, is hardly completely isolated from the environment, which is also a quantum mechanical system, so the interaction between the two can cause some unexpected action leading to a different set of operations affecting the initial state. This leads to four main actions that can occur inside our error block that could affect our perfect initial state:

- Nothing: $|\psi\rangle$
- Bit flip: $X|\psi\rangle$
- Phase flip: $Z|\psi\rangle$
- Both: $Y|\psi\rangle$

In 1995, Peter Shor (*Shor 1995*) suggested using 9 physical qubits so that any arbitrary change would be detected and corrected, extending previous works on single qubit bit flip and sign changes. *Figure 9.3* shows the underlying circuit for one of those logical qubits following Shor's scheme. The E block points to where the error might take place:

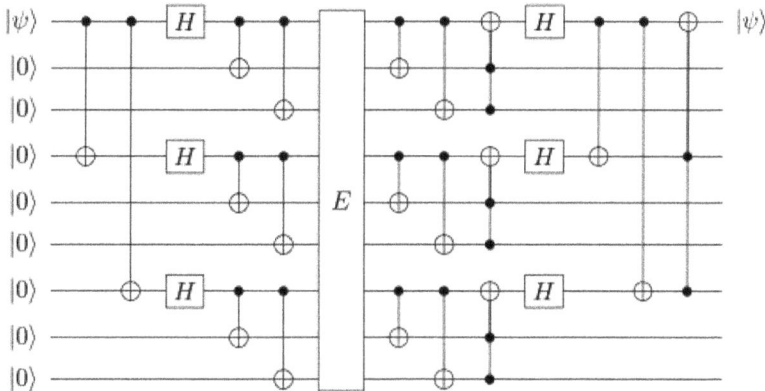

Figure 9.3 – Implementation of 9-qubit physical code for bit flip detection and correction (Shor)

This field of study has been extended to the current status, where some really interesting techniques have appeared. Surface codes (*Fowler 2012*), from the original work on toric codes (*Bravyi and Kitaev 1998*), have recently emerged, trying to create a more generic approach to these techniques on a 2D lattice setup. Indubitably a research field will be enabling agnostic algorithmic setups once it is fully developed and quantum hardware can deliver the required number of physical qubits.

Of course, this takes us to the limit on how many physical qubits we would require to implement a logical qubit that relies upon all the interferences and error sources a realistic system might face. Error-resilient quantum computation might require quite a few physical resources. It is suggested that the order of physical qubits is placed around 1,000 qubits per logical qubit, although this figure may vary for specific implementations.

Once again quoting Peter Shor and his famous algorithm for prime factorization, to effectively decode an RSA 2,048-bit integer in 8 hours (*Gidney & Ekerå 2021*), we would need to provide a quantum machine in the order of 20 million physical qubits due to the usage of logical qubits to overcome hardware-generated errors. From this, it is evident that we are far from a realistic realization of said approaches under the current noise regime and physical constraints.

The use of logical qubits for circuit implementation also poses a challenge in terms of the scalability of resources. Blindly trying to apply them will force hardware providers to scale up to the million-qubit regime, which seems a long-term bet, even if it's feasible for some of the currently available hardware (*Fellous-Asiani 2021*).

Some providers believe this is the approach to follow, which is why their product roadmaps aim to deliver millions of qubits, despite the decrease in the fidelity of operations it might create when working at larger scales. Google is one of those providers that is aiming to build six-figure qubit devices, as evidenced by their roadmap (`https://quantumai.google/learn/map`).

Fault-tolerant approaches

Extending the notion of quantum error detection and correction, fault-tolerant quantum computation broadens the scope of some of the techniques known in classical computation. A fully fault-tolerant system (*Paler and Devitt, 2015*) should look for errors at the physical qubit level and system level so that our circuits can run, even though they would need to switch hardware instances at a given point in time. This general overview is a key factor when we want to leap from theory to actual field usage for the techniques and examples shown in previous chapters.

As we already discussed, some errors in the quantum regime can be detected and corrected. Other errors may come from systematic defects, as is the case of readout errors, which we will discuss later. But some errors will come from the fact that these machines may fail at a service level. Most of the quantum devices that are used are at a laboratory status, so they may have lower availability than we are used to in other classical services.

We will experience queuing times and non-operational periods during which these quantum devices will not be that useful from an operational perspective

	Quantinuum Quantinuum	Quantum Computing	Azure Quantum Credits	✓	Degraded	
	quantinuum.hqs-lt-s1 ☐				Degraded	<1m
	quantinuum.hqs-lt-s1-apival ☐				Available	<1m
	quantinuum.hqs-lt-s2 ☐				Unavailable	N/A ◷
	quantinuum.hqs-lt-s2-apival ☐				Available	<1m
	quantinuum.hqs-lt-s1-sim ☐				Available	<1m
	quantinuum.hqs-lt-s2-sim ☐				Available	<1m

Name		Qubits	QV	CLOPS	Status	Total pending jobs
ibm_washington	Exploratory	127	64	850	● Online - Queue paused	998
ibmq_montreal		27	128	2K	● Online	85
ibmq_mumbai		27	128	1.8K	● Online	256
ibm_cairo		27	64	2.4K	● Online	18
ibm_auckland	Exploratory	27	64	2.4K	● Online - Queue paused	0
ibm_hanoi		27	64	2.3K	● Online - Queue paused	704
ibmq_toronto		27	32	1.8K	● Online	50
ibmq_guadalupe		16	32	2.4K	● Online - Queue paused	114
ibm_perth		7	32	2.9K	● Online - Queue paused	33
ibm_lagos		7	32	2.7K	● Online	47

Figure 9.4 – Availability and queuing time on Azure and IBM cloud services

Productive environments need to be aware of the problems the whole chain of actions may entail, from data collection to results to preprocessing. Specific problems may also exploit the need for bigger systems that are often scarcer and, therefore, harder to get computing time available.

In some cases, we might be able to fit our problems into different devices to parallelize the workload. Still, those different devices will come with different error mitigation and correction techniques, leading to small discrepancies. This makes distributed quantum computation (*Häner et al. 2021*) a field needed but still in its infancy.

One key requirement to get all the advantages would be a technology capable of interconnecting those devices without losing the quantum advantage. This could be achieved by using fiber optics and Bell states as communicating states, entering the promising land of quantum communications and the quantum internet (*Kimble 2018*).

On a more practical note, providers such as IBM have proposed using the existing communication networks and knowledge from classical distributed systems to not achieve the theoretical gain a quantum networking system could provide but surpass the barrier of single-chip computations that nowadays limit the capacity of our exercises.

Circuit knitting

Circuit knitting was proposed recently (*Piveteau and Sutter 2022*), given the complexity of providing larger chips without introducing large amounts of errors. Instead of aiming for larger, fully quantum chips, you could think of distributed resource systems where these instances are classically connected.

This type of architecture has been exploited in the field of distributed GPU computing (*Gu et al. 2019*), distributed computing for big data (*Zaharia et al. 2012*), and even edge computation (*Shi 2016*). However, it does not entail a paradigm shift from classical to quantum as all these resources work, let's say, at the same physical level.

The main difference between those approaches and circuit knitting is the need to split a quantum circuit that would classically communicate with other parts of the circuit. Assuming there is a group of gates that could minimize the cut between two groups of more densely connected operations, you could split the circuit into two groups, replacing those quantum interactions connecting the two groups by classical means, as shown in *Figure 9.5*, where two CNOTs can be reshaped into two splittable circuits (classically connected):

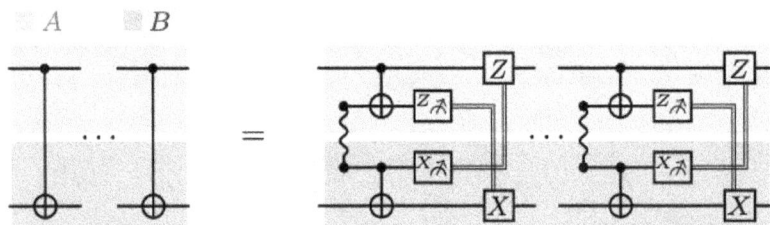

Figure 9.5 – Two CNOT gates split into blocks of classically connected circuits

You need to reflect on how the quantum advantage is compromised when taking the complexity of quantum states to classical bits and bytes and back again. You must also reflect on the ability to split the initial design into blocks of densely and weakly connected circuits.

For sparsely connected examples, it could be that these schemes provide a significant advantage. Still, some of the examples we have seen require all-to-all connectivity between qubits, making it more complicated to split and not lose the actual computational gain quantum hardware aims for.

Error mitigation

Some common sources of error can be more systematically tackled since measuring the classical outcome of quantum hardware is not free of errors. Luckily, this type of error can be tackled by observing the common errors that are made upon readout and compensating for post-processing the outcome.

If we look into our IBM Quantum Experience service once more, we could request the readout error for a given device. In *Figure 9.6*, we can observe how any operation that's done on qubits 10 and 15, upon measurement, could be misinterpreted:

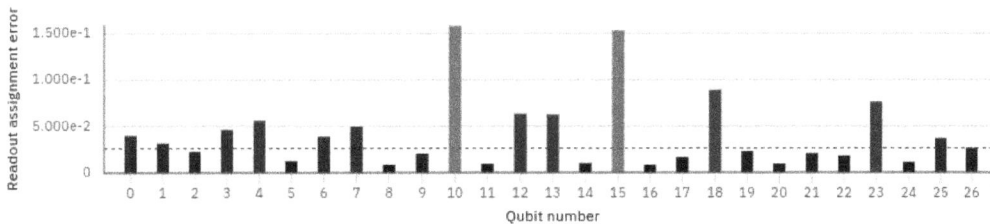

Figure 9.6 – Readout error on IBM's Toronto device (27 superconducting qubits Falcon r4)

These statistics can be derived by the simple act of placing an operation whose outcome is known (for example, $X|\psi\rangle$) and recording the discrepancies upon measuring it for a significant number of tryouts. If those statistics are known, you can compensate for the measurements that are obtained for an experiment by knowing this systematic error.

Let's consider a simple scenario. Imagine we encode all possible combinations on a two-qubit case separately. These states are prepared using an X gate on the corresponding qubit, and we measure the following outcome for 10,000 shots in each case:

```
Prepared state: 00 Measured:          {'01': 102, '11': 3, '10': 97, '00':
9798}
Prepared state: 01 Measured:becomes   {'00': 92, '11': 102, '01':
9806}
Prepared state: 10 Measured:becomes   {'01': 5, '00': 99, '11':
106, '10': 9790}
Prepared state: 11 Measured:becomes   {'01': 99, '10': 97, '11':
9804}
```

We can see that the output is almost always right, measuring close to 9,800 times out of the 10,000 circuit runs in the state we were aiming to prepare by applying X gates. But it is not a perfect statistic as, more or less, 1-2% of the time, we get an unexpected bitstring upon measurement (that is, measuring 11 when we prepared the $|00\rangle$ state). What would you think if, for the device we used in the previous experiment, we got the following output on 100 shots?

```
{'01': 2, '11': 52, '10': 2, '00': 46}
```

Half of the time, we obtained 11 bit strings and 00 for the other half in some minor cases, where we measured 01 and 10. We already know that the device has a 1-2% error rate of flipping qubit states from our previous exercise. So, could we assume a superposition between the $|00\rangle$ and $|11\rangle$ states? Maybe a Bell state?

By understanding the systematic error a given device introduces compared to the ideal representation of operations when preparing the state, we could characterize its error and mitigate it by the inverse effect. By setting a matrix conversion that would do this operation mapping prepared states with measured states, we could error correct upon measurement of every experiment done on a device.

Qiskit already provides some of these functionalities within its experimental package:

```
from qiskit_experiments.library import CorrelatedReadoutError
qubits = [0,1]
num_qubits = len(qubits)
exp = CorrelatedReadoutError(qubits)
for c in exp.circuits():
    print(c)
```

The preceding code will plot the circuits that have been created to calibrate the readout error as shown in *Figure 9.7*.

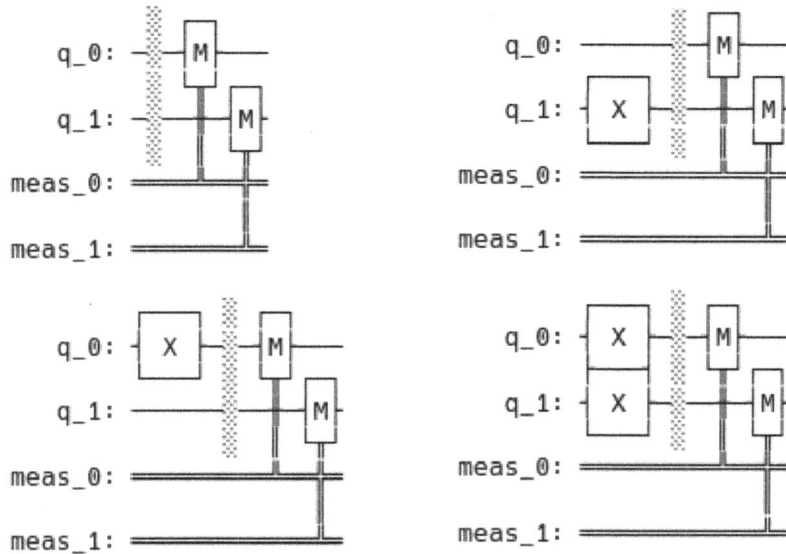

Figure 9.7 – Calibration circuits for a two-qubit device

In this manner, by just invoking the calibration upon a noisy backend, we would get the matrix that's needed to mitigate the readout error.

As an example, if we took the case of a |00⟩ state on the ibmq_lima device, which would be like the first circuit shown in the preceding plots, we would expect only a 00 bitstring to be read. However, we would see that its plot would differ from the expected outcome, plotting some unwanted or unexpected bitstrings:

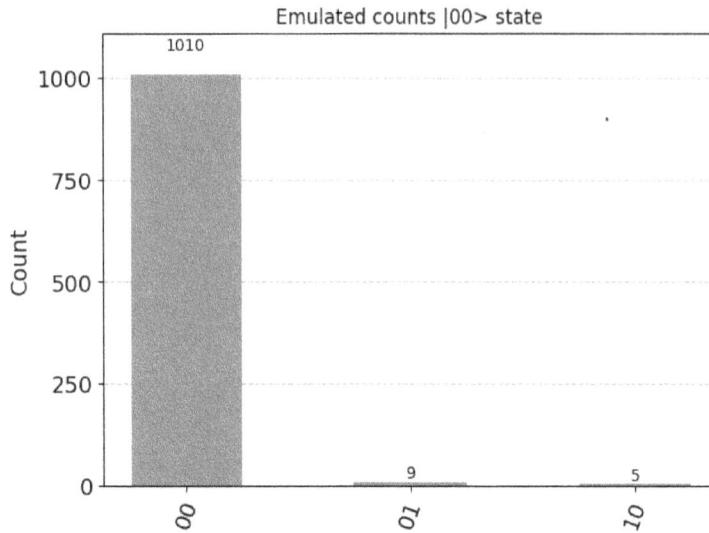

Figure 9.8 – Estimation of the |00⟩ state after 1,024 shots

Here, we can calibrate the systematic error on the device by using the previous circuits shown in *Figure 9.7*:

```
result = exp.run(emulator)
mitigator = result.analysis_results(0).value
result.figure(0)
```

By doing this, we would obtain a matrix similar to the following that applies to previous counts of measured bitstrings. By doing this, it would be able to correct this device's systematic error upon measurement. By plotting this matrix, we would see that apart from obvious maps between prepared and measured states shown in black, gray areas appear as well, representing the transition some states make from the prepared state to the measured one. This is what is called a mitigation matrix as it allows us to map the systematic transitions that occur between states. It can reverse or at least compensate for the effects caused by errors occurring within the device once applied after the measurement:

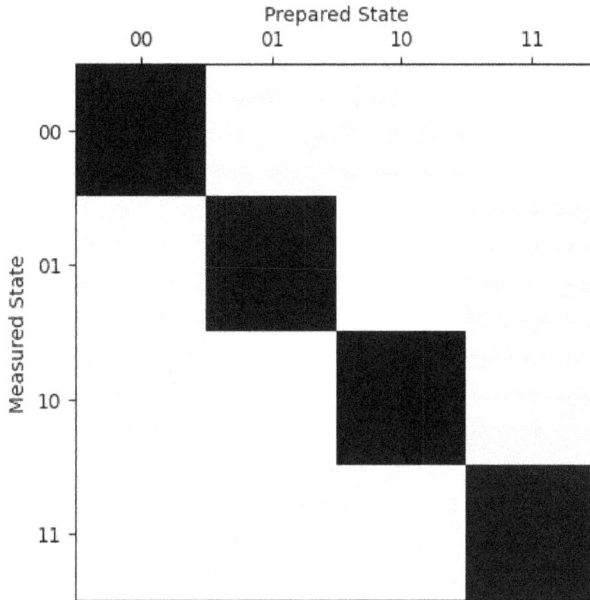

Figure 9.9 – Mitigation matrix for the |00⟩ state

This way, we could compare the plots showing the mitigated and unmitigated results. This matrix is going to be able to extract a probability distribution with negative probability values so that, once it's applied to the outcome probabilities of bitstring upon measurement, the compensation of it will plot the quasi-probabilities of measurements. Here, quasi-probability refers to the relaxation over conventional probability distributions as negative values may be reflected in the outcome:

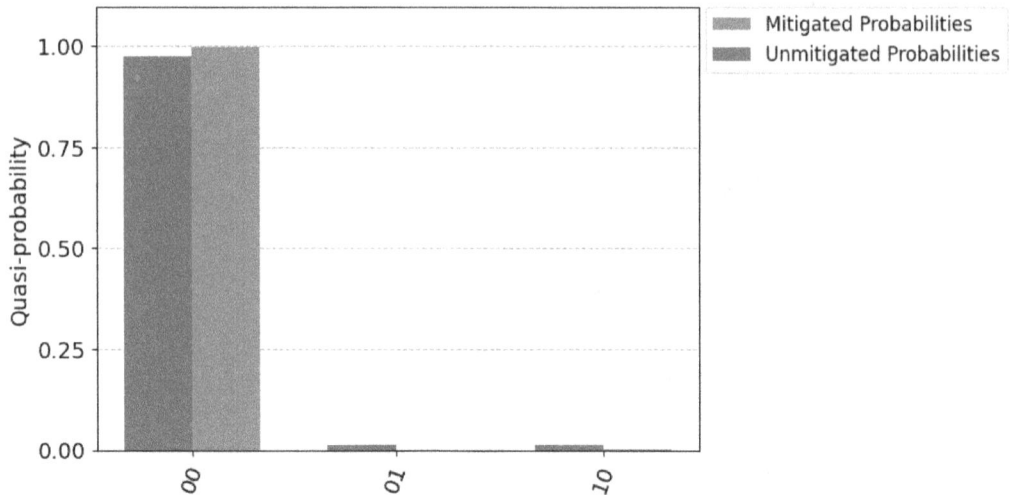

Figure 9.10 – Probability to obtain the state |00⟩ with and without error mitigation

Note that this technique will not play well when scaling to bigger devices (more qubits) as we would need to characterize all possible combinations for the number of qubits available in the system to obtain such statistics. That is why different methods for error mitigation on large-scale devices (devices with many qubits) have been suggested that will perform much better at those scales. Let's look at some of those early-stage research areas digging deeper into error mitigation:

- **Probabilistic error cancellation** (*Pashayan et al. 2015*) is one technique that tries to characterize the outcome probability of ideal gate sets, so this can be considered an error cancellation technique for a more general case. The concept holds the same description as the error mitigation described above, where an outcome probability wants to be set and corrected for a specific device, but in this case Monte Carlo averaged probabilities are used.

- **Zero noise extrapolation** (*Giurgica-Tiron et al. 2020*) is more suited to when the expectation value is used. The error is modeled by running the hardware and increasing its noise factor (λ) so that a curve can be fitted. If hardware noise is set to $\lambda = 1$, then the model can be used to estimate the expectation value at $\lambda = 0$, since this is our error-mitigated expectation value.

- **Dynamical decoupling** (*Viola et al. 1999*) is a technique that takes place almost at the lowest level of the hardware. Each gate we have talked about takes a different physical meaning. In the case of IBM, for example, these are pulses that, depending on the gate, could have a longer or shorter duration (depending on the operation being performed). Given these disparities between the length of the instructions, when certain qubits idle for a while, other qubits are acted on. These idle qubits are prone to errors due to interactions with the environment. By introducing sequences of operations that would not affect the outcome of the problem, we can keep those qubits active, diminishing the idling error that's generated.

If you do not want to go that far in terms of the electronics of the hardware being used, the Mitiq framework has enabled a digital dynamical decoupling package so that we can abstract from the complexities of those DD schemes (`https://mitiq.readthedocs.io/en/stable/guide/ddd-5-theory.html#common-examples-of-ddd-sequences` and (`https://mitiq.readthedocs.io/en/stable/guide/ddd-3-options.html`).

Given the complexity and specific knowledge required to apply most of the previously described techniques, many companies have included a hardware/software middle layer in their roadmap that takes care of these techniques. Companies such as IBM have included these techniques within their recently released Qiskit Runtime or partnered with technology providers such as Riverlane, who aim to build the perfect abstraction layer between algorithm developers and hardware providers.

Some important changes will need to be made in the medium term regarding how these errors are handled and how users abstract from them. However, at the time of writing, some attention is needed from early adopters to select the set of techniques that will allow them to squeeze the most out of hardware providers.

Annealers and other devices

We have mostly talked about digital quantum computers, which are computers that use the abstraction of gates to operate on qubits. But quantum annealers such as those used in *Chapters 5* to *7* (D-Wave's quantum annealers) are also subject to errors and problems when dealing with larger-scale problems, mainly when increasing the number of assets involved in our operations.

If we take the example of portfolio optimization, D-Wave provides up to 5,000 qubit chips, which could potentially mean up to 5,000 asset portfolios having to be optimized.

Annealers require problems to be encoded or mapped onto their hardware, which involves representing the assets using the QUBO or Ising models and assigning them to specific qubits on their chips. Then, relationships between those variables are mapped to the couplings between qubits. Those links will carry the parameters associated with a given pair, which is often represented by J_{ij} in the canonical form of an Ising type of problem, as shown here:

$$H(\sigma) = - \sum_{\langle ij \rangle} J_{ij} \sigma_i \sigma_j - \mu \sum_j h_j \sigma_j,$$

Here, σ_j will be the variable that's mapped to a qubit in the device. This linking cannot always be present as the device itself may lack some of those connections in an all-to-all connected problem.

In fact, in 2019, Venturelli and Kondratyev were able to embed up to 60 asset portfolios in a DW 2000Q system thanks to them leveraging minor-embedding compilation techniques. This allowed them to place a 1D string in all assets so that they could be placed on a Chimera chip. Due to the embedding technique's overhead, this was the maximum they could achieve, even for a 2,000-qubit system. This limitation is visible if you look at the chip architecture in *Figure 9.11*:

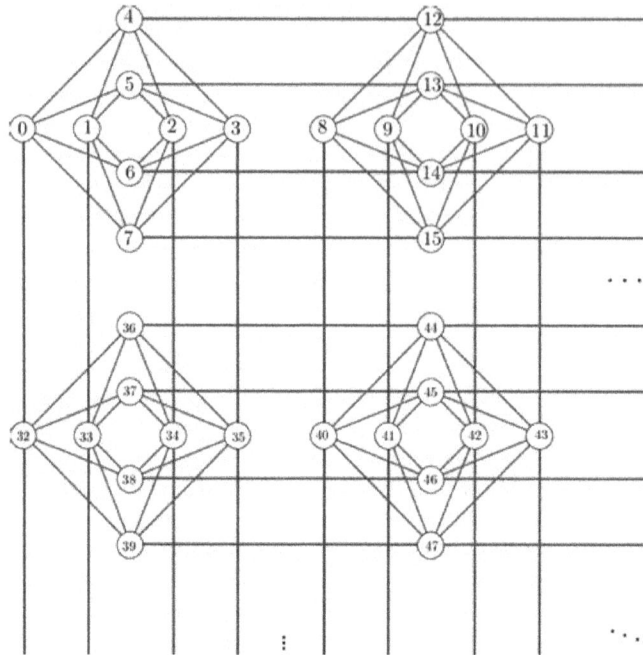

Figure 9.11 – D-Wave's Chimera chip's qubit architecture and coupling map (32 qubits square)

In the preceding Chimera graph, we can see how each qubit is directly connected to another 5 or 6 qubits in general. This means that if a qubit representing a variable requires more connections than the ones it has, you would need to chain more than one qubit instance as they would represent the same variable of the problem – hence the name chain, which means two qubits behave as a single unit. That way, by losing a single coupler, a qubit could almost double its connection capacity.

This is what D-Wave refers to as a chain. This is established by setting a strong coupling between those two units so that they will return the same value (remember, they refer to the same qubit). In this case, those two physical qubits represent (or should represent) the same logical unit or qubit.

However, this chain can be broken. Generally, the strength of those couplings is higher than those referenced by the specific problem being embedded. However, they could return different values upon readout, meaning the chain was broken, and the obtained solution may not be valid according to our problem definition. To dig deeper into this concept of chains, D-Wave's documentation offers plenty of information on it (`https://docs.ocean.dwavesys.com/en/stable/concepts/embedding.html`). In the end, many of the limitations we find in the general cases for quantum devices can also be found in specific machines, as in the case of quantum annealers.

Summary

In this chapter, we explored the challenges that working on real hardware may pose. Depending on the specific nature of the hardware, regardless of whether it is purpose-specific, as in the case of quantum annealers, or one of the many implementations of digital quantum computers, these concepts are still hard to omit.

Being aware that the mapping for a given problem is being done at a hardware level, paying attention to which qubits are used, their associated error, and how this will be reflected in the outcome, you can implement countermeasures so that the results still offer enough resolution. That way, the advantage that's expected from quantum computation can still be significant.

By understanding the different challenges and how they may affect a given problem setup, you can choose the appropriate hardware that can better accommodate the problem.

Annealers can be used for large problems but not as large as you might think in terms of embedding restrictions and the type of problems this may solve. D-Wave is still in the order of thousands of qubits compared to other providers, and it is likely to provide close to 8,000 qubits by 2023/2024. But still, this might not be sufficient to encode some of the problems at the scale that the industry requires.

Digital quantum hardware comes with different types of physical implementations to choose from, from superconducting chips such as the ones offered by IBM to Cold Atoms by QuEra or Topological Qubits, Microsoft's bet.

Undoubtedly, each technology will offer different coupling architectures or error levels for operation fidelity or readout accuracy. Having a minimal understanding of how this can be leveraged will be critical in the short term, so it might be necessary for the adventurous to educate themselves on those hardware specifications. Luckily, the active effort done by IBM on both Qiskit Runtime and circuit knitting techniques may soon abstract you from needing to understand how to optimally embed a problem into your device. However, it is still in its infancy, looking to provide significant advances while trying to come close to the numbers available at D-Wave (`https://www.ibm.com/quantum/roadmap`).

Google is also continuing at a steady pace, focusing on enlarging their devices to the range of millions of qubits, surpassing competitors, and trying to achieve the scale required for error-corrected qubits. So far, they have progressed at a steady pace but to work with their existing devices, you need to make it onto the list of privileged collaborators (`https://quantumai.google/hardware`).

Lastly, ion-trap providers such as IonQ and Quantinuum are focusing on providing the best hardware available. Their quality is a major milestone for them providing consistent improvements in the number of operations they can put together while providing meaningful results (`https://www.quantinuum.com/news/quantum-volume-reaches-5-digits-for-the-first-time-5-perspectives-on-what-it-means-for-quantum-computing`).

You should never forget that this is an actively researched field where scientific breakthroughs are expected. It could very well happen that some limitations on scalability-specific technologies may be solved in the next decade, so do not hesitate to experiment with all those different options so that you're prepared. Thanks to cloud service providers, this is easier than ever. One important key to partnering or betting on an appropriate provider is to balance the size of your problems, connectivity, and accuracy to provide meaningful results. This will most likely drive your decisions in the near future.

Further reading

It is worth highlighting that the techniques we discussed in this chapter require less technical detail to grasp their advantage fully. Interestingly, the work by Huang et al. 2022 cites the whole path from algorithm definition to lower-level action on devices, with some detailed information on how previously discussed error mitigation techniques can be used:

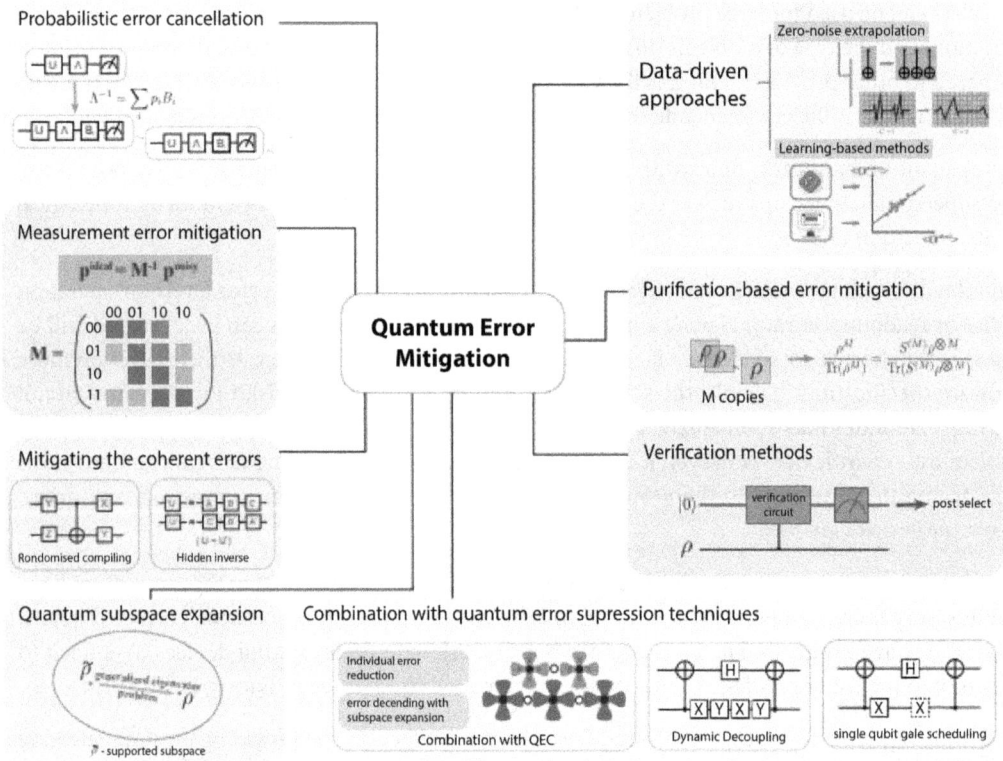

Figure 9.12 – Landscape of quantum error mitigation techniques

You can also benefit from the implementations available in the open source community so that you can apply them without requiring deep technical knowledge to code what can be found in the literature. It is pretty common nowadays that an implemented version of the published results is made available to the public.

Qiskit, one of the most mature frameworks for quantum computing, has extensive documentation and practical tutorials that will make understanding those concepts much easier.

Hardware-related tutorials and lower-level experiments, such as the ones we have tackled in this chapter, can be found in their experimental library documentation: `https://qiskit.org/documentation/experiments/tutorials/index.html`.

Another interesting resource is the Mitiq package, which is supported by the non-profit organization Unitary Fund. This resource not only implements some of the already discussed techniques in different hardware and cloud service providers but also offers extensive documentation and a vibrant community that you can join to discuss any topic related to efficient quantum computing: `https://mitiq.readthedocs.io/en/stable/index.html`.

References

Bravyi, S. B., & Kitaev, A. Y. (1998). Quantum codes on a lattice with boundary. arXiv preprint quant-ph/9811052.

Bravyi, S., Gosset, D., & König, R. (2018). Quantum advantage with shallow circuits. Science, 362(6412), 308-311.

Fellous-Asiani, M., Chai, J. H., Whitney, R. S., Auffèves, A., & Ng, H. K. (2021). Limitations in quantum computing from resource constraints. PRX Quantum, 2(4), 040335.

Fowler, A. G., Mariantoni, M., Martinis, J. M., & Cleland, A. N. (2012). Surface codes: Towards practical large-scale quantum computation. Physical Review A, 86(3), 032324.

Gidney, C., & Ekerå, M. (2021). How to factor 2,048-bit RSA integers in 8 hours using 20 million noisy qubits. Quantum, 5, 433.

Giurgica-Tiron, T., Hindy, Y., LaRose, R., Mari, A., & Zeng, W. J. (2020, October). Digital zero noise extrapolation for quantum error mitigation. In 2020 IEEE International Conference on Quantum Computing and Engineering (QCE) (pp. 306-316). IEEE.

Gu, J., Chowdhury, M., Shin, K. G., Zhu, Y., Jeon, M., Qian, J., ... & Guo, C. (2019). Tiresias: A {GPU} cluster manager for distributed deep learning. In 16th USENIX Symposium on Networked Systems Design and Implementation (NSDI 19) (pp. 485-500).

Hamming, R. W. (1950). Error detecting and error correcting codes. The Bell system technical journal, 29(2), 147-160.

Häner, T., Steiger, D. S., Hoefler, T., & Troyer, M. (2021, November). Distributed quantum computing with qmpi. In Proceedings of the International Conference for High Performance Computing, Networking, Storage and Analysis (pp. 1-13).

Huang, H. L., Xu, X. Y., Guo, C., Tian, G., Wei, S. J., Sun, X., ... & Long, G. L. (2022). Near-Term Quantum Computing Techniques: Variational Quantum Algorithms, Error Mitigation, Circuit Compilation, Benchmarking, and Classical Simulation. arXiv preprint arXiv:2211.08737.

Kimble, H. J. (2008). The quantum internet. Nature, 453(7198), 1023-1030.

Lindblad, G. (1999). A general no-cloning theorem. Letters in Mathematical Physics, 47(2), 189-196.

Paler, A., & Devitt, S. J. (2015). An introduction to fault-tolerant quantum computing. arXiv preprint arXiv:1508.03695.

Pashayan, H., Wallman, J. J., & Bartlett, S. D. (2015). Estimating outcome probabilities of quantum circuits using quasiprobabilities. Physical review letters, 115(7), 070501.

Peres, A. (1985). Reversible logic and quantum computers. Physical review A, 32(6), 3266.

Peres, A. (1996). Error correction and symmetrization in quantum computers. arXiv preprint quant-ph/9611046.

Piveteau, C., & Sutter, D. (2022). Circuit knitting with classical communication. arXiv preprint arXiv:2205.00016.

Shi, W., & Dustdar, S. (2016). The promise of edge computing. Computer, 49(5), 78-81.

Shor, P. W. (1995). Scheme for reducing decoherence in quantum computer memory. Physical review A, 52(4), R2493.

Venturelli, D., & Kondratyev, A. (2019). Reverse quantum annealing approach to portfolio optimization problems. Quantum Machine Intelligence, 1(1), 17-30.

Viola, L., Knill, E., & Lloyd, S. (1999). Dynamical decoupling of open quantum systems. Physical Review Letters, 82(12), 2417.

Zaharia, M., Chowdhury, M., Das, T., Dave, A., Ma, J., Mccauley, M., ... & Stoica, I. (2012). Fast and interactive analytics over Hadoop data with Spark. Usenix Login, 37(4), 45-51.

10

Business Implementation

Zapata Computing issued its first annual report in December 2021. They reported the results of a poll of over 300 leaders (CTOs, CIOs, C-level, and VP-level executives). Even if you remove the possible bias of a quantum ecosystem participant such as Zapata Computing, the result still gives useful and interesting information about how quantum computing is used.

Even though some businesses have wanted to use quantum technologies for a while, the bridge between them and quantum hardware hasn't been finished. Software applications should be that bridge to connect the two worlds. According to a report by Zapata Computing, 74% of respondents agree that companies that don't adopt quantum computing solutions will fall behind soon. Additionally, 29% of respondents are already in the early or advanced stages of adopting quantum computing, and another 40% was expected to follow in 2022. Also, 96% of the executives who were asked agreed they needed a reliable partner or vendor to help them overcome the quantum barrier.

On the other hand, the Capgemini Research Institute issued a report titled *Quantum technologies: How to prepare your organization for a quantum advantage now in 2022*. One of the most important insights was that 23% of firms are utilizing quantum technology or plan to do so. However, many have yet to undergo testing or piloting. Also, according to a Goldman Sachs prediction from 2021, quantum computing could begin to yield a quantum advantage in practical financial applications within the next five years, and the majority of surveys indicate an expectation of practical and commercial usage of quantum solutions (in particular use cases) within the next three to five years. Of the 857 organizations surveyed by Capgemini, 10% of them anticipate that quantum technology will be accessible for use in at least one important commercial application within the next three years.

There are dozens of reports, such as the aforementioned ones, plus others from McKinsey, BCG, Accenture, and EY, that show how companies are igniting their quantum journeys in different ways. Most of them have also encountered some main obstacles, which are typically as follows:

1. The complexity of IT integration
2. Security concerns
3. Lack of advanced internal capabilities
4. Lack of expertise or talent

5. Lack of clear use cases

6. Internal skepticism

7. Lack of budget or funding for these initiatives

8. Lack of market maturity on hardware

The report *The Road to Quantum Supremacy* from Quantum.Tech and Honeywell, in collaboration, has a few more things to say about the difficulties of putting quantum computing solutions into place. They conducted a poll of 100 quantum program leaders. This survey asked, *What is your greatest impediment to using quantum technologies?* The majority of respondents cited *Cost* (23%), *Establishing the Right KPIs* (18%), *Convincing Stakeholders* (13%), *Unknown Value/ROI of Technology* (12%), and *Fear of Failure* (5%) as the most significant challenges.

As previously stated, the market appears to be moving toward a quick-wins requirement for quantum computing and attempting to overcome some of the barriers mentioned in various reports. Quantum software development can be the key to partially unlocking these challenges. We previously knew that investment in quantum technologies increased between 2018 and 2021, but it now appears to be slowing down and undergoing a transition as well. In 2021, the direct investment in quantum computers was $1.67 billion, and the direct investment in software was $168 million, representing 77% and 7% respectively of the total. In 2022, there was $942 million in quantum computers (45%) and $785 million in software (38%). The total investment in 2022 is only 93% of what it was in 2021. This is a well-known slowdown in the market (*The Quantum Insider, December 2022*).

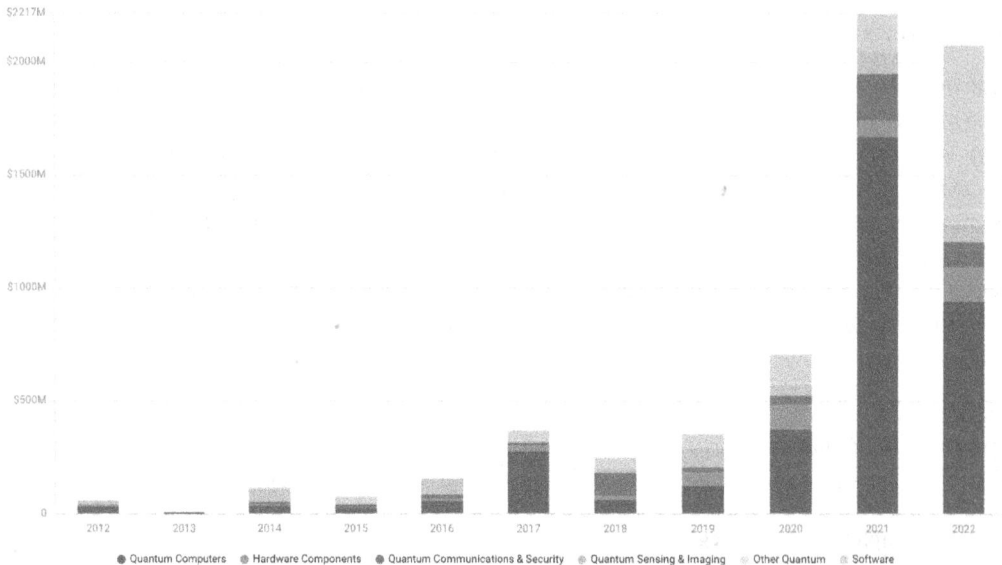

Figure 10.1 – Investment evolution in quantum technologies (The Quantum Insider, December 2022)

The market is reaching the point where applying quantum software to real-world problems and demonstrating more quantifiable and wider advantages may be more important than discussing them. Researchers and quantum startup teams are always searching for examples of how the features of these systems might be applied in the current commercial environment. This can raise investment and clarify what can be accomplished within a few months, years, or decades.

This chapter will walk you through some use cases and strategies to overcome most of the challenges and myths associated with quantum computing implementations in financial institutions:

- The quantum workforce barrier
- Infrastructure integration barrier
- Identifying the potentiality of quantum advantage with QML
- Funding or budgeting issues
- Market maturity, hype, and skepticism
- Roadmap for early adoption of quantum computing for financial institutions
- Quantum managers' training

The quantum workforce barrier

The development of human resources to operate quantum computers is an important aspect of the growth and adoption of quantum technologies. As quantum computers become more prevalent, there will be a growing demand for professionals skilled in working with these systems.

Organizations may invest in training programs and educational initiatives to develop these skills. These programs may include specialized courses in quantum computing principles and algorithms, training in programming languages and software development tools, and cloud infrastructure implementations that work with quantum computers.

In a report developed by QTEdu and Quantum Flagship and funded by the European Union, called *Qualification Profiles for Quantum Technologies* from 2022, several types of **quantum positions** are mentioned. Some are new roles that have arisen, since this technology and market are evolving. Of course, engineers are requested for hardware and software development, but the Quantum technology strategist position appears in the middle of highly specialized profiles. The report defines these strategists this way:

Such a person who has explored all basic quantum technologies and at least heard about more specific aspects, hardware, and enabling technologies. Through their education, they have explored the basic concepts, heard about the physical foundations of quantum technologies, and closely linked these to the application-oriented aspects.

The use of simulators can represent a good cost-efficient option, since the quantum algorithms can run faster (in the case of a small number of qubits), are cheaper, can respond in a real-time manner, and can do so without errors (depending on the setup and the parameters that the user wants to apply). The training process of QML models in a real quantum computer can take days to finish due to queue waiting times for each job or training iteration, compared with a simulator that, for the same challenge, could take a couple of hours.

Another advantage of using simulators is that the software will be ready in any case for future improvements with the quantum computers since most of the quantum SDKs (e.g., Qiskit or PennyLane) can handle the change of *backends* easily. So, switching between simulators and official quantum hardware can be as simple as adapting a couple of lines.

With regards to simulators, there are several options, but the most popular and easiest to use are the ones integrated into well-known clouds. AWS Braket, Azure Quantum, Google (Quantum AI), and IBM Quantum are the most straightforward to be used since they are available under classical companies' infrastructure. In Amazon Web Services, the braket_sv, braket_dm, SV1, DM1, and TN1 simulators can be found; in IBM, statevector, stabilizer, extended stabilizer, MPS, and QASM. Google also has an interesting approach, providing qsim (an optimized quantum circuit simulator) and the **Quantum Virtual Machine** (**QVM**), which emulates a Google quantum computer. Depending on the type of simulator, users can execute circuits with a handful number of qubits up to even more than a 100 (in the case of MPS).

When a universal quantum computer is not available, and optimization is the problem to solve, quantum annealers can be the best option. This technology can be considered more mature since companies such as D-Wave have spent more than 20 years exploring solutions using a non-circuit-based QC and they are the first to commercialize this technology.

For example, D-Wave's machine has a set of solvers carrying out the quantum annealing process. Similar approaches have been used in literature when dealing with large and complex optimization problems inspired by the annealing processes in metallurgy (*Bertsimas and Tsitsiklis, 1993*).

Following the adiabatic process, D-Wave's machine starts on an already known problem, the Transverse Field Ising model, and little by little, modifies its shape toward a target problem known to be more complicated. The overall idea is that if the machine starts with the solution of a simpler problem and we slowly change its shape towards a more complicated one, at the end of the process, the machine will have evolved from the solution for an easy problem to one of the complicated problems that users need to be solved.

Given that the machine is already encoded to follow that procedure, the user interacting with it would only be required to provide a target problem so that the D-Wave's machine can produce its magic. This is the case, for example, with the portfolio optimization problem. By providing a mathematical description of how the assets in our portfolio interact with one another, the D-Wave machine is meant to follow that process.

D-Wave is not the only resource in its category, as more and more, other companies are broadening the options in this spectrum. This is the case of Fujitsu's Digital Quantum Annealer (`https://www.fujitsu.com/global/services/business-services/digital-annealer/index.html`). The trick here is that it is quantum-inspired, meaning that classical computing technology is used following quantum-inspired processes (such as the quantum annealing one) but, as it happens with quantum simulators above, makes this technology available to a broader audience and in most of the cases much more cost-effective.

Case study

CaixaBank is one of the largest financial institutions in Spain. It is composed of a variety of different verticals in the financial sector, but one of the most relevant business units for the group is their insurance branch, VidaCaixa.

Part of their activity revolves around selecting the best investment portfolio to increase profitability. We covered the case of how this could be done in *Chapter 5*. Still, it is interesting to see a real-life example where using a D-Wave Hybrid solver (a combination of classical and quantum solver), they were able to produce portfolios much faster (hours to minutes), saving up to 90% computing time, increasing 10% the **Internal Rate of Return** (**IRR**), and even being able to pose more complex constraints than they were able to before (`https://www.caixabank.com/comunicacion/noticia/caixabank-group-d-wave-collaborate-on-innovative-new-quantum-applications-for-finance-industry_en.html?id=43342`). The idea of the hybrid solver is indeed a sensible one, as classical resources are used where they are proven to be more reliable. In contrast, quantum processing is left to those areas where it can bring benefits compared to the fully classical approach. One can see this type of example in Variational Algorithms or even the famous Shor's algorithm, where the quantum procedure is just part of the complete factorization scheme.

Being innovative is always challenging, as it requires a sensible risk acceptance, but focusing on the core activities of a company, such is the case of VidaCaixa, even a brand-new technology with much room for improvement still can show the path towards the best coupling of problem and technology in comparison with the business-as-usual approach many companies fall into.

Identifying the potentiality of advantage with QML

When the subject is QML, there are several potential applications in finance, as was outlined in the previous chapters. The following are a few examples:

- Risk analysis and management
- Trading
- Fraud detection
- Credit scoring
- Churn prediction

It is important to note that while there are many potential applications of quantum machine learning in finance, the field is still in its early stages. It is unclear how these algorithms will perform in practice and what the companies can expect from the QML implementations. With this in mind, analyzing how to measure the success of a quantum project can be challenging.

Despite the previously described concern, one of the interesting points about exploring quantum machine learning challenges is that popular Python SDKs such as Qiskit (IBM), TensorFlow Quantum (Google), and PennyLane (Xanadu) enable the users and quantum developers to compare "apples with apples" when the project reaches the point to be evaluated. Considering this, a typical machine learning project can be followed to provide structure, stages, and milestones, and the measurement can be compared to demonstrate which approach is performing better.

Cloud tools such as Amazon SageMaker can be used for classical machine learning development or quantum experiments and explorations. Considering this and the use of Python, Jupyter Notebooks, and partially, some current machine learning infrastructure to create QML solutions, the barrier can be considered less complex regarding the current data science knowledge and the roadmaps attached to that area of research.

Taking the overlap between data science and quantum machine learning development into consideration, a classical ML approach for project management can be implemented as follows:

1. Collect data
2. Prepare data
3. Select and engineer features
4. Preprocess the data
5. Choose the best model
6. Train the model
7. Evaluate the results
8. Adjust parameters and iterate over the outcome
9. Put the model in backtesting
10. Execute quality assurance
11. Deploy in a production environment

The backtest will be critical in the NISQ era due to the necessity of discovering the right place to include quantum technologies in the current company pipelines. QML methods can be used as a main algorithm to create the predictions, as kernels to analyze the data points and their separability, or as an ensemble architecture combining several algorithms (classical and quantum) to create one prediction (*Grossi et al., 2022,* `https://arxiv.org/abs/2208.07963`).

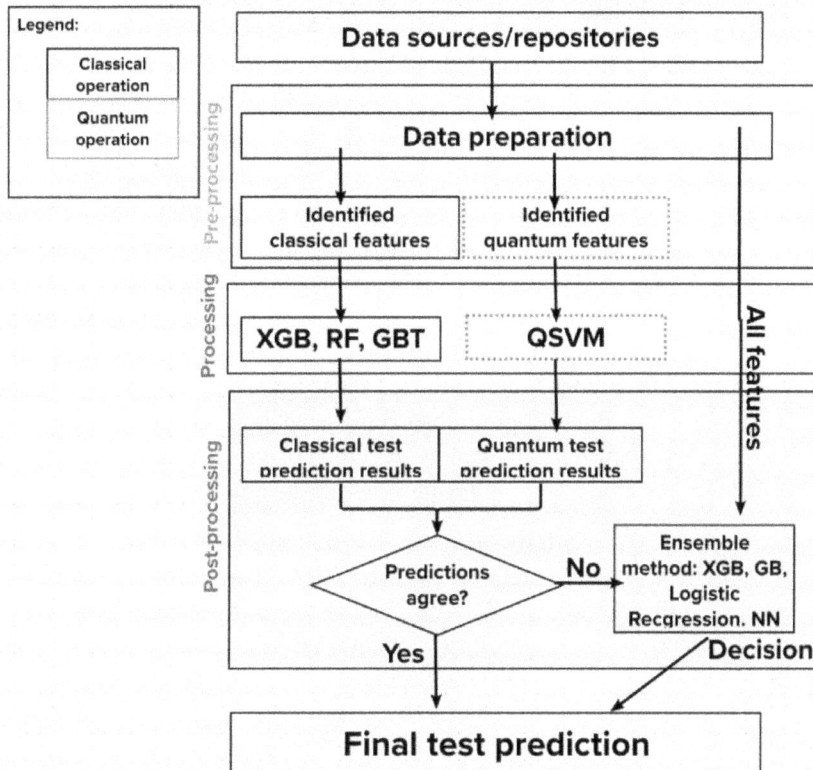

Figure 10.2 – Flow chart of a combined classical and quantum approach for a single prediction

Image source: From the paper *Mixed Quantum-Classical Method for Fraud Detection with Quantum Feature Selection,* available at `https://arxiv.org/abs/2208.07963`

Comparing the results of classical and quantum models will demonstrate that for specific cases, the quantum "add-on" could be useful and can become a productive solution even in the noisy era.

The implementation of PoCs and the identification of advantages around quantum technologies are not isolated cases but a rising trend that is constantly growing. **Boston Consulting Group (BCG)** shared some interesting findings at the Q2B 2022 event. These can be summed up as follows:

- End-user experiments with quantum computing are taking off – there are more than 100 active end-user PoCs in 2022, representing a 3X increase compared with 2020.

- 80% of the companies currently spending USD 5 millon and more on quantum computing plan to increase that spending in the following years.

- There is a disproportionate share of the value for early adopters in this field. This is due to the construction of IP capabilities and securing contracts and partnerships with relevant providers that can later increase their prices and contract requirements.

BCG emphasized that in the R&D phase that we are currently in, businesses can capture a lot of value when quantum adoption starts growing. In a few years or even months, when the value might finally be confirmed widely, the compute resources will stay limited, the pricing could get higher, and a custom quantum solution will take time to be produced and launched in a productive ecosystem.

Case study

Itaú Unibanco, the largest bank in Latin America, started a journey with QC Ware (quantum software and services development company) to improve their churn models by including quantum machine learning methods. The partnership aims to comprehend the potential of quantum algorithms and prepare Itaú Unibanco for the future usage and deployment of quantum banking systems.

Itaú Unibanco provided QC Ware with two years of anonymized user data and over 180,000 data points to better comprehend which clients were likely to quit the bank within the following three months. QC Ware developed quantum-based training architectures based on determinant sampling methods for customer retention models (QML). The quantum software company discovered, during the research and development phase, a way to implement a variation of these approaches on today's classical computers, therefore enhancing Itaú Unibanco's model by increasing the number of withdrawals caught by 2% and the model's overall precision from 71% to 77.5%.

In this case, one of the most important things to discuss is how scalable the bank's algorithms are. Even though their current quantum models run on classical machines, they can be quickly changed to run on real quantum hardware when it is ready and fits the problem the bank is trying to solve. If this happens, the speedup and benefits from these algorithms can go even further.

Funding or budgeting issues

Many organizations already count on Data and Analytics departments using all the information companies have available to derive insights and drive business revenue. But not long ago, all those initiatives were accessory projects that were part of innovation funnels or just simple attempts led by key organizational actors. It was mostly a vision that needed to be proved as a business asset.

Support from C-level executives is key, but most of the time, these innovation projects must overcome a significant lack of resources and resistance to change within an already settled organization. Most importantly, these initiatives must track expenditure and **return on investment** (**ROI**). This is one crucial aspect that many initiatives cannot overcome, which is of the utmost importance given the cost of some of the available quantum hardware. *Figure 10.3* shows an example of Quantinuum and IonQ's hardware cost in Azure for dedicated workloads.

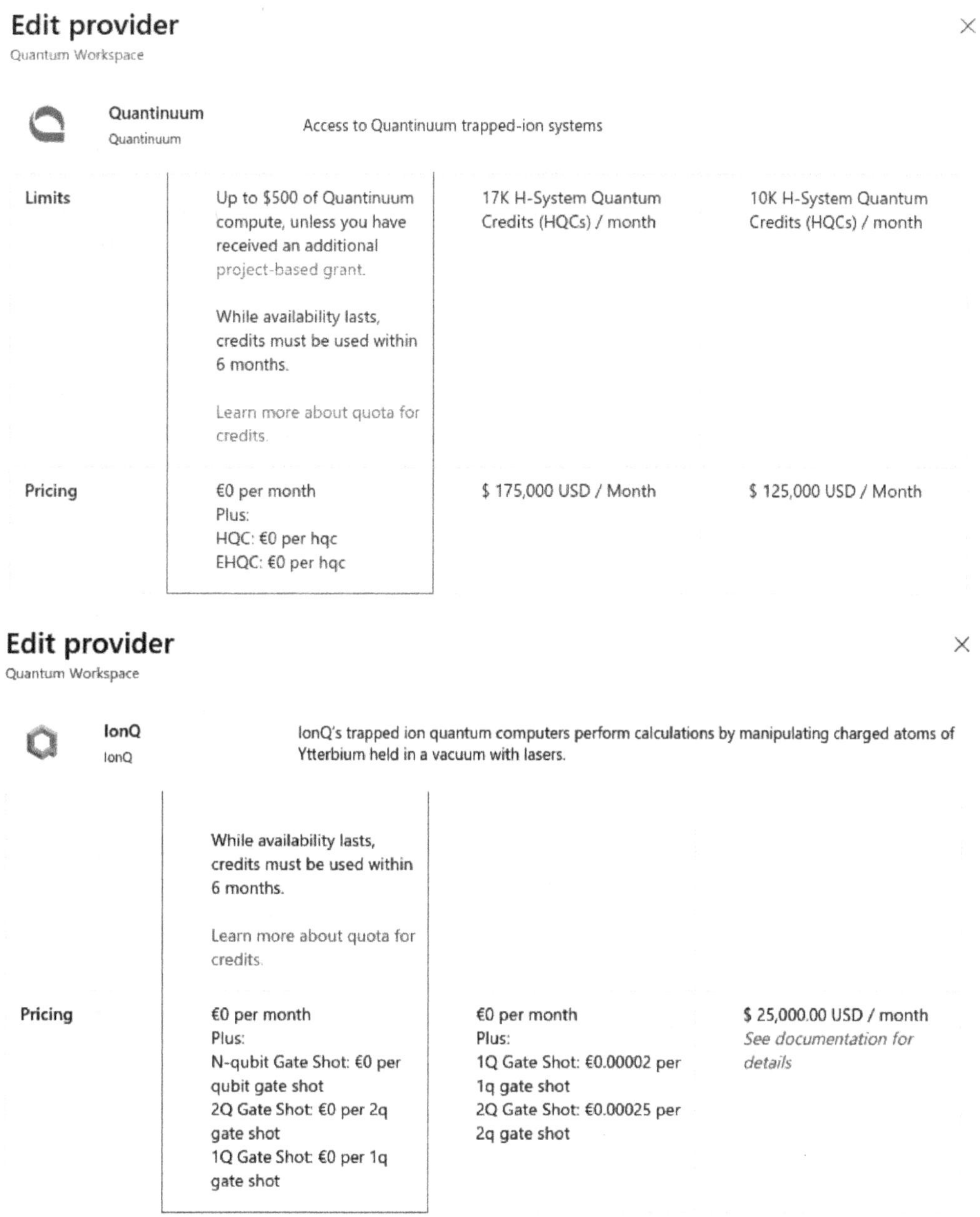

Edit provider   ✕

Quantum Workspace

Quantinuum
Quantinuum   Access to Quantinuum trapped-ion systems

Limits	Up to $500 of Quantinuum compute, unless you have received an additional project-based grant.	17K H-System Quantum Credits (HQCs) / month	10K H-System Quantum Credits (HQCs) / month
	While availability lasts, credits must be used within 6 months.		
	Learn more about quota for credits.		
Pricing	€0 per month Plus: HQC: €0 per hqc EHQC: €0 per hqc	$ 175,000 USD / Month	$ 125,000 USD / Month

Edit provider   ✕

Quantum Workspace

IonQ
IonQ   IonQ's trapped ion quantum computers perform calculations by manipulating charged atoms of Ytterbium held in a vacuum with lasers.

	While availability lasts, credits must be used within 6 months.		
	Learn more about quota for credits.		
Pricing	€0 per month Plus: N-qubit Gate Shot: €0 per qubit gate shot 2Q Gate Shot: €0 per 2q gate shot 1Q Gate Shot: €0 per 1q gate shot	€0 per month Plus: 1Q Gate Shot: €0.00002 per 1q gate shot 2Q Gate Shot: €0.00025 per 2q gate shot	$ 25,000.00 USD / month *See documentation for details*

Figure 10.3 – Costs for Quantinuum and IonQ services in Azure as of winter of 2022

So, it seems evident that these initiatives involving QC should also have a sensible roadmap to demonstrate their feasibility regarding business interests.

Many initiatives often start with simulations so that only existing allocated resources are used. But going for large system sizes might also require quite some infrastructure, as we saw on the AWS simulation for 44 qubits. Along with hardware access, many providers offer device noise models so one can load and mimic the response of the real devices using classical means. This will help the company's visionary devise a plan to guide management and ensure the project can grow in terms of resources and money. A key aspect indeed.

The prudent approach may necessitate demonstrating the benefit of including quantum algorithms in the mix of classical solutions. Depending on the size of the problem we would like to solve (for example, 100-asset portfolio optimization), we might need to discuss with some providers whether they would be interested in collaborating on our project. Many companies have embraced collaborations with academic institutions or early **innovation-driven enterprises** (**IDEs**) to access and receive support in their quantum journey. It is an interesting approach, as it allows the organization to be at the cutting edge of innovation and train its internal people while risking the minimum number of resources.

Once the project is successful, other departments such as corporate architecture, security, or financial services in charge of operational costs might also want to be included in the discussions. Given the maturity of the technology and the complexity of the business solutions, this could take longer, so rushes and hype should be avoided in favor of a longer marathon when it comes to cultural changes regarding technology.

Case study

For example, companies such as Credit Agricole have joined forces with Pasqal and Multiverse Computing. Between the three, they can unravel the intricate mixture of classical and quantum resources for risk analysis and capital market management (`https://pressroom.credit-agricole.com/news/credit-agricole-cib-explores-quantum-computing-applications-in-partnership-with-pasqal-and-multiverse-computing-5121-94727.html`). They took advantage of the European Quantum Flagship initiative to form this consortium. Hence, their main contribution to the project is their domain knowledge about the problem to be solved. It is important that domain experts other than physicists and software developers focus on and take the solution along the right path so that the outcome can be used in real environments.

Ali El Hamidi, Crédit Agricole CIB's project sponsor, had this to say:

Quantum computing is radically different from almost everything we know and use today, in terms of theory, hardware, and algorithms. This project will assemble many different competencies around the table: bankers, physicists, mathematicians, computer scientists, IT architects, all cooperating on this remarkable journey. This is a huge challenge, and we are confident we will make it a success, jointly with our talented partners Pasqal and Multiverse Computing.

This is not the only example. One might believe these opportunities are only available to large corporations. The QC community is open and willing to be challenged with use cases. Therefore, large service providers such as Microsoft offer research credits to projects in collaboration with research institutions, and the AWS Braket team will be more than willing to help. Even niche players such as Strangeworks offer backstage passes with credits for AWS services.

Finally, free access are also a possibility. Two of the most known ones are IBM's free access to small-ish devices and D-Wave's free minutes each month, allowing you to use their annealers for some time without any other access restriction. Azure and AWS have also enabled some free credits, even though they may not last long.

Market maturity, hype, and skepticism

Quantum computing is not the first tech revolution we face. Big data, the cloud, remote workforces, and even the internet have completely changed how we work and do business. In particular, we have gone from office-based services to app-first strategies and prospective service management in the financial sector.

We live in a business environment where it is common that we don't know our customers' faces. Still, we can forecast their earnings, plot their consumption profile, or even recommend how to change their habits to save money. This is an intriguing setup that would not be possible without all the technology surrounding us. But there was skepticism on those fronts, at least in the early days:

After two decades online, I'm perplexed. It's not that I haven't had a gas of a good time on the Internet. I've met great people and even caught a hacker or two. But today, I'm uneasy about this most trendy and oversold community. Visionaries see a future of telecommuting workers, interactive libraries, and multimedia classrooms. They speak of electronic town meetings and virtual communities. Commerce and business will shift from offices and malls to networks and modems. And the freedom of digital networks will make government more democratic.

Baloney. Do our computer pundits lack all common sense? The truth is no online database will replace your daily newspaper, no CD-ROM can take the place of a competent teacher and no computer network will change the way government works.

This text is the beginning paragraph of a Newsweek article titled *Why the Web Won't Be Nirvana* from 1995 (https://www.newsweek.com/clifford-stoll-why-web-wont-be-nirvana-185306). They did not even believe there would be an online market for purchasing books or newspapers over the internet. They were wrong.

At the edge of a breakthrough, it is hard to tell if there is more than meets the eye. Sales representatives will always try to highlight the good things while omitting the not-so-good bits of their services or products, and that has not changed that much. That is why one must maintain positive skepticism about breakthroughs. They may apply to our business opportunities; they may bring novelty but not a significant change in the market. What is most important is that we check and validate the technology to gain knowledge and make appropriate decisions.

Gartner's hype cycles and reports about them could be a good way to learn about how the field is changing from the point of view of large businesses, even though reports and charts from these prestigious companies can be surpassed by the talent, creativity, and constant R&D from the private sector.

A significant portion of this exploration within the company is conducted by innovation departments or pilot initiatives, allowing us to test and compare our existing resources. This scheme allows the management of risk and protects the operational business. Not only that, but as described by MIT, innovation ecosystems allow for long-term interaction among interested parties, allowing us to expand beyond the scope of traditional business.

Depending on the nature of our institution, we could play the role of a large organization, a small startup (fintech), or a risk capital funder investing in an initiative from the five stakeholders highlighted by MIT, as shown in *Figure 10.4*, needed for a sustainable ecosystem for innovation. These different roles will have very different implications. Still, all will better understand the market and potential solutions from a potentially groundbreaking technology or development.

MIT's five stakeholders in an Innovation Ecosystem

Figure 10.4 – Five stakeholders of the Innovation Ecosystem framework of MIT

Image source: https://innovation.mit.edu/assets/MIT-Stakeholder-Framework_Innovation-Ecosystems.pdf

Case study

Based on the Hyperion survey in 2022, it is expected that quantum computing is in the early adoption phase. The survey found that 34% of the 485 organizations that took part are looking into their options and monitoring technology to adopt QC technologies. In the survey, it was said that early adopters see the possibility of speeding up existing classical workloads by using quantum computers or simulators to share a wide range of computational workloads, such as finance-oriented optimization and logistics and supply chain management.

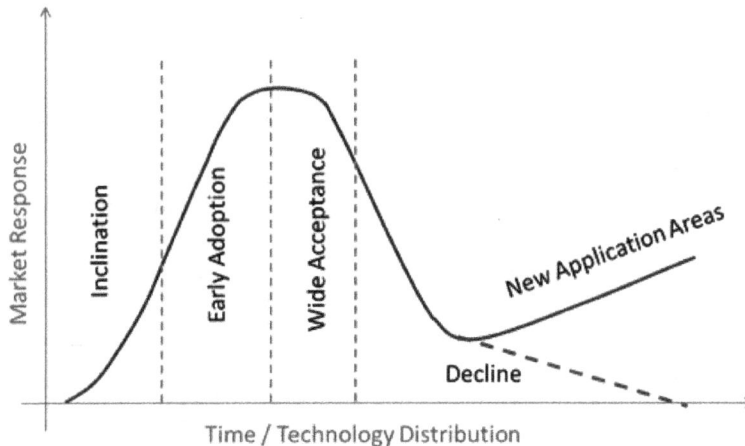

Figure 10.5 – Product lifecycle related to Quantum computing adoptions

The chart shows that a technology product goes through four stages: introduction, early growth, growth, and maturity:

1. During the introduction phase, a new technology is put on the market. Usually, only a few researchers and organizations can use it at this point.

2. During the early growth phase, the technology becomes more common and easier to use, and some commercial applications emerge.

3. As technology moves into the growth phase, it becomes more common and is used increasingly in many industries.

4. When the technology finally reaches maturity, it becomes a mainstream technology many people use.

Goldman Sachs is an example of a company looking into how quantum computing could be used, even though it is still in its early stages. The company has been working with D-Wave to investigate how quantum computers could be used in finance for portfolio optimization and risk analysis. Using quantum computing technology early on, Goldman Sachs will gain a competitive edge and discover its possible benefits before most other companies do.

Several important things have led to the quantum computing market's current level of growth:

Criteria	Description
Cost	How much does the technology cost to implement and maintain?
Benefits	What benefits will the technology bring to the organization, such as increased efficiency or competitiveness?
Feasibility	Is the technology ready for practical use, or is it still in the early stages of development?
Compatibility	Will the technology work with the organization's current infrastructure and processes, or will it require major changes?
Risk	What are the possible risks of using the technology, such as problems with security or dependability?
Expertise	Does the organization have the necessary expertise to implement and use the technology effectively?
Support	Is there sufficient support available for the technology, such as training or technical assistance?

The quantum computing market is still in the early stages of development. It will likely take several more years before quantum computers become widely available and widely used for a wider range of applications. However, based on expert advice and after the study of use cases, the authors have found that companies have been using quantum computers to overcome these limitations.

Challenge	How quantum computing can help	Example
Complexity	Quantum computers are able to handle complex problems that are beyond the capabilities of classical computers, due to their ability to perform many calculations in parallel.	Goldman Sachs is using quantum computers to optimize portfolios, which involves analyzing large amounts of data and making complex calculations.
Speed	Quantum computers can perform certain tasks much faster than classical computers, making them suitable for time-sensitive applications.	JPMorgan Chase is using quantum computers to perform real-time risk analysis, which requires processing large amounts of data quickly.
Accuracy	Quantum computers have the potential to produce more accurate results than classical computers, due to their ability to process more data and account for more variables.	Credit Suisse is using quantum computers to model financial instruments and improve the accuracy of pricing and hedging.

Security	Quantum computers may be able to provide improved security for sensitive data, as it is difficult to intercept or tamper with quantum information.	Wells Fargo is exploring the use of quantum computers to enhance the security of data storage and transmission.
Energy efficiency	Quantum computers may be more energy efficient than classical computers for certain tasks, as they can perform certain calculations using less energy.	UBS is using quantum computers to optimize energy consumption in data centers.
Cost	While quantum computers may be more expensive to purchase and maintain than classical computers, they may be able to deliver cost savings over time by improving efficiency and reducing the need for manual labor.	Morgan Stanley is using quantum computers to automate certain processes and reduce the need for manual labor, which may result in cost savings.

Companies can use the special features of quantum computers to solve hard problems that would be impossible to solve with traditional computers. Make by making software and algorithms that work well with quantum computers.

Use Case	Business Function	Timeline	Company
Portfolio optimization	Investment management	5-10 years	Goldman Sachs, JPMorgan Chase
Risk analysis and modeling	Risk management	5-10 years	Bank of America, Citigroup
Credit scoring and fraud detection	Credit and lending	5-10 years	American Express, Visa
Pricing and hedging of financial instruments	Trading and market making	5-10 years	Barclays, Deutsche Bank
Asset and liability management	Treasury and capital management	5-10 years	HSBC, Wells Fargo
Supply chain finance	Trade finance	5-10 years	Alibaba, Citi
Regulatory compliance	Compliance and reporting	5-10 years	UBS, Morgan Stanley
Predictive analytics	Data analysis and decision-making	5-10 years	BlackRock, Fidelity Investments

Road map for early adoption of quantum computing for financial institutions

The financial institution might use a cloud-based quantum simulator to model and test quantum algorithms for risk analysis and portfolio optimization tasks. This allows the institution to evaluate the potential benefits of quantum computing without investing in its quantum hardware.

Once the institution has found a promising quantum algorithm, it can test and improve it using a cloud-based quantum simulator. This can involve running simulations on different datasets and tweaking the algorithm to make it work better and more accurately.

Once the institution is satisfied with the performance of the quantum algorithm, it can use quantum hardware to run the algorithm on real data. The institution can then use the results of the quantum computation to help them make decisions or improve their risk analysis, portfolio optimization, or other financial operations.

Case study

This is not directly related to quantum computing, but it is interesting to understand some of the mindset shifts the financial sector has faced before. It is particularly interesting in the case of cloud services.

Capital One faced serious issues while moving its services to cloud (`https://www.occ.treas.gov/news-issuances/news-releases/2020/nr-occ-2020-101.html`). Even though cloud computing was expected to increase the bank's agility and revenue, the rush for cloud adoption left them facing serious fines from the **Comptroller of the Currency** (**OCC**). Forbes pointed out the concern around cybersecurity requirements for banks' strategies while moving their services to the cloud.

Meanwhile, Santander Bank moved its core banking to the cloud in 2022 and created a platform whose core will be made accessible to others via Google Cloud to facilitate this core banking transition.

It is interesting to see how the same activity had quite a different outcome in both cases. In fact, strategy and planning ahead seem to be the big conclusions we can derive here and are extensible to almost any other technology adoption we have seen before. Many companies have deployed complex distributed computing infrastructures that are expensive to maintain in-house, while only a few could take advantage of them.

Finding the right balance between early adoption and late arrival of a key technology will help drive these innovative approaches while the market matures, minimizing the risk to our organization. Technology awareness and market research are key pieces in regulating this balance. That is why strategy consulting companies such as Gartner or McKinsey for larger organizations or niche market consulting firms such as Stafford Computing can become valuable allies in this journey.

Quantum managers' training

Managers who are responsible for handling and managing quantum computing resources must have a comprehensive understanding of quantum computing's underlying principles, as well as the technical capabilities and limitations of quantum hardware and software. This might require specialized education and training in fields such as quantum mechanics, quantum algorithms, and quantum error correction.

In addition to technical expertise, managers will require solid project management skills and the capacity to coordinate the efforts of multiple teams and stakeholders. This may involve establishing objectives and priorities, allocating resources, and monitoring progress against milestones. Managers may need strong communication skills to explain the possible benefits and risks of quantum computing to a wide range of audiences, including technical and non-technical stakeholders.

Various educational and training programs can equip managers with the skills and knowledge to handle and manage quantum computing resources. There may be degree programs in quantum computing or computer science, as well as courses and workshops for professional development at universities, research institutions, and private companies.

Case study

Birla Institute of Management Technology (**BIMTECH**), started in 1988, is one of the best business schools in Delhi. They developed a 12-week course in 2022 called *Quantum for Managers*, an online course offered in collaboration with QKRISHI.

The course costs close to $500, and it is delivered through 36 hours of live sessions with quantum experts from academia and industry. The program is designed to walk professionals through different stages of relevant information about quantum computing, starting with linear algebra and ending with presenting a capstone project on how these technologies can be applied to any company or startup.

Regarding platforms and content delivery, this course is straightforward. They use Zoom for the lessons, Google Classroom for the materials, assignments, and course content, and WhatsApp to keep in touch. The program has an extraordinary number of subject matter specialists. You may take classes from renowned experts and researchers from IBM, AWS, and other universities, organizations, and businesses associated with quantum computing.

Conclusions

It can be proven that there are barriers to putting quantum computing solutions into place in any kind of business. What is also true is that for each barrier or obstacle, there is a parallel set of tools, strategies, and solutions that constantly evolve to provide the right package to overcome the adoption issues.

As we mentioned, the ecosystem is naturally evolving with more investment in and development of quantum software to deliver the quick wins required for the NISQ era. In the same way, training methods, simulation techniques, literature, and many other fronts of the technology ecosystem will grow rapidly to meet the challenges of a company's quantum journey robustly.

References

Bertsimas, D., & Tsitsiklis, J. (1993). Simulated annealing. Statistical science, 8(1), 10-15.

Index

M

machine learning and quantum machine learning

data preparation 142, 143

implementing, for credit scoring case 141

preprocessing stage 143-146

Machine Learning (ML) 32, 59, 80

geometric Brownian motion (GBM) 80-84

limitations 80

merger and acquisition (M&A) life cycle 60

Microsoft Quantum 46, 47

ML and QML models

case, of study 140

data preprocessing 137, 138

data, provider 141

feature analysis 136, 137

features 141

real business data 138

synthetic data 139

ML model

execution, preparing 136

modern portfolio theory (MPT) 106

money market funds (MMFs) 58

Money Market Funds Regulation (MMFR) 58

Monte Carlo simulation 111-113

technique 113

N

net asset value (NAV) 59

no-cloning theorem 220

noise models

local simulation 204-209

Noisy Intermediate-Scale Quantum (NISQ) 18, 23

NP problems

cryptography 8

optimization 8

pattern recognition 8

simulation 8

O

Open Quantum Assembly Language (OpenQASM) 168

P

Parameterized Quantum Circuit (PQC) 24, 33, 127, 153

PennyLane 40

physical qubits

versus logical qubits 220-224

Platform as a Service (PaaS) 17, 45

portfolio management, with traditional machine learning algorithms

classical implementation 116-120

probabilistic error cancellation 232

Q

qGANs for price distribution loading

using 90-98

QIR Alliance

reference link 210

Qiskit 39, 40

quantum computing, implementation 84-90

reference link 39

Qiskit implementation 125-131

QML methods 135

QML model

execution, preparing 136

quadratic programming 115

V

Z

‹packt›

Subscribe to our online digital library for full access to over 7,000 books and videos, as well as industry leading tools to help you plan your personal development and advance your career. For more information, please visit our website.

Why subscribe?

- Spend less time learning and more time coding with practical eBooks and Videos from over 4,000 industry professionals

- Improve your learning with Skill Plans built especially for you

- Get a free eBook or video every month

- Fully searchable for easy access to vital information

- Copy and paste, print, and bookmark content

Did you know that Packt offers eBook versions of every book published, with PDF and ePub files available? You can upgrade to the eBook version at packtpub.com and as a print book customer, you are entitled to a discount on the eBook copy. Get in touch with us at customercare@packtpub.com for more details.

At www.packtpub.com, you can also read a collection of free technical articles, sign up for a range of free newsletters, and receive exclusive discounts and offers on Packt books and eBooks.

Other Books You May Enjoy

If you enjoyed this book, you may be interested in these other books by Packt:

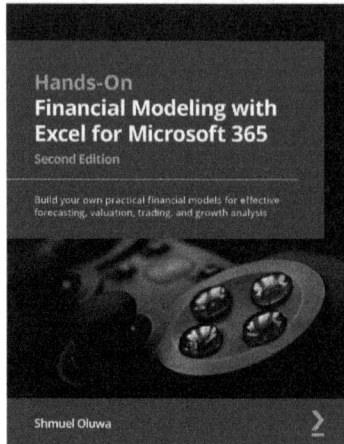

Hands-On Financial Modeling with Excel for Microsoft 365 - Second Edition

Shmuel Oluwa

ISBN: 9781803231143

- Identify the growth drivers derived from processing historical data in Excel
- Use discounted cash flow (DCF) for efficient investment analysis
- Prepare detailed asset and debt schedule models in Excel
- Calculate profitability ratios using various profit parameters
- Obtain and transform data using Power Query
- Dive into capital budgeting techniques
- Apply a Monte Carlo simulation to derive key assumptions for your financial model
- Build a financial model by projecting balance sheets and profit and loss

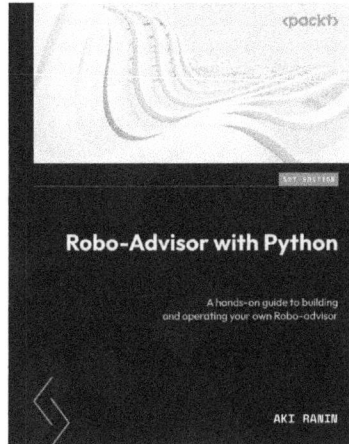

Robo-Advisor with Python

Aki Ranin

ISBN: 9781801819695

- Explore what Robo-advisors do and why they exist
- Create a workflow to design and build a Robo-advisor from the bottom up
- Build and license Robo-advisors using different approaches
- Open and fund accounts, complete KYC verification, and manage orders
- Build Robo-advisor features for goals, projections, portfolios, and more
- Operate a Robo-advisor with P, rebalancing, and fee management

Packt is searching for authors like you

If you're interested in becoming an author for Packt, please visit `authors.packtpub.com` and apply today. We have worked with thousands of developers and tech professionals, just like you, to help them share their insight with the global tech community. You can make a general application, apply for a specific hot topic that we are recruiting an author for, or submit your own idea.

Share Your Thoughts

Now you've finished *Financial Modeling using Quantum Computing*, we'd love to hear your thoughts! Scan the QR code below to go straight to the Amazon review page for this book and share your feedback or leave a review on the site that you purchased it from.

`https://packt.link/r/1-804-61842-X`

Your review is important to us and the tech community and will help us make sure we're delivering excellent quality content.

Download a free PDF copy of this book

Thanks for purchasing this book!

Do you like to read on the go but are unable to carry your print books everywhere? Is your eBook purchase not compatible with the device of your choice?

Don't worry, now with every Packt book you get a DRM-free PDF version of that book at no cost.

Read anywhere, any place, on any device. Search, copy, and paste code from your favorite technical books directly into your application.

The perks don't stop there, you can get exclusive access to discounts, newsletters, and great free content in your inbox daily

Follow these simple steps to get the benefits:

1. Scan the QR code or visit the link below

https://packt.link/free-ebook/9781804618424

2. Submit your proof of purchase
3. That's it! We'll send your free PDF and other benefits to your email directly

www.ingramcontent.com/pod-product-compliance
Lightning Source LLC
Chambersburg PA
CBHW080518220326
41599CB00032B/6124